The Maastricht Treaty: Second Thoughts after 20 Years

The Maastricht Treaty, signed in 1992 and ratified in the following year, is widely seen as a landmark in the evolution of the European Union. It introduced into the treaty framework revolutionary new elements such as the co-decision procedure between the Council and the European Parliament, cooperation in the area of Justice and Home Affairs, the Common Foreign and Security Policy and the 'Euro' as a single currency for the majority of the then member states. It also introduced the concept of European citizenship into the treaty, reflecting the rising expectations of both citizens and decision-makers in the European project, and upgraded the role of the European Council at the summit of the EU's institutional structure.

Twenty years later, each of these innovations remains of central importance for the process of European integration, while current developments provide a valuable opportunity to reflect on the historical decisions taken in Maastricht in order to assess their significance and examine the subsequent evolution of the Union.

This volume brings together an international group of leading scholars in the field in order to provide such an assessment, with each chapter both looking back over the developments within each of these domains as well as looking ahead to the way in which the EU is positioned to address current challenges.

This book was published as a special issue of the *Journal of European Integration*.

Thomas Christiansen is Jean Monnet Professor of European Institutional Politics at Maastricht University. He is Co-Director of the Maastricht Centre for European Governance (with S. Vanhonacker) and Executive Editor of the *Journal of European Integration* (with S. Duke). He has published widely on different aspects of the institutional politics of the EU.

Simon Duke is a Professor at the European Institute of Public Administration (EIPA), Maastricht, Netherlands. He has published several monographs and his work has also appeared in numerous academic journals including the *Journal of Common Market Studies, International Politics, European Foreign Affairs Review* and the *Hague Journal of Diplomacy*.

The Maastricht Treaty: Second Thoughts after 20 Years

Edited by
Thomas Christiansen and Simon Duke

LONDON AND NEW YORK

First published 2013
by Routledge
2 Park Square, Milton Park, Abingdon, Oxfordshire OX14 4RN

Simultaneously published in the USA and Canada
by Routledge
711 Third Avenue, New York, NY 10017

First issued in paperback 2014

Routledge is an imprint of the Taylor and Francis Group, an informa business

© 2013 Taylor & Francis

This book is a reproduction of the *Journal of European Integration*, vol. 34, issue 7. The Publisher requests to those authors who may be citing this book to state, also, the bibliographical details of the special issue on which the book was based.

All rights reserved. No part of this book may be reprinted or reproduced or utilised in any form or by any electronic, mechanical, or other means, now known or hereafter invented, including photocopying and recording, or in any information storage or retrieval system, without permission in writing from the publishers.

Trademark notice: Product or corporate names may be trademarks or registered trademarks, and are used only for identification and explanation without intent to infringe.

British Library Cataloguing in Publication Data
A catalogue record for this book is available from the British Library

ISBN 978-0-415-64126-5 (hbk)
ISBN 978-1-138-85051-4 (pbk)

Typeset in Times New Roman
by Taylor & Francis Books

Publisher's Note
The publisher would like to make readers aware that the chapters in this book may be referred to as articles as they are identical to the articles published in the special issue. The publisher accepts responsibility for any inconsistencies that may have arisen in the course of preparing this volume for print.

Contents

Citation Information	vii
1. Understanding and Assessing the Maastricht Treaty *Thomas Christiansen, Simon Duke & Emil Kirchner*	1
2. Still Rooted in Maastricht: EU External Relations as a 'Third-generation Hybrid' *Michael Smith*	15
3. Justice and Home Affairs: The Treaty of Maastricht as a Decisive Intergovernmental Gate Opener *Jörg Monar*	33
4. Twenty Years of Co-decision Since Maastricht: Inter- and Intrainstitutional Implications *Anne Rasmussen*	51
5. The Maastricht Treaty and the European Council: The History of an Institutional Evolution *Wolfgang Wessels*	69
6. The Maastricht Treaty at Twenty: A Greco-European Tragedy? *James A. Caporaso & Min-Hyung Kim*	85
7. 'Maastricht Plus': Managing the Logic of Inherent Imperfections *Kenneth Dyson*	107
8. Post-Maastricht Civil Society and Participatory Democracy *Beate Kohler-Koch*	125
9. In the Face of Crisis: Input Legitimacy, Output Legitimacy and the Political Messianism of European Integration *J. H. H. Weiler*	141
10. The Arc of Institutional Reform in Post-Maastricht Treaty Change *Desmond Dinan*	159
Index	175

Citation Information

The chapters in this book were originally published in the *Journal of European Integration*, volume 34, issue 7 (November 2012). When citing this material, please use the original page numbering for each article, as follows:

Chapter 1
Understanding and Assessing the Maastricht Treaty
Thomas Christiansen, Simon Duke & Emil Kirchner
Journal of European Integration, volume 34, issue 7 (November 2012) pp. 685-698

Chapter 2
Still Rooted in Maastricht: EU External Relations as a 'Third-generation Hybrid'
Michael Smith
Journal of European Integration, volume 34, issue 7 (November 2012) pp. 699-716

Chapter 3
Justice and Home Affairs: The Treaty of Maastricht as a Decisive Intergovernmental Gate Opener
Jörg Monar
Journal of European Integration, volume 34, issue 7 (November 2012) pp. 717-734

Chapter 4
Twenty Years of Co-decision Since Maastricht: Inter- and Intrainstitutional Implications
Anne Rasmussen
Journal of European Integration, volume 34, issue 7 (November 2012) pp. 735-754

Chapter 5
The Maastricht Treaty and the European Council: The History of an Institutional Evolution
Wolfgang Wessels
Journal of European Integration, volume 34, issue 7 (November 2012) pp. 753-768

Chapter 6
The Maastricht Treaty at Twenty: A Greco-European Tragedy?
James A. Caporaso & Min-Hyung Kim
Journal of European Integration, volume 34, issue 7 (November 2012) pp. 769-790

CITATION INFORMATION

Chapter 7
'Maastricht Plus': Managing the Logic of Inherent Imperfections
Kenneth Dyson
Journal of European Integration, volume 34, issue 7 (November 2012) pp. 791-808

Chapter 8
Post-Maastricht Civil Society and Participatory Democracy
Beate Kohler-Koch
Journal of European Integration, volume 34, issue 7 (November 2012) pp. 809-824

Chapter 9
In the Face of Crisis: Input Legitimacy, Output Legitimacy and the Political Messianism of European Integration
J. H. H. Weiler
Journal of European Integration, volume 34, issue 7 (November 2012) pp. 825-842

Chapter 10
The Arc of Institutional Reform in Post-Maastricht Treaty Change
Desmond Dinan
Journal of European Integration, volume 34, issue 7 (November 2012) pp. 843-858

Understanding and Assessing the Maastricht Treaty

THOMAS CHRISTIANSEN, SIMON DUKE & EMIL KIRCHNER

ABSTRACT   This article introduces the collection of articles of the special issue and provides a discussion of the common themes linking these contributions. The article stresses the continuing significance of the Maastricht Treaty and illustrates the various ways in which the key reforms of the early 1990s still matter today. This includes not only the bearing that the decisions at the time of the Maastricht Treaty have had on the current crisis of the Eurozone, but also the developments in the areas of foreign policy and justice and home affairs. Indeed, the very move towards 'pillarisation' as well as key institutional changes such as the creation of the co-decision procedure and the elevation of the European Council all continue to play an important role today. The article concludes with some reflections about the legacy of the Maastricht Treaty, highlighting both the achievements of the treaty but also the shortcomings in terms of enhancing democratic legitimacy and engagement with civil society — indicating the key challenges that the Union still faces today.

Introduction

The purpose of this volume is to reflect on the continuing significance of the Maastricht Treaty, some 20 years after it was signed in 1992. It brings together a group of prominent scholars to discuss the most significant aspects of that historical reform and developments since. Each author was invited to consider the treaty's importance within their respective area of expertise, in order to arrive at a comprehensive assessment of the contribution that the treaty has made to the process of European integration. In conceiving this special issue, the editors decided to focus on what are generally considered to be the main areas of reform in the treaty, commissioning contributions on the key policy-areas and institutional changes alongside the obvious contemporary importance of addressing the economic and monetary aspects. This brief introduction will attempt to give an overview of the principal issues or themes addressed, the main arguments presented and the conclusions arrived at. It will also draw together a number of common themes from these diverse contributions, one of which was apparent in the response by the authors to the editor's invitations — namely, that we are still feeling the repercussions of the Maastricht decisions today, and that it is therefore still necessary to strive to understand the implications of this important treaty.

In the following we first discuss the historical context in which the Maastricht Treaty negotiations were conducted, which undoubtedly had an impact on the shape of the ensuing agreement, before examining a number of key aspects of the treaty which are discussed in much greater depth in the contributions to this volume: the creation of separate pillars for the Common Foreign and Security Policy (CFSP) and Justice and Home Affairs (JHA); institutional reforms, in particular the strengthening of the European Council and the introduction of the co-decision procedure in the adoption of legislation; the creation of the single currency and the provisions for Economic and Monetary Union (EMU). A final section of this chapter then discusses the impact that the treaty had on democratic accountability, civil society and legitimacy more broadly.

Historical Context

Twenty years ago, Europe — and indeed the world — were very different places. It is worth recalling that the treaty was conceived in the immediate aftermath of the Cold War and the collapse of the Soviet Union. This changed the conceptions of international relations and removed many of the certainties, however unpleasant, of the Cold War era with its bipolar structure and nuclear alliances. This was replaced with something altogether more difficult to understand, let alone categorise. The end of the Cold War also changed the conceptions of a Europe which had been divided by the Iron Curtain for the better part of four decades. The Europe that emerged in the aftermath of the implosion of the Soviet Union was surprisingly unchaotic, with the notable exception of the violent break-up of the former Yugoslavia. Mounting tension in the Western Balkans eventually led to war in 1991. The subsequent bloodshed, refugee movements across international borders, US backed military interventions and eventual (but uneasy) diplomatic settlements, were one of the main external catalysts for the creation of a CFSP, and thereby laid the foundations for the European Security and Defence Policy (ESDP) that followed a few years later.

These major events during the 1980s and early 1990s grabbed the headlines, but the European Community was also confronted with the implications of its development as an international actor in its more 'normal' business, such as trying to reach a successful outcome to the GATT Uruguay Round, contributing to the Middle East Peace Process or upgrading relations with important partners such as Japan. The external challenges collectively led to renewed interest in the idea of European Political Union which had been raised tentatively almost two decades before.

Another parallel development, promoted by a decision in 1985 to complete the Internal Market by removing all physical, technical and fiscal barriers by the end of 1992, led to the first concrete proposals for EMU in 1989. The two processes, political and monetary union, would become inextricably linked, most notably in the context of German unification.

Desmond Dinan's contribution to this volume views the Maastricht Treaty as part of a continuum or process. As he observes a number of themes that surfaced in the intergovernmental conference and the treaty itself were recognised refrains in the language of European integration, such as questions of democratic legitimacy, supranationality, enlargement and more efficient decision-making. These are themes that are very much alive and well today, notwithstanding the merits or demerits of the Maastricht Treaty. The factors shaping the treaty were therefore the result of complex internal debates and positions, as well as attempts to react to a number of external shocks.

It was against the background of these international and internal developments that the Maastricht Treaty, or the Treaty on European Union (TEU) as it is formally called, was agreed at the December 1991 European Council. It was subsequently signed in Maastricht on 7 February 1992 and came into effect in November 1993. As it happens, the ratification of the treaty was something of a baptism of fire for the new 'European Union' since Denmark only ratified the treaty after a second referendum, following a first negative vote and the subsequent agreement on a number of opt-outs. A referendum in France in September 1992 supported the treaty only by the barest of margins, while in the United Kingdom demands for opt-outs from some of the social provisions almost cost the Prime Minister, John Major, his position after a bitterly fought vote of confidence. In Germany, ratification was held up until the Constitutional Court in Karlsruhe had approved it. These difficulties in ratification, unparalleled in the history of treaty reform, signalled the end of the so-called 'permissive consensus' of the European populations and spawned two decades of debates about the Union's 'democratic deficit'.

The bearing of the various internal and external factors on the shaping of the Maastricht Treaty have been subject to vigorous, if inconclusive, academic debate. Suffice it to say that the contributions to this volume suggest that the resulting treaty was shaped by a *combination* of internal, external and national impetuses. For some the treaty may be located within the context of the onward logic of European integration, while for others the progression towards monetary, or political, union did not represent universally desired ends but the state of thinking within the Franco–German engine in the early 1990s. As was observed above, the struggle to ratify the treaty suggests that even if there were universally desired ends, they were diluted significantly by the introduction of a number of national opt-outs as the price levied for eventual ratification.

'Pillarisation'

One of the key novelties of the Maastricht Treaty was the creation of distinct 'pillars' with differing decision-making procedures. Essentially, the purpose of creating pillars for the Common Foreign and Security Policy

(CFSP) of the Union and for Justice and Home Affairs (JHA) was to make the expansion of Union competences in these areas possible without applying the 'Community method' to these. In other words, the initiating role of the European Commission, the involvement of the European Parliament and recourse to the European Court of Justice were all extremely limited or excluded altogether. The new second and third pillars were conceived as intergovernmental arenas next to the supranational logic of the 'Community method'.

In the case of CFSP, the emergence of a new 'pillar' raised a number of specific issues, as well as some broader questions about the nature of the Union's actorness on the international stage. Michael Smith argues convincingly in this volume that the Maastricht Treaty, 'institutionalised and embedded in the EU framework a hybrid structure of external relations which has fundamentally conditioned all subsequent attempts to establish an integrated EU 'foreign policy'. Although later efforts were made, notably in the Lisbon Treaty, to tame the hybrid nature of the Union's external relations it has retained much of its character from the Maastricht Treaty.

The 'hybrid' nature of the EU's external relations, drawing upon heterogeneous sources or elements, was not entirely due to the Maastricht Treaty since the informal process of European Political Cooperation (EPC) — consisting of regular meetings of the Community's foreign ministers outside of the formal structures — was the pre-cursor to CFSP. The Community elements of EU external relations, such as trade and development policy, were present at the inception of the Community and were therefore well-established by the early 1990s. The treaty therefore reflected and solidified the 'mixed actor system' it had inherited from earlier periods. It was clear in the intergovernmental conference preceding the adoption of the treaty that the foreign and security elements were of immense sensitivity to the member states and there was little change of them being *communautarised*. As the relevant chapter notes, the Maastricht Treaty embodied and magnified a number of competing logics with the effect that mean that the 'EU occupies an essentially ambiguous position on key questions of world order'.

This essential ambiguity proved to be platform for subsequent attempts in Amsterdam, Nice and Lisbon, to resolve some of the underlying dilemmas posed by the treaty. These included how to provide the resources necessary for CFSP (and later ESDP/Common Security and Defence Policy [CSDP]); how to link the relevant parts of the pillars as well as the policies and instruments towards common goals; how the Western European Union (WEU) should complement or be associated with the EU; how to link together the different actors responsible for EU external relation; and determining at the strategic level what kind of goals and interests the EU wishes to promote and defend on the international scene.

In external relations terms the Maastricht Treaty has been conceived of as the 'root stock', onto which successive grafts have been attempted, all of which have attempted to address the effects of the EU's 'embedded hybridity' in its external relations. The latest graft is obviously the Lisbon Treaty which attempts to bridge the pillars by introducing the High

Representative who is also a Vice President of the Commission, as well as the European External Action Service (EEAS). Although the potential for more coherence, efficiency and visibility is present in the Lisbon Treaty, there are still the shadows of the Maastricht Treaty and the presence of a distinct second pillar which, as the Lisbon Treaty notes, is subject to 'special rules and procedures'. While it would be easy to retrospectively criticise the flawed hybridity of the Maastricht Treaty, the treaty represents the consensus at that time and what was possible. The hybridity of the pillarised EU external relations established by the Maastricht Treaty has, however, proven enduring and been extended, or grafted, upon.

Moreover, despite this long standing hybrid framework and the associated ambiguities or lack of coherence which such a complex policy setting provokes, there has been considerable success in EU actorness in this field, as demonstrated, for example, by the over twenty CSDP missions which the EU has undertaken since 2000 with regard to peace keeping and peace building efforts in Europe, Africa and Asia. While the Lisbon Treaty clearly has echoes of the Maastricht Treaty in this context, the evolution of CSDP and the fact that the hitherto silent 'D' in CSDP is now included more explicitly in the treaty, is indeed testimony to the vigour of the necessary hybridity.

The Maastricht treaty also introduced a third 'pillar' to the European Union, JHA, which the Amsterdam Treaty subsequently renamed and refined to Police and Judicial Cooperation on Criminal matters (PJCCM). The third pillar designated asylum policy, immigration, as well as judicial, customs and policy cooperation, as areas of 'common interest'. The Amsterdam Treaty would give the EU's institutions full control over specific JHA policy areas like asylum and immigration.

Jörg Monar's contribution acknowledges that of the three pillars, the third pillar was the thinnest, especially with the above refining in mind. Yet, this was also the policy area that spurned a dedicated Council formation, two Commissioner portfolios, two Commission Directorate-Generals and a dedicated European Parliament committee. One of the more remarkable facets of the Maastricht Treaty is that it formally introduced the Area of Freedom Security and Justice (AFSJ) into the EU based on what appeared to be inauspicious foundations marked by compromise on basic principles, non-binding texts and questionable parliamentary and judicial control. Somewhat perversely, it may be that the very weaknesses of the Maastricht Treaty amply demonstrated that this area of EU policymaking 'needed clearer objectives, more effective instruments and — for the sake of its legitimacy — better parliamentary and judicial control'.

Despite its initial limited provisions, it would be wrong, as Monar suggests in his paper, to view 'the Maastricht "third pillar" as a sort of failed first attempt'. He goes on to argue that 'throughout the history of the European construction treaty reforms have played an important role as 'enablers' of its further development, and this is even more true in a case like the given one where a whole new policy field has been formally introduced by a treaty reform'. While most text adopted under the Maastricht provisions were non-binding, the Maastricht Treaty, as Monar points out, brought JHA cooperation decisively within the EU system and laid the foundations on which the area of freedom, security and justice (AFSJ) could be built after the Amsterdam Treaty reforms. As a consequence, the EU has asserted a kind of autonomy with the progressive harmonisation of judicial and penal law within the Union and the creation of legal instruments valid throughout the EU, particularly the European arrest warrant, the European evidence warrant, and the guaranteed mutual access to a standardised criminal database (Lavenex and Wallace 2006). Complementing these legal instruments are agencies such as Europol and Eurojust as well as the Police Chiefs' Task Force.

Beyond creating specific conditions for decision-making in different areas, the pillarisation of the Union that was established by the Maastricht Treaty has also been as a fragmentation of the hitherto uniform development of the Community. For instance, we have already seen that the price of ratification were the opt-outs negotiated by Denmark and the United Kingdom. Denmark negotiated four opt-outs (EMU, CSDP, JHA and EU citizenship) as one of the necessary concessions for the eventual successful referendum on the treaty in 1992. The United Kingdom negotiated an opt out from the Social Charter in 1991 (although this was later abolished in 1997 by the incoming Blair government but others were added). There are now five countries with opt-outs (in addition to Denmark and the United Kingdom, Poland, Ireland and Sweden have opt-outs although in the case of the latter it is of a specific nature). The idea of opt-outs went against the functionalist logic of European integration by opening up the possibility of a variable speed Europe and, with the 2004 enlargement in mind, raised the spectre of double-standards since for the new EU members opt outs were not an option (whereas lengthy transition periods for labour market access for workers from the accession states were introduced). In his contribution Desmond Dinan presciently observes that the Maastricht Treaty stands out not only for its 'inherent importance but also because of the public reaction it generated' which signalled a 'growing unease with the nascent EU'.

A further notion introduced by the Maastricht Treaty, which also proved contentious, was the principle of subsidiarity. The principle states that:

> ... the Community shall take action... only if and in so far as the objectives of the proposed action cannot be sufficiently achieved by the member states and can therefore, by reason of the scale or effects of the proposed action, be better achieved by the Community. Any action by the Community shall not go beyond what is necessary to achieve the objectives of this treaty.

Although the principle existed implicitly prior to the Maastricht Treaty, its explicit recognition in the treaty was to open up debates about whether this strengthened the states, regions or even local government vis-à-vis the EU, or vice versa.

Institutional Reform

The 'pillars' of the Maastricht 'temple' were meant to be held together by an institution — the European Council — that had been previously present but which received much greater significance from the 1990s. As Wolfgang Wessels points out in his contribution, the European Council was not listed in the treaty among the institutions of the Community — and as such was also exempt from judicial review of its actions — but was designed as an over-arching structure that would hold together the various elements of the Union. Thus it can both be seen as a symptom of pillarisation and as an attempt to overcome the problems arising from it.

With Maastricht, the European Council's role at the summit of the Union's architecture was confirmed and expanded. Not only did the European Council continue to set the broad agenda and strategic direction for the Union's legislative programme, but it also became the ultimate decision-making body with regard to both CFSP and EMU. Wessels' contribution charts the gradual evolution and growth of the institution, in which Maastricht was a significant event. While summitry in the area of CFSP proved to be uncontroversial, the European Council's elevated role in decision-making about the Euro would in time turn it into the crucial forum for crisis- management. As will be discussed below, in recent years the cooperation among Heads of State and Government in the context of the European Council was essential in dealing with the fall-out of the sovereign debt crisis. Wessels detects already at the time of Maastricht evidence for the emergence of a 'presidency model' in the work of the European Council, something which is reinforced after the Lisbon Treaty when Herman van Rompuy took up his position as President of the European Council, replacing the rotating Presidency at this level. Dinan goes to suggests that the European Council emerged 'as the centre of political gravity', in no small part due to the Eurozone crisis and the frequent meetings.

Besides an expansion of Qualified Majority Voting (QMV) and the establishment of a European citizenship, a profound change was introduced by the treaty with respect to the co-decision procedure, making the European Parliament a co-legislator with the Council of Ministers (or the Council). As Dinan reminds us, this was due in part to the recognition of the principle of democratic legitimacy which underlay earlier efforts to strengthen the role of the European Parliament. The co-decision procedure did more than anything else to transform the role of the European Parliament vis-à-vis the other institutions. Although there is disagreement about the relative balance between the institutions, the very fact that post-Maastricht the Council and European Parliament were required to agree on almost all of the legislative compromises, ushered in a far closer working relationship between the bodies.

The procedure undoubtedly introduced complexity into the Union's procedures, with up to three readings being necessary for a legislative deal on occasion. However, as the chapter on co-decision notes, it worked 'surprisingly well' and did not result in 'chaos and stalemate'. Although the procedure has been developed since the Maastricht Treaty, since the treaty only introduced a restricted version of co-decision (applying to only 15 legal bases whereas today it applies to nearly all areas where the Council decides by qualified majority voting), it nevertheless stands as one of the most far-reaching institutional innovations of the treaty. The foundations of co-decision in the Maastricht Treaty would eventually lead to the development of trialogues (involving the European Parliament, the Council and the Commission) which gradually became standard practice at all stages of co-decision. As Rasmussen's contribution makes clear, the literature suggests that the introduction of co-decision heralded 'fundamental changes in the EU construction' but has also led to concerns about the potential for abuse in the 'shielded negotiation forums' that comprise much of the co-decision procedures.

Besides the record on monetary policy, CSDP and JHA, it is important to note the institutional innovations that the Maastricht Treaty has made in terms of improving EU decision-making and advancing EU democracy and a common European identity. Among these were an expansion of Qualified Majority Voting (QMV), the introduction of the co-decision procedure, and the establishment of a European citizenship. It is the expansion of QMV and especially the co-decision method which have made significant contributions to more efficiency, more transparency in inter-institutional relations and greater democracy in EU decision-making.

Some of those changes brought about by the co-decision procedure have affected the balance of power between the EU institutions and their organisations internal decision-making in a fundamental way. Co-decision has implicitly introduced a clientealistic relationship based on trade-offs between the EU peoples' direct and indirect representatives. The fact that decisions have eventually to be taken for reasons of efficiency, has resulted in a constant bargain between the EP and the Council which does not totally reflect the ethos of democratic politics and may even lead to decisions which may not correspond to the public demand. As pointed out by Rasmussen, the joint legislation formula between EP and Council has made the Commission the loser since its formal powers are reduced in this procedure compared to previous legislative procedures. But the Commission still has the sole right of initiative in EU legislation.

The co-decision procedure has implications for EU democracy, the promotion of the concept of European citizenship and the forging of a European identity. This link is particularly well documented in the contribution by Beate Kohler-Koch on the role of European civil society organisations at European level. As Kohler-Koch argues, the Maastricht Treaty was instrumental in inducing civil society organisations to flock to Brussels and for EU institutions to become committed to involve civil society in governance. In her view, civil society was seen as a beacon of hope for reducing the democratic deficit by advancing participatory democracy. But, as she shows, reality turns out to be otherwise in that increased non-governmental organisation (NGO) participation in EU governance did not render political representation in the EU more democratic because of failing to bring about the democratic empowerment of citizens or equal and effective participation. Whether the European Citizens' Initiative, launched under the Lisbon Treaty and, which require the signatures of one million citizens from at least one quarter of the EU member states to interfere in EU governance will be a more effective vehicle for overcoming the apparent EU democratic deficit than NGO activities is unclear at this stage. Doubts might even be raised over its future, as according to a survey 64 per cent of EU citizens think have expressed their view in a survey that they are it quite unlikely to ever make use of the ECI initiative (Eurobarometer 2010).

Economic and Monetary Union

Dinan argues in his contribution to this volume that, as significant as the two new intergovernmental pillars (CFSP and JHA) were, the commitment to Economic and Monetary Union (EMU) 'set the Maastricht Treaty apart from previous and future landmarks in the history of European integration'. Of course, the notion of landmark can be understood either positively or negatively representing either a significant leap forward or a notable folly.

The current financial and sovereign debt crisis in the Eurozone has to much debate about the logic, or lack thereof, of attempting to create a monetary union in the absence of the accompanying political infrastructure and enforcement mechanisms. The contribution by James Caporaso and Min-hyung Kim concurs with Andre Sapir who noted the absence of any real transferral of competence from the member states to the EU, with 'no significant EU budget, no integrated financial supervision, no strong political counterpart to the central bank nor any provisions for crisis resolution'. If only for this reason, it is important to look back at the Maastricht Treaty as many are wondering how such a precarious creation could have been endorsed, with such apparent faith, by the EU's leaders at that time in an area that involved one of the Union's core freedoms of movement (capital). How could monetary integration have been endorsed without the accompanying fiscal integration? Was it assumed that this would follow later or that the European economies, propelled and safeguarded by the German economy along with a German-inspired Maastricht 'add-on', in the form of the 1997 Stability and Growth Pact (SGP), would facilitate the stability and longer-term viability of EMU?

As with other policy areas, it is all too easy with hindsight to be harsh on the decisions taken in the context of the treaty and to overlook its strengths. One of these is that, as Caporaso and Kim observe, 'the Treaty did recognize that economic homogeneity, particularly with regard to inflation rates, budget deficits, and accumulated public debt, was highly desirable'. Yet, the authors conclude that notwithstanding the strength and vision of the treaty, the foundations for EMU represent a 'transnational Greek tragedy' based on the inherent flaws of the treaty. One of the most notable 'character flaws' of the treaty and the subsequent SGP (with its inherent bias towards price stability) was the provision for a common currency without a common economic governance structure or uniform banking regulations. A further issue is identified as the concentration on fiscal irresponsibility to the exclusion of other issues, such as those deriving from loosely regulated capital flows. The treaty itself, along with the capital liberalisation directive, was seen as providing 'the permissive conditions for capital movements across countries'.

The extent to which the current problems of the Eurozone crisis might be found in a flawed conception present in the Maastricht Treaty is debatable, especially since many of the contributory factors to the 2008 financial crisis lay beyond the collective borders of the EU. Dyson's contribution suggests that regardless of any external aspects, the treaty was conceptually flawed in one fundamental aspect: the 'desire to keep financial/fiscal authority at the national level is incompatible with the objectives of having capital mobility and financial stability all at the same time'. The flaws of the Maastricht Treaty were then compounded by subsequent complacency during the years of economic growth, especially on the periphery of what became the Eurozone. This lesson appears to have been learned, but what it implies in practical terms for the resolution of the current Eurozone crisis is far from clear.

A number of complementary themes resurface in the chapter on the Supreme Emergency Exemption. The key argument of Dyson's contribution is that the 'creditor power' represented, most notably, by Germany was supposed to set standards of appropriateness and the parameters of reform trajectories in European economic governance. As we now know, with the benefit of hindsight, the lack of a Supreme Emergency Exemption from 'its stability-oriented paradigm of sound money and finance in the interests of Treaty-guaranteed irreversibility of EMU', proved to be flaw. In spite of open differences in the literature as to the nature of the inadequacies of the Maastricht Treaty, based on neo-classical or neo-Keynesian assumptions, there is broad consensus that 'the institutional arrangements and policy instruments of the new economic constitution were inadequate for a sustainable monetary union'. As Dyson notes, although efforts were made in the Amsterdam, Nice and Lisbon treaties to compensate for the deficiencies of the Maastricht Treaty, they did so 'in ways that sought to satisfy the Bundesbank and the ECB that the Maastricht 'monetary constitution' remained fully intact'.

As these contributions by Dyson and by Caporaso and Kim make abundantly clear, the TEU drafting of the text on monetary union and the additional SGP provisions, failed to incorporate corresponding central fiscal or banking authorities to those existing in the monetary field, as represented by the European Central Bank (ECB). Despite its design faults, the ECB has been able to deliver on the provision of price stability, and the Euro, after an initial fall in value with respect to the US dollar, demonstrated considerable strength in the currency markets in the decade after its introduction. Nonetheless, the failure by some countries to observe the SGP rules, the unwillingness by the member states in the Council to enforce these and the underlying flaws in the overall design of economic and EU monetary policy, proved to be too strong and resulted in serious questions being raised about the future of the Eurozone in 2011/12.

At the time of writing in the summer of 2012, it is too early to make a considered judgement on the future of the Eurozone, but it is evident and acknowledged by policy-makers and observers alike that the institutional framework for managing a stable Euro has been insufficient.

The Legacy of Maastricht

The common theme that appears across all of the contributions to this volume is that the treaty is perhaps best conceived of as a foundation. Indeed, as Dinan argues, the treaty could be seen as a 'watershed' since it transformed the Community 'in ways that seemed unimaginable less than a decade before'. Although the many aspects of the treaty had their origins in discussions in past intergovernmental conferences and numerous reports, the treaty's importance lies in its codification of EMU, CFSP, JHA and co-decision — to name the most obvious examples. In each of these cases subsequent intergovernmental conferences, or the Convention on the Future of Europe, would develop the basic frameworks and structures established in the Maastricht Treaty. The image of a 'graft' is a particularly appropriate one, with the Maastricht Treaty as the rootstock. This has both positive connotations, in the sense that hybrids can often prove surprisingly hardy, as well as less positive ones where the initial flaws of the treaty are proving far harder to ignore or amend.

Asking whether the Maastricht Treaty provisions have ultimately worked or not raises three different but interrelated lines of enquiry: first, the context in which the Maastricht Treaty was conceived; second, the ingenuity and foresight of the treaty provisions themselves; and third, the circumstances which have followed from the implementation of those provisions and subsequent EU treaty alterations. As posited by George Ross:

> ... the historical circumstances and conditions of the times set limits on what is possible, just as the consequential actions themselves alter these circumstances, shaping them into something which they were not before — and perhaps creating the very limits of what can be done. (Ross 1995)

The restoring, if not advancing, of EU economic success in the late 1980s, uncertainties surrounding the collapse of the Cold War, anxieties linked with the re-unification of Germany, and the challenges posed by globalisation were influential factors in the forming and setting of the Maastricht Treaty. To transpose those different factors into agreeable and workable treaty provisions was the challenge faced by the leaders of the EU and the European Commission. A central aim of the treaty promulgation process was how to move the EU's economic mandate towards broader, federalising or state-building goals.

With hindsight, whereas certain treaty provisions have proved to be inadequate, or harboured the seeds of output failure, others have stood the test of time well in terms of performance. What undoubtedly affected the success of treaty provisions were events and circumstances post-Maastricht, three of which are particularly noteworthy. First, the general economic situation took a decisive turn for the worse, caused partly by the burdens of re-unification for Germany. Second, major parts of the European monetary system broke apart, for instance the demise of the European Monetary System (EMS) in September 1992. Third, the 1992 referenda in Denmark and France on ratifying the Maastricht Treaty indicated that public opinion on European integration had changed from being broadly supportive to being sceptical and nationalistic; not only in Denmark and France but in most of the EU. Moreover, all of the aforementioned factors were contributing factors for member states to lose enthusiasm for "European" solutions and retreat towards national remedies (Ross 1995, 14).

In this context, Dinan's contribution is valuable since the real importance of the Maastricht is to be found in what in some cases was initiated by the treaty, or codified in others, and how it shaped subsequent attempts to reform the EU. His article shows that Maastricht was not only a 'watershed' in the history of the European Union, but also the beginning of an almost continuous effort at further institutional reform of the Union's ever since. In charting this 'arc' of institutional reform since the early 1992, Dinan points to the efforts of further reform that involved the subsequent treaty changes at Amsterdam, Nice and Lisbon, each of which included further modifications to key aspects of the institutional architecture, be it the co-decision procedure, the size of the European Commission or the reform of the rotating Presidency. This 'story' is not complete without the experience of the failed Constitutional Treaty, as Dinan shows how the outcome of the negotiations in the Convention were closely linked to the developments and reforms that occurred both previously and subsequently, and how open questions still remain at this point. All this demonstrates 'the inherently untidy nature of formal institutional change in the ever-evolving EU', indicating that the process is far from finished and has, in certain respects, still to play itself out in the future.

It appears that, even twenty years after its signing, some of the key Maastricht reforms are still work in progress, with the assessment of what these changes agreed in 1992 actually mean for Europe being difficult. What can be said with greater confidence is that the calls at Maastricht for a European citizenship and the forging of a European identity have remained both vague and elusive, though they have become significantly more important in later phases of supranational integration. At the same time the highly relevant debates on the existence of a European public sphere and a European demos — relevant because they are directly linked to the creation of a shared European identity — were absent from the Maastricht Treaty. Of course, the European Union has come a long way since part of the original impetus for solidarity revolved around the European idea of a common future for the European countries. Generational change and increasing historical distance from the cataclysmic factors that formed the European idea have inevitably weakened it. Attachment to the vision of a shared European future has survived better among elites than mass publics but it has recently suffered considerable erosion even among political elites. This tendency will not be helped by the current Eurozone crisis, which has dealt a huge blow to solidarity. It has divided the creditor nations from the debtor nations and, in a peculiar sense, has created solidarity among both the creditor nations and among the debtor ones thus dividing the one group from the other. This condition can, potentially aggravate the 'input' legitimacy problem indicated by Fritz Scharpf (2003).

Joseph Weiler's piece in this volume addresses the question of legitimacy head-on, identifying the weaknesses of both 'input' and 'output' legitimacy: input legitimacy is lacking in a European Union that, according to Weiler, 'did not have democracy in its DNA' and were little or no political accountability is attached to the performance of the main institutions (including the European Parliament). Output legitimacy — the provision of prosperity, stability and security — is also weak, and in the context of the current crisis demonstrates the fragility of the European construction. 'The worst way to legitimate a war is to lose it', and the EU, in not winning against the attacks on the Eurozone, is facing failure and hence delegitimation. Weiler adds a third type of legitimacy, that of political messianism to the mix. This involves the original aspirations of the founding fathers and subsequent elites to put the past behind them and work towards a better future, a 'promised land'. This promise of future reconciliation, of peace and prosperity has lost its appeal in more recent times, partly because of the actual success of integration, and partly because of changing societal attitudes. But Weiler also points to a deeper problem with this type of legitimation which inevitably wanes as the ultimate goal keeps receding into the distance.

His conclusion is that the solution to the EU's legitimacy crisis will have to come from within the member states: 'it will be national parliaments, national judiciaries, national media and, yes, national governments who will have to lend their legitimacy to a solution which inevitably will involve yet a higher degree of integration'. In a reversal of Milward's 'European rescue of the nation state', it will have to be member states rescuing the European Union in order to overcome the crisis facing the Union today.

Clearly, the place of the Maastricht Treaty in the history of European integration will continue to generate debate in years to come. With the benefit of hindsight the strengths and weaknesses of the treaty will tend to depend very much on the perspective of the viewer — something illustrated nicely in this volume. If EMU was indeed the distinguishing feature of the treaty, its legacy might well be judged tainted. Even if the outcome of the ongoing Eurozone crisis are not entirely apparent, it is more than an economic or financial crisis since, whatever happens, there will be profound repercussions for the confidence of European citizens in European integration generally and the EU more specifically, the Union's long-term economic competitiveness and its international standing. Indeed, in the face of the current crisis, the same macro-question asked prior to the Maastricht Treaty — what kind of Union do we want? — is still being asked today.

When seen from an institutional perspective, the Maastricht Treaty could be lauded for its attempts to strengthen the role of the European Parliament, to engage citizens and the emergence of the European Council as an increasingly influential 'non-institution' (until the Lisbon Treaty). Nevertheless, the intergovernmental conference preceding the Maastricht Treaty recognised that issues surrounding institutional reform were long-term agenda items and even provided for a further intergovernmental conference to discuss institution reform prior to any further rounds of enlargement. A more critical reading of the treaty's legacy might suggest that if it marked two steps forward, there was at least one step back: the growing public alienation from the EU and a series of negative referendum results on not only the Maastricht Treaty, but also subsequent ones, alongside a series of national 'opt-outs' in key policy areas. The degree to which the publics' enthusiasm for European integration or their trust in the Union's institutions, can be regained, remains the key challenge for the future.

References

European Commission, Eurobarometer 73, November 2010.
Lavenex, S., and W. Wallace. 2006. Shifting up and out: the foreign policy of European immigration control. *West European Politics* 29, no. 2: 329–50.
Ross, G. 1995. *Jacques Delors and European integration*. Cambridge: Polity Press.
Scharpf, F. 2003. Problem-solving, effectiveness and democratic accountability in the EU, *MPIFG Working Papers* — an electronic source.

Still Rooted in Maastricht: EU External Relations as a 'Third-generation Hybrid'

MICHAEL SMITH

Department of Politics, History and International Relations, Loughborough University, Loughborough, UK

ABSTRACT This article argues that EU external relations since the Maastricht Treaty have constituted the Union as a hybrid international actor, reflecting a number of tensions built into the roots of the treaty. These tensions — reflected in the international roles and status of the EU — arise from the logics expressed in institutions and policies, and the ways in which those logics interact with each other when confronted with situations in which diplomatic, economic and security concerns are entangled. The result is that the EU has an ambiguous relationship to issues of European and world order. Since Maastricht, successive grafts in treaties and other forms have added elements to the EU's external relations, but have not resolved the basic issues and ambiguities attending hybridity. The article explores these issues and ambiguities and relates them to four key roles claimed by the EU in the world arena: those of market actor, security actor, diplomatic actor and normative actor.

Introduction

The Maastricht Treaty (TEU — Treaty on the European Union) represents a key juncture in the development of European Union (EU) external relations. It not only introduced the Common Foreign and Security Policy (CFSP) to the institutional architecture of the Union, but also laid the first foundations for what later became the European Security and Defence Policy (ESDP). Additionally, it introduced to the EU framework a number of policy areas (for example, the 'third pillar' of Justice and Home Affairs and more specific policy areas such as environmental policy) that have come to have major external relations dimensions in the world arena of the early twenty-first century.

The treaty, though, did more than this. It institutionalised and embedded in the EU framework a hybrid structure of external relations which has fundamentally conditioned all subsequent attempts to establish an integrated EU 'foreign policy', and which is visible in the post-Lisbon era as much as it was in the early 1990s. By 'hybrid' in the context of this article I mean a political, institutional and legal structure derived from heterogeneous sources, or composed of elements of different or incongruous kinds.[1] This structure was not created simply by the TEU — it drew upon and consolidated tendencies that were apparent in some cases from the 1970s onwards — but the treaty was a crucial formative moment in the process of hybridisation, since it crystallised and cemented in a number of key assumptions and sets of preferences.

These assumptions and preferences were partly political — that is to say, they were rooted in the aims and activities of political actors within the EU context (and more specifically, within the negotiating context for the treaty itself). As Andrew Moravcsik has argued, the TEU is one of a series of intergovernmental bargains that have incrementally increased the scope and depth of coordination between member states and European institutions in the field of external relations (Moravcsik 1993, 1998). Others have argued equally powerfully that account needs to be taken of a range of other actors in the negotiating process, and of the effect of institutional engagement itself in generating treaty change for the external relations domain (Smith 2003). Leaving aside the differences of approach and methodology, all would agree that political influences in EU external relations have strong elements of hybridity as defined above, arising from the operation of a 'mixed actor system' and reflecting heterogeneity of political influences. Not surprisingly, this political hybridity was reflected in the TEU's institutional provisions for external relations, and also expressed what might be described as the competing cultures of external relations emanating not just from member states but also from the European institutions and from different areas within them.

In terms of the definition given above, it is thus clear that on the one hand the framework set out in the TEU reflected heterogeneous sources, and on the other it consisted of different and what might be seen as 'incongruous' elements. It is also important to be aware that it reflects a number of co-existing logics in the European integration process (Smith 2009). On the one hand, there is the logic of integration, in which the developing architecture of external relations is a key contribution to the development of the EU itself; in other words, the process through which external activity and presence contributes to the legitimacy and consolidation of the European construction, and is also subject to the progress or the tribulations of integration. At the same time, a different logic takes effect — that of external structure, and the opportunities and constraints that it creates, whereby the evolution of the world arena provides openings or limits for the assertion of a specifically 'European' form of actorness. Finally, it is important to recognise the operation of a third logic, which conditions and is conditioned by the first two — the logic of European identity and the search for a 'certain idea of Europe' in and through external relations, which has been a powerful driver of EU engagement in the world arena.

The two tendencies identified so far — the growth of hybridity and the operation of powerful and intersecting logics in the development of EU external relations — mean that the EU occupies an essentially ambiguous position on key questions of world order. As I have argued elsewhere (Smith 2007), there are important contradictions and tensions in the EU's approach to European order (where it can be seen as possessing formidable structural and ideational power) and the broader world order (where it can be seen as embodying structural and procedural ambiguities that limit its potential and its actual impact). These ambiguities are also apparent in the EU's approach to new centres of power and 'strategic partners' (or rivals) in the changing world arena of the twenty-first century.

Much of the literature produced on the subject of 'European foreign policy' and EU external relations over the past twenty years reflects a series of attempts to wrestle with the coexisting logics shaping EU external policies, the implications of the consequent hybridity and the ambiguities of the EU's role in the world arena (see, for example, White 2001; Keukeleire and MacNaughtan 2008; Hill and Smith 2005, 2011; Smith 2002; Smith 2008; Peterson and Sjursen 1998; Bretherton and Vogler 2006; Bickerton 2011a, b; Youngs 2010). This is not the place for a detailed review of this literature, which has come to be one of the most dynamic areas in the study of the EU, but it is important to the argument in this article that no treatment has yet managed entirely to square the circle constituted by these three intersecting forces — the debates continue, and this article is a further attempt to contribute to them. The article itself explores the problem in three stages. First, it identifies the roots of the problem of hybridity and its embodiment in the TEU. Second, it analyses the ways in which successive grafts onto the root stock of the TEU, mainly but not only in the treaties of Amsterdam, Nice and Lisbon, have added to the problem of hybridity and extended it into new areas of external policy, creating what I term a 'third-generation hybrid'. Third, it assesses the implications of the underlying hybridity for the EU's roles in the world arena, and specifically for four types of role: the EU as a market actor, as a security actor, as a diplomatic actor and as a normative actor. The article concludes that the EU has learned to live with hybridity — that it is in fact fundamental to the EU's international existence — but that current conditions in the world arena impose particular strains and pose particular challenges for the EU's hybrid external relations system.

Maastricht: The Root Stock

A sense of context is vital to understanding how hybridity became a central component of the Maastricht Treaty. The end of the Cold War created new uncertainties and new challenges even as it seemed to open up new opportunities for the European project (Laffan, O'Donnell, and Smith 2000). The European Community (EC) stood tall in the confusion of the early 1990s as a stable 'community of law' reflecting the twin assets of democracy and prosperity; not surprisingly, the new or newly liberated states of central and eastern Europe looked upon it as the potential guarantor of these three sought-after qualities — stability, democracy and prosperity — and their view was shared by others such as the United States. It appeared in terms of our earlier discussion that the internal logic of integration through the Single Market and other channels was positive, that the logic of the external opportunity structure was equally positive, and that in a continent where identities were contested and confused, the EC could provide an ideational anchor for those searching for a new European vocation.

The negotiations for the TEU, though, revealed something else. Although all three of the surrounding logics pointed in a positive direction, this was not enough to dictate a dramatic or transformational outcome for the Treaty (Laursen and Vanhoonacker 1992). The result was, as previously noted, the institutionalisation of hybridity. The Union framework was not a 'tree' but a 'temple', with three apparently distinct pillars under a common roof and a multiplicity of modes of policy-making, many of them retaining a key role for the member states. In external relations, this was especially apparent; trade policy was firmly in 'pillar one' and subject to the 'Community method', CFSP in 'pillar two' with an essentially intergovernmental character, JHA (with its major potential resonances for European order) in 'pillar three' with a strong intergovernmental element, and a significant number of major policy areas such as development poised uncomfortably somewhere in between. The treaty, that is to say, not only institutionalised hybridity, it actually magnified it by increasing the scope of the areas in which it could be found, and by linking this to the development of the fundamental integration project in a new and demanding way.

The implications of this situation were not hard to discern, especially given the key challenges to which the EU was exposed even before the treaty came into operation in 1993. The Gulf conflict of 1990–1991 showed the problems faced by the soon-to-be Union in the context of the 'new world order' and the tension between member state foreign policies and a collective European stance, whilst the breakdown of former Yugoslavia showed the tensions built into the foundations of the new European institutional architecture even whilst the treaty itself was being ratified and brought into operation. At the same time, the problems attending a collective European stance in the Uruguay Round of trade negotiations (for example in the negotiations relating to agriculture or to the 'cultural exception'), and the linked consideration of issues relating to a changing global economic order, showed that even in the more long established areas of Community competence and in areas where the Europeans collectively held a substantial amount of institutional and resource power, there were problems to be confronted (Woolcock 1993; Woolcock and Hodges 1996). The period of negotiation, ratification and implementation of the TEU was one in which the external opportunity structure for the nascent Union was 'open' if confused, but in which issues around the nature and scope of integration in external policy and the nature and limits of a common European consciousness remained unresolved.

As a result of this rather painful germination and rooting process, the strengths and weaknesses of the Maastricht bargain on external relations were being questioned even before the treaty came into operation. Once it was in effect, the debates did not subside, and the problems of collective action, resources and impact that were exposed in the early 1990s formed part of the context for the Reflection Group established in 1995. Most significantly, though, in terms of the argument here, there was no suggestion that the treaty should be uprooted or abandoned; rather, the debate was about how it might be refined and strengthened especially in the operational sense. The roots were established — the question was how the hybrid structures that had been set up could be made to work more effectively and coherently.

The Negotiation of Hybridity: From Amsterdam to Lisbon

The decade between the preparations for the Amsterdam Treaty and the negotiation of the Lisbon Treaty was a constant if punctuated effort to grapple with the implications of the hybrid external relations structures that had emerged from the early 1990s. It was argued earlier that these structures brought together both well-established areas of external relations and novel domains of external activity, and that the three-pillar structure embodied in the TEU constituted in a very direct sense the institutionalisation of hybridity. Here, I focus on three sets of efforts to negotiate this set of structures, and on a further set of forces that strongly shaped the context in which these efforts took place.

The first explicit attempt to work through the implications of the hybrid structures established in the TEU was the IGC of 1995–1997, which led to the Amsterdam Treaty. As has been well documented, these negotiations led to what was almost a set-piece confrontation between those espousing a 'maximalist' and a 'minimalist' version of further development — the former stressing the need for further transfers of activities and powers to the EU level, the latter emphasising the retention of a strong if not central role for member states (Westlake 1998). The treaty itself embodied what at the time appeared to be an uneasy compromise between these two positions, with the consolidation of the resource base for CFSP, the establishment of the position of High Representative, the introduction of the potential for closer cooperation and for some element of qualified majority voting in CFSP, and the potential for absorption of the Western European Union (WEU) into the Union structures. Alongside this, the scope of the Common Commercial Policy in 'pillar 1' was extended subject to certain restrictions, and the attempt to achieve greater coherence of policy between the different pillars of the Maastricht structure was continued. This was in many ways an incremental set of developments, working on the areas of tension identified in the existing structures but not placing the structures themselves into question, and with the negotiators playing the role of 'blind watchmakers' as argued by Martin Westlake (2008, chapter 2). Even the British, who constituted the core of the 'minimalist' camp within the negotiations, did not suggest that the structures should be uprooted and re-planted — rather, they suggested that the equivalent of a bit of trimming and weeding would be sufficient, given the relatively recent growth in the structure itself.

The point about Amsterdam, though, as of the Nice Treaty that followed in 2000, was that this was not just incremental growth and extension. The treaty rather grafted into the Maastricht root-stock a set of new qualities and characteristics, with the aim of making the whole structure more stable and sustainable. By doing so, both Maastricht and Nice created the potential for further growth and development into new and perhaps unanticipated areas — especially in the context of new external challenges and opportunities. Nowhere was this more apparent than in the Treaty of Nice, which was explicitly shaped by the external experiences of former Yugoslavia and the external challenge of dealing with the implications of enlargement to central and eastern Europe. The development of the European Security and Defence Policy after the St Malo meeting between France and the UK in 1998, followed by the elaboration of new structures for the management of security issues in the wake of the Kosovo conflict of 1999, created new dimensions for the conduct of 'European foreign policy' (Howorth 2000, 2007). At the same time, the demands of enlargement lent new urgency to the achievement of consistency across a wide range of other external policy issues, and the continuing pressures of commercial policy in a partly globalised world arena meant that further extension of the Common Commercial Policy was a high priority.

By the end of the 1990s, it could thus be argued that substantial progress had been made in extending and integrating key areas of EU external relations. This had been achieved not simply through the negotiation and renegotiation of treaty provisions, which often followed developments in the operational area rather than initiating them. Rather, it had been developed on the basis of successive grafts onto the structure of EU external relations established initially at Maastricht in 1991–1992. The structure was still there — but it had had a number of new instruments and attributes grafted onto it, which had changed both the appearance of the structure, and more importantly the dynamics of its operation. By the early part of the twenty-first century, at least part of the 'maximalist' agenda from Amsterdam had been achieved, and more was to follow, by a process of evolution rather than revolution, without disturbing the roots laid down at Maastricht.

This remains an accurate description of what has been achieved in the structures of EU external relations, even after the abortive Constitutional Treaty and the Lisbon Treaty. Despite the grand ambitions of some for the development of a unified EU foreign policy, what has resulted from nearly a decade of negotiation and ratification (or non-ratification) remains recognisably a structure rooted in Maastricht. Although the pillar structure in external relations has in principle been abolished, it still exists in many areas, and the practices of policy-making are strongly influenced by it. Further grafting operations have produced the role of High Representative for Foreign and Security Policy/Vice-President of the Commission

(HRVP), which in many ways crystallises the underlying hybridity of CFSP in particular, but adds to it responsibilities in security and defence policy and development policy which are not often found in national diplomatic services. Major areas of external relations such as trade and investment, not to mention international monetary policy for at least the Eurozone states, remain subject to distinctive policy-making processes, whilst areas such as development policy in general, environmental policy and others remain stubbornly mixed in formal allocations of competences and in informal policy-making processes. Financial, human and institutional resources are as much a focus for contestation as they are for coordination, although it is tempting sometimes to overstate the contestation that does take place, and to miss the mass of everyday coordination processes that take place.

My point is a simple one, but one that requires further argumentation and exemplification: the development of the structures, expectations and practices surrounding the broad domain of EU external relations is still rooted in the Maastricht Treaty, which after twenty years remains the root-stock of the EU's role(s) in the world arena. This root-stock has been the subject of almost continuous grafting processes, most obviously through the negotiation of successive treaty provisions for a wide variety of areas in EU external relations These negotiations have fallen into two major periods, those of Amsterdam and Nice and of the Constitutional Treaty and Lisbon. It is thus appropriate to see the current framework for EU external relations as representing a 'third-generation' hybrid'. Equally obviously, over the twenty-year period, the negotiation (formal and informal) of EU external relations institutions and practices has been affected continuously by the evolution of the external opportunities and constraints generated by the world arena. And finally, the successive graftings and re-graftings to which EU external relations have been subject must be seen in the light of a continuous search for elements of European identity. So the three logics of development in EU external relations to which I drew attention earlier have existed in a continuous and fluctuating balance, surrounding the development of EU external relations and permeating its constant re-negotiation. In the next part of the article, I will pursue this argument further, by exploring the ways in which hybridity has shaped the development of the EU's roles in four areas: as a market actor, a security actor, a diplomatic actor and a normative actor.

The EU's Roles in the World Arena

As Ole Elgström and myself have pointed out (Elgström and Smith 2006, introduction; see also Aggestam 2008; Knodt and Princen 2003), the analysis of the EU's roles in the world arena rests on a combination of material and ideational factors. On the one hand, material factors such as institutions, resources and operational processes form an indispensable part of what is possible. On the other hand, ideational factors such as images, expectations and discourses of EU international action are indispensable to an understanding of the ways in which role conceptions are formed and EU actions are 'received' in the world arena. The combination of these factors enables us to penetrate not only the processes by which understandings of role(s) are shaped and elaborated, but also the ways in which roles are performed and evaluated within and outside the EU. The concept of role thus provides us with a way of furthering the argument in this article, by exploring the ways in which the logics of EU external action and the hybridity of the structures set up and elaborated since Maastricht feed into specific domains of EU activity. As noted above, four such domains will be explored here, with an emphasis not only on the dominant roles in each area but also on some of the tensions within each area that further reflect the impact of hybridity.

The first of these is the domain of the EU as a market actor. Since the inception of the European Coal and Steel Community and the European Economic Community in the 1950s, this has been the core of the EU's international presence and external activity. The regulation of the European internal market and the projection of the EC's market power were for many years almost the entirety of its international activity, with add-ons from development policy still strongly affected by the exercise of market power and the granting of market access. The legal and institutional base for this lay in the Common Commercial Policy and its grant of extensive competence to the Community, with the Commission as a powerful agent of international commercial action in defence of promotion of the Community interest. With the development of new dimensions of external commercial policy, especially from the 1980s onwards, it was clear that there would be pressure to extend the reach of the CCP, for example into trade in services, the treatment of intellectual property issues and the handling of regulatory matters at the global or the regional level (Smith 2004).

The process of extension of the CCP, however, was not trouble-free. During the 1990s, the pressures created by the pursuit of the EC's Single Market Programme combined with the extension of global trade negotiations into new areas, to create the demand for a more 'complete' CCP. This was met with resistance — or at least questioning — by a number of member states, who were suspicious of the ways in which their interests might be handled in areas such as services (financial, audio-visual and others) or intellectual property. The politicisation of global trade negotiations through links with human rights or environmental issues during the 1990s also posed its own set of challenges. As a result, the question 'who speaks for Europe?' in commercial policy remained open, and the EU could be presented as a 'conflicted trade power' (Meunier and Nicolaïdis 1999, 2006).

The net result of this set of intersecting pressures was paradoxical. At one level there was a progressive 'completion' of the CCP, which might be seen also as a progressive reduction in the level of hybridity in EU external commercial policy. Through the 1990s, the extension of Community competence into areas such as trade in services and intellectual property was steady and broadly uncontested, whilst the Lisbon Treaty effectively rubber-stamped the extension of the CCP to all matters involving external commerce and for good measure also gave competence for the first time in international investment policy (art. 207 TFEU). It might be concluded that this effectively eliminated any remaining aspects of hybridity in the pursuit of external commercial policy, but such a conclusion would be misleading. The EU is undoubtedly a leading market power in the global arena (Damro 2012; Woolcock 2011), but it is still not a completely unified one. The persistence of commercial diplomacy at the level of EU member states is one area in which this remaining hybridity can be glimpsed; at the same time, the continuing development of the linkages and transnational forces characterising globalisation means that the CCP in itself must be pursued in the context of the internal integration process as well as coexisting and often contending processes of regionalisation, securitisation and broader politicisation. As we shall see shortly, this has profound implications for some of the other roles the EU has acquired in the world arena.

One of these other roles — and arguably the one with the most marked development during the twenty years since the TEU — is that of the EU as security actor. This is not to argue that the European integration process before Maastricht was not at least indirectly a process with security implications; rather, it is to note as many others have done that it was at Maastricht that security policy became an essential part of the way in which the European integration process was constituted and understood by those involved in it (Howorth 2007; Hyde-Price 2006, 2007; Nuttall 2000). In the 20 years since then, the framing of what has become the European Security and Defence Policy has been a continuous process and one with major implications for the EU's role in the world arena.

Unlike the EU's role as a market (especially commercial) actor, where the notion of exclusive Community competence was established at an early stage, its development as a security actor has from the outset been explicitly and indelibly marked by high levels of hybridity. The ESDP institutions remain intergovernmental rather than supranational, the resources and specifically the military capabilities on which operations rest are controlled at the national level in member states, and the context in which it operates is permeated by vital national interests, especially those of the major EU member states. Nonetheless, the development of military planning and (for example) crisis management procedures at the EU level have proceeded inexorably during the past decade at least, resulting in a decidedly mixed picture both at the level of overall strategic concerns and at the level of operations. Not only this, but interaction with the other key European military organisation, the North Atlantic Treaty Organisation (NATO) has been elaborated and sets of rules have been developed in the cause of managing that element of hybridity — which of course also has a strong transatlantic dimension (Rees 2011a).

The development of the ESDP has thus led to a series of institutional and operational innovations in the cause of managing hybridity and containing the potential problems that lie in the continuing dominance of national military structures and of particular member states. But of course this is not the whole of the story about the EU as a security actor. The changing nature of security challenges in the world arena has led away from purely or even predominantly military structures, and towards an increasingly mixed picture in which national and transnational forces with both military and civilian 'faces' are heavily mutually engaged (Howorth 2011; Rees 2011b). At its simplest, this situation means that the 'third pillar' of Justice and Home Affairs established at Maastricht (and subsequently at least partly absorbed into the 'first pillar') has become increasingly relevant to the EU's external relations. Not only this, but the demands posed by new and newly securitised areas of international activity have created further pressures to add to the EU's role as security actor: the increasing linkages between 'traditional' security and challenges such as those of terrorism, the environment, energy and human rights have become apparent and have challenged the EU to move beyond the initial assumption that conventional military structures might be displaced from the national to the European level. Indeed, it might be argued that ESDP in this 'conventional' sense has stalled since the mid-2000s, but that the other and arguably more challenging aspects of security in the contemporary era have become the dominant focus of EU activities.

The new security challenges of the post-Cold War and post-Maastricht eras have thus been a key factor driving the development of hybridity in the EU's security and defence policies, and in securitising ever-increasing areas of the European integration process. The problems thus created are not simply confined to a small Brussels elite of 'securocrats'; increasingly they have attracted the attention of the European Parliament and of a wide variety of pressure groups and non-governmental organisations (NGOs). The notion in the Maastricht Treaty that there would be a kind of deliberative process through which the CFSP would develop gradually into a common defence policy and then in the fullness of time into a 'common defence' has been continuously challenged since the very time at which the Treaty was being negotiated, with former Yugoslavia, '9/11' and the Arab Spring of 2011 as key punctuation marks (Allen 2012, forthcoming). As a result, treaty provisions have been supplemented — and perhaps transcended — by fixes for immediate challenges and responses to external demands. At many points, these have also come into conflict with the EU's continuing self-assessment as a 'force for good' and a 'civilian power' (see below), thus providing further evidence for the policy impact of hybridity in the EU's security policy structures. This stands as a rather dramatic example of the ways in which the three logics of EU external relations — internal integration, external challenge and opportunity, and the search for identity — can come together and shape the evolution of the EU's hybrid policy structures.

Implicit in the discussion above has been an understanding about development in another key area of the EU's international role(s): that of the EU as a diplomatic actor. In some ways, this was the key to the Maastricht Treaty provisions on the CFSP: as a development of the existing European Political Cooperation (EPC) process, the CFSP was implicitly conceived as a set of provisions for more effective diplomatic coordination among the member states. As such, it was of course also a key response to the challenges of the post-Cold War era, as seen in 1991–1992. The mechanisms that were set up or consolidated at Maastricht were thus hybrid from the outset, given that one of their key aims was the more effective accommodation and coordination of member state positions; we have already noted the constraints placed on the development of 'supranational' mechanisms such as majority voting or the power of initiative for the Commission in this area. Not for nothing did Christopher Hill and William Wallace refer to the 'hydra of European foreign policy' as it had developed by the mid-1990s, referring thereby to its 'mixed system of common actions, shared competences, joint declarations and transgovernmental cooperation' (1996, 3). The key roles were to be played by national foreign ministers and by national diplomatic representatives in third capitals, and also by the rotating presidency of the Council of Ministers (Nuttall 2000; Smith 2001), but within a setting where their interactions in themselves might generate new forms, levels and understandings of cooperation.

This essentially evolutionary approach to the development of the EU as a diplomatic actor was subject to challenge from the outset, but there were powerful forces lined up to defend it. As noted earlier, the pressure to complete the unfinished business of the TEU on such matters as the resources available to the CFSP, the provision of continuity in coordination and the development of a 'European' diplomatic presence made itself felt in the Amsterdam Treaty especially, and led to rapid evolution in the late 1990s. The establishment of the office of High Representative for the CFSP, and its occupation by Javier Solana, was a major element in raising the profile of this area of diplomatic coordination, and the division of labour between Solana and Chris Patten as Commissioner for External Relations the subject of much analysis (Allen 2012, forthcoming). From the perspective of the argument here, this is strong evidence of the persistence (but also of the changing nature and impact) of hybridity in the EU's role as diplomatic actor. Not only in the relationship between EU-level diplomacy and national diplomacy, but also in the division of labour between 'intergovernmental' and 'supranational' elements of the policy structures in Brussels itself, there was a distinctive set of tensions and intersections.

This element of hybridity has if anything become more prominent since the late 1990s. Most obviously, the Lisbon Treaty had as one of its key elements the transformation of EU external action, through the creation of a new set of services and internal roles. The office of High Representative was bolstered in such a way as to make it effectively something in between the head of a diplomatic service and a foreign minister, and to make an organic link between the new European External Action Service (EEAS) and the Commission's services through the HR's role also as Vice-President of the Commission. The new office of President of the European Council was also given diplomatic functions, in the shape of an obligation to ensure the representation of the EU externally and at its level (i.e., in relations with heads of state and government both inside and outside the EU). The rotating presidency of the Council, at least in diplomatic matters, was to become rather less prominent but nonetheless to operate in coordination with the EEAS and the HRVP (Duke 2009; Joint Study 2010).

This novel set of relationships within the EU's external relations structures is of course still in its bedding-in period. Without entering into a detailed analysis of the problems that emerged during the first year of operation of the EEAS, it is important here to note that the Lisbon Treaty in fact further entrenched hybridity — albeit in a distinctive form — within the EU's external relations structures. The HRVP was in some ways the encapsulation of this and of the problems it could create; an overloaded job description, a demanding policy agenda and the pressure of establishing a diplomatic service from scratch, drawing upon personnel from the Commission, the Council Secretariat and national diplomatic services, would have taxed anybody inserted into this post (Balfour, Bailes, and Kenna 2012; Hemra, Raines, and Whitman 2011; Lehne 2011). When to this is added the changing nature of diplomacy itself — with increasing attention to transnational processes, to the eruption and accommodation of new quasi-diplomatic actors and to the linkages between areas such as commercial policy, environment, energy, development and security — then the challenge could be seen as insuperable (Hocking and Smith 2011; see also Emerson *et al.* 2011 on specific ways in which this relates to the representation of the EU externally). The development of rules and conventions for handling relations between the EEAS and other Brussels services has been a major preoccupation, and has consumed much energy, quite apart from the development of new ways of dealing with member states, some of whom have high expectations of the EEAS and others of which harbour deep suspicions. This could be seen as a disabling manifestation of hybridity, and of the three logics to which I have drawn attention in this article; but the point needs to be made that in many ways these needs for adjustment and innovation have been faced by all diplomatic services, not just by the Brussels machinery.

The fourth role for the EU in its external relations to be examined here is in some ways different from the others examined so far. Whilst these dealt with (admittedly broad and changing) areas of external activity, the notion of the EU as a normative actor poses distinctive questions. In some ways at least, these questions pervade the other three areas we have explored, because they relate to the EU's self-identification as a 'different' form of power in the world arena. This self-identification has not only been powerful as an influence on policy discourses — it has also attracted a large and growing number of scholars to the field (for example, Manners 2002, 2006; Scheipers and Sicurelli 2007; Whitman 2011). It shares with the areas explored above the fact that it became more explicit and more formalised in the Maastricht Treaty, which set out for the first time a set of principles on which EU external action was to be based. These principles embodied multilateralism, development, the peaceful handing of disputes and a range of other normative positions. They were not of course unheralded or unprecedented, since the notion of the EC as a 'civilian power' with distinctive approaches to international issues had been advanced since the 1970s. The principles were further developed in the Amsterdam Treaty, which formally incorporated the so-called 'Petersberg tasks' dealing with conflict resolution, peace-keeping, peace-building and the like, and further elaborated during the late 1990s and 2000s with reference to areas such as democratisation, human rights, good governance and associated normative concerns.

From this brief and crude outline, it might be assumed that 'normative power' is part of the essence of the EU, and that it is therefore constitutive of the European integration process. To paraphrase Ian Manners (2002), the EU is a normative actor not only because of what it does, but also because of what it is — a shining example of the norms that it seeks to propagate in the wider world arena. It might also be contended, however, that the focus on normative concerns is (a) not as distinctive as it appears, given that many major actors might claim to be 'normative powers' in one way or another; and (b) little more than a rationalisation of the fact that the Europeans are relatively weak and unable to wield other types of power in the world arena (see for example Kagan 2003). In penetrating this set of contending arguments, the notion of hybridity is helpful, since it gives us some clues as to the limits of 'normative power Europe' as well as to the strength of this conception.

The fact is that the EU is a normative hybrid as well as a hybrid in terms of institutions and political processes. What does this mean? One dimension of the matter is that whilst there is a normative layer at the EU level consisting of elements to which all EU member states subscribe (and by implication their publics as well), this layer is uneven and sometimes remarkably 'thin'. Thus, all relevant actors in the EU might subscribe (as they do) to the abolition of the death penalty, but this is qualified either by other EU norms (for example, stability and a market economy) or by material considerations to do with commercial advantage. Equally, all relevant actors in the EU subscribe to norms of multilateralism in global governance, to such an extent that the EU might be described as a compulsive multilateralist (Smith 2012, forthcoming), but these are qualified and can be marginalised by the EU's material interests in commercial advantage or in 'trade defence'. The tension between the EU as 'market power' and the EU as 'normative power' is clear in such cases, but parallel tensions can and do exist in respect of the EU's role as a security actor and as a diplomatic actor.

Whilst this version of hybridity is distinct from those encountered in the EU's roles as market actor, security actor and diplomatic actor, it clearly emanates from at least some of the same roots as those other forms — and of course it intersects with them and coexists with them at many points. The explicit statements of principle in the Maastricht, Amsterdam and successive treaties — synthesised in considerable detail in the Lisbon Treaty — form the core of the EU's self-identification as a normative power, but they come up against powerful structural and external imperatives as well as against the demands of the integration process itself in a globalised economic and security arena.

This means that rather than a set of clear-cut and distinct roles for the EU in the world arena, we are confronted with a considerable level of role confusion, reflecting at least in part the impact of the three underlying logics of EU external relations. Although in this part of the discussion I have identified four rather broad roles, it is also evident that there can be conflicts, tensions and uncertainties within the four areas: thus for example, there are tensions between the EU's role as 'liberalising' and 'protectionist' market actor, between the 'civilian' and 'martial' tendencies in security policy, between the multilateralist and unilateralist tendencies in diplomacy, and as already noted between the materialist and the ideational in the EU's self-perception as a normative power. This is an international actor — to put it crudely — that at certain key points either forgets or cannot articulate its script, or seems to speak with a forked tongue. Such a tendency is a reflection of the demands of the integration process, the fluctuating challenges and opportunities produced by a rapidly changing external context and the 'thin' self-identification of the EU as a normative actor. Most importantly, for the purposes of the argument here, the tendency is rooted in successive attempts to deal with hybridity in the structures of the EU's external relations, starting with Maastricht.

Conclusion

A number of significant conclusions flow from the arguments presented here. The first is that the Maastricht 'root stock' has had a potent effect on all subsequent efforts to define and redefine the EU's external relations. This is not to say that all subsequent efforts have been prisoners of the TEU, but it is to say that those efforts have been working within and trying to grapple with a set of political, institutional and cultural constraints that were embedded in and by the Maastricht Treaty.

A second and linked conclusion is that there have been successive grafts onto the Maastricht root stock, and that these have created new dynamics and tensions of their own by constituting the current framework for EU external relations as a 'third-generation hybrid'. As noted earlier, each of the Amsterdam, Nice, Constitutional and Lisbon Treaties has attempted to deal with the effects of embedded hybridity in the EU's external relations, and the two key phases of negotiation and renegotiation have each added to the scope and scale of that hybridity without resolving the essential problems to which it gives rise. Partly this is because the context within which the successive treaties have been negotiated has not transcended the interaction of the three logics that lie at the core of this article. They have had to cope with the fluctuations of the integration logic, the external logic and the identity logic whilst also dealing with the intersections and interactions between them. And as noted at the outset, the treaties themselves have then fed back into the subsequent operation of these three logics to create a new context for subsequent (re)negotiation of the external relations structures.

A third conclusion is that the Maastricht root stock has proved robust and resilient in the face of radical contextual change. One reason for this is that the successive grafts noted above have contributed to a modification of (although not a reduction of) hybridity. Most notably, the 'three pillars' and the 'temple' structure that served as a compelling image of the Maastricht outcome have been changed: what we see now is like a set of three major tree trunks growing from a common root, in which the branches have become entangled so that in some areas at least it is difficult to distinguish what relates to one trunk and what to another. This is still an essentially hybrid structure, for example when compared to the image of a single tree with different branches that was also canvassed at Maastricht. The three trunks derive from the same roots, were trained to grow in different directions, but have grown together to create a complex and resistant whole, without significantly undermining the hybridity established and made explicit by Maastricht.

What further conclusions can we draw from this for the present and future of the EU's external relations? First, they are robust and vigorous and this is partly because of their hybrid nature. Second, they can be adapted to changing circumstances without losing their essentially hybrid nature, and they thus constitute a stable and persistent pattern of relations despite the fact that they exist in a different world from that of the TEU. Third, it is more profitable to work with the hybridity — to look for means of coordination and coalition-building within the structure — rather than to look for grand transformations into some purer state. The EU's external relations continue to be hard work, and continue to be criticised externally for incoherence and inconsistency, but that is part of their essence, not something to be wished away. In the current state of the integration project, challenged from within by crisis and from without by an increasingly multipolar world, and subject to problems of identity and legitimacy at several levels, it might be reassuring to reflect on the robustness and vigour of the hybrid established 20 years ago.

Note

1. This basic dictionary definition of hybridity is adopted for the purposes of the argument here, but it should be noted that there is a significant literature within Comparative Politics on the features and dynamics of hybrid regimes. See for example Diamond (2002), Wigell (2008), Brownlee (2009), Bogaards (2009), Molino (2009) and Levitsky and Way (2010). More recently, this set of approaches has been extended into consideration of issues such as peace-building: see for example the special issue of *Global Governance* (18(1), 2012) and particularly the articles by Jarstad and Belloni (2012) and Belloni (2012). The comparative politics literature focuses especially on the phenomenon of 'competitive authoritarianism' or 'defective democracy', where elements of democratic rule such as elections co-exist with a wider authoritarian structure; the peace-building literature focuses especially on related issues of 'hybrid peace governance' in political orders where contrary elements coexist and the possibility of violence is high. These approaches also raise the issue of stability — are such regimes or orders in transition, or can they be stable and persist for extended periods? The latter question will be examined with respect to the EU's external relations in the Conclusion to this article, since it is clearly significant to the argument advanced here.

References

Aggestam, L. 2008. Introduction: ethical power Europe. *International Affairs* 84, no. 1: 1–11.
Allen, D. 2012. The common foreign and security policy. In *The Oxford handbook of the European Union*, eds. E. Jones, A. Menon, and S. Weatherill, 643–59. Oxford: Oxford University Press.
Balfour, R., A. Bailes, and M. Kenna. 2012. *The European External Action Service at work: how to improve EU foreign policy*. Brussels: European Policy Centre.
Belloni, R. 2012. Hybrid peace governance. its emergence and significance. *Global Governance* 18, no. 1: 21–38.

Bickerton, C. 2011a. Towards a social theory of EU foreign and security policy. *Journal of Common Market Studies* 49, no. 1: 171–90.

Bickerton, C. 2011b. *European Union foreign policy: from effectiveness to functionality.* Basingstoke: Palgrave Macmillan.

Bogaards, M. 2009. How to classify hybrid regimes? Defective democracy and electoral authoritarianism. *Democratization* 16, no. 2: 399–423.

Bretherton, C., and J. Vogler. 2006. *The European Union as a global actor.* London: Routledge.

Brownlee, J. 2009. Portents of pluralism: how hybrid regimes affect democratic transitions. *American Journal of Political Science* 53, no. 3: 515–32.

Damro, C. 2012. Market power Europe. *Journal of European Public Policy* 19, no. 5: 682–99.

Diamond, L. 2002. Thinking about hybrid regimes. *Journal of Democracy* 13, no. 2: 21–35.

Duke, S. 2009. Providing for European-level diplomacy after Lisbon: the case of the European External Action Service. *The Hague Journal of Diplomacy* 4, no. 2: 211–33.

Elgström, O., and M. Smith. 2006. *The European Union's roles in international politics: concepts and analysis.* London: Routledge.

Emerson, M., R. Balfour, T. Corthaut, J. Wouters, P. Kaczynski, and T. Renard. 2011. *Upgrading the EU's role as global actor: institutions, law and the restructuring of European diplomacy.* Brussels: Centre for European Policy Studies.

Hemra, S., T. Raines, and R. Whitman. 2011. *A diplomatic entrepreneur: making the most of the European External Action Service.* London: Chatham House.

Hill, C., and M. Smith. 2011. *International relations and the European Union.* Oxford: Oxford University Press.

Hill, C., and M. Smith. 2005. *International relations and the European Union.* Oxford: Oxford University Press.

Hill, C., and W. Wallace. 1996. Introduction: actors and actions. In *The actors in Europe's foreign policy*, ed. C. Hill, 1–16. London: Routledge.

Hocking, B., and M. Smith. 2011. An emerging diplomatic system for the EU? Frameworks and issues. *Cuadernos Europeos de Deusto* 44, 19–43.

Howorth, J. 2000. *European security and defence. the ultimate challenge?* Chaillot paper no. 43. Paris: EU Institute for Security Studies.

Howorth, J. 2007. *Security and defence policy in the European Union.* Basingstoke: Palgrave Macmillan.

Howorth, J. 2011. The EU's security and defence policy: towards a strategic approach. In *International relations and the European Union*, eds. C. Hill and M. Smith, 2nd edn., 197–225. Oxford: Oxford University Press.

Hyde-Price, A. 2006. Normative power Europe: a realist critique. *Journal of European Public Policy* 31, no. 2: 217–34.

Hyde-Price, A. 2007. *European security in the twenty-first century: the challenge of multipolarity.* London: Routledge.

Jarstad, A., and R. Belloni. 2012. Introducing hybrid peace governance. impact and prospects of liberal peacemaking. *Global Governance* 18, no. 1: 1–6.

Joint Study. 2010. *The Treaty of Lisbon: a second look at the institutional innovations.* Brussels: CEPS/Egmont/EPC.

Kagan, R. 2003. *Of Paradise and Power: America and Europe in the New World Order.* New York: Knopf.

Keukeleire, S., and J. MacNaughtan. 2008. *The foreign policy of the European Union.* Basingstoke: Palgrave Macmillan.

Knodt, M., and S. Princen. 2003. *Understanding the European Union's external relations.* London: Routledge.

Laffan, B., R. O'Donnell, and M. Smith. 2000. *Europe's experimental union.* London: Routledge.

Laursen, F., and S. Vanhoonacker. 1992. *The Intergovernmental Conference on Political Union: institutional reforms, new policies and international identity of the European Community.* Maastricht: European Institute of Public Administration.

Lehne, S. 2011. *More action, better service: how to strengthen the European External Action Service.* Brussels: Carnegie Europe.

Levitsky, S., and L. Way. 2010. *Competitive authoritarianism: hybrid regimes after the Cold War.* Cambridge: Cambridge University Press.

Manners, I. 2002. Normative power Europe: a contradiction in terms? *Journal of Common Market Studies* 40, no. 2: 235–58.
Manners, I. 2006. Normative power Europe reconsidered: beyond the crossroads. *Journal of European Public Policy* 13, no. 2: 182–99.
Meunier, S., and K. Nicolaïdis. 1999. Who speaks for Europe? The delegation of trade authority in the EU. *Journal of Common Market Studies* 37, no. 3: 477–501.
Meunier, S., and K. Nicolaïdis. 2006. The European Union as a conflicted trade power. *Journal of European Public Policy* 13, no. 6: 906–25.
Molino, L. 2009. Are there hybrid regimes? Or are they just an optical illusion? *European Political Science Review* 1, no. 2: 273–96.
Moravcsik, A. 1993. Preferences and power in the European Community: a liberal intergovernmentalist approach. *Journal of Common Market Studies* 31, no. 4: 473–524.
Moravcsik, A. 1998. *The choice for Europe: social purpose and state power from Messina to Maastricht*. Ithaca, NY: Cornell University Press.
Nuttall, S. 2000. *European foreign policy*. Oxford: Oxford University Press.
Peterson, J., and H. Sjursen. 1998. *A common foreign policy for Europe? Competing visions of the CFSP*. London: Routledge.
Rees, W. 2011a. *The US–EU security relationship*. Basingstoke: Palgrave Macmillan.
Rees, W. 2011b. The external face of internal security. In *International relations and the European Union*, eds. C. Hill and M. Smith, 2nd edn., 226–45. Oxford: Oxford University Press.
Scheipers, S., and D. Sicurelli. 2007. Normative power Europe: a credible utopia? *Journal of Common Market Studies* 45, no. 2: 435–57.
Smith, H. 2002. *European Union foreign policy: what it is and what it does*. London: Pluto Press.
Smith, K. 2008. *European Union foreign policy in a changing world*. Cambridge: Polity Press.
Smith, M. 2001. European foreign and security policy. In *Governing the European Union*, ed. S. Bromley, 255–86. London: Sage.
Smith, M. 2004. The European Union as a trade policy actor. In B. Hocking and S. McGuire, 2nd edn., 289–303. London: Routledge.
Smith, M. 2007. The European Union and international order: European and global dimensions. *European Foreign Affairs Review* 12, no. 4: 437–56.
Smith, M. 2009. Between "soft power" and a hard place. European Union foreign and security policy between the Islamic world and the United States. *International Politics* 46, no. 5: 596–615.
Smith, M. 2012. The EU, the US and China: strategic engagement, political commitment and diplomatic interaction in multilateral arenas. In *China, the EU and the US: partners and competitors*, ed. J. Men. Cheltenham: Edward Elgar.
Smith, M.E. 2003. *Europe's foreign and security policy: the institutionalization of cooperation*. Cambridge: Cambridge University Press.
Westlake, M. 1998. *The European Union beyond Amsterdam: new concepts of European integration*. London: Routledge.
White, B. 2001. *Understanding European foreign policy*. Basingstoke: Palgrave.
Whitman, R. 2011. *Normative power Europe: empirical and theoretical perspectives*. London: Routledge.
Wigell, M. 2008. Mapping hybrid regimes: regime types and concepts in comparative politics. *Democratization* 15, no. 2: 230–50.
Woolcock, S. 1993. The European *acquis* and multilateral trade rules: are they compatible? *Journal of Common Market Studies* 31, no. 4: 539–58.
Woolcock, S. 2011. *European Union economic diplomacy: the role of the EU in external economic relations*. Aldershot: Ashgate.
Woolcock, S., and M. Hodges. 1996. EU policy in the Uruguay round: the story behind the headlines. In *Policy-making in the European Union*, eds. H. Wallace and W. Wallace, 4th edn., 301–24. Oxford: Oxford University Press.
Youngs, R. 2010. *The EU's role in world politics: a retreat from liberal internationalism*. London: Routledge.

Justice and Home Affairs: The Treaty of Maastricht as a Decisive Intergovernmental Gate Opener

JÖRG MONAR

College of Europe, Bruges, Belgium; Sussex European Institute, University of Sussex, Brighton, UK

ABSTRACT   The introduction of 'cooperation in the fields of justice and home affairs' in the guise of Title VI of the Treaty on European Union can be regarded as one of the most momentous innovations of the Treaty of Maastricht. In 20 years it has turned from a loosely framed and largely intergovernmental cooperation framework into a fundamental treaty objective which has generated over 1400 texts adopted by the Council and a range of new EU institutional structures such as Europol and Eurojust. This article will show that the Treaty of Maastricht — although it did not provide for clear objectives, adequate legal instruments and effective decision-making procedures in the JHA domain — nevertheless marked at decisive breakthrough for this policy-making domain. It did so by opening the entire domain for regular institutionalised cooperation between the member states, allowing for the development of a common perception of the challenges and a gradual agreement on basic objectives and principles which a few years later — when the Treaty of Amsterdam had removed some of the legal and institutional obstacles left in place by the Maastricht Treaty — allowed for an extraordinarily rapid development of what is now the Union's 'area of freedom, security and justice'.

Introduction

Those who have been working on the development of EU justice and home affairs (JHA) since the beginning of the 1990s may today re-read the provisions of old Title VI TEU of the Maastricht Treaty on 'cooperation in the fields of justice and home affairs' with some emotion as — in a sense — that is 'where it all began'. They may also do so with some degree of amazement: compared with today's 23 much more substantial and precise articles of Title IV of the third part of the TFEU on the EU's 'area of freedom, security and justice' (AFSJ) the old 'third pillar' introduced by the Treaty of Maastricht appears in retrospect a very 'thin' basis indeed for starting what has become one of the major policy-making domains of the EU with a special Council formation, two Commissioner portfolios, two Commission Directorate-Generals and a European Parliament Committee dedicated to it, a continuously expanding range of agencies and data-bases, significantly expanded budget lines and over a hundred new texts approved by the JHA Council annually every year since 1999.

Having been by far the 'thinnest' of the Maastricht 'pillars' and the object of widespread criticisms already shortly after its establishment (Curtin and Pouw 1995; Monar 1996; Pauly 1996) has not helped the Maastricht Treaty getting much credit for being at the origin of today's AFSJ, and neither has the fact that its 'third pillar' was substantially reformed and partially dismantled by the Amsterdam Treaty reforms just a few years later. Yet discarding the Maastricht 'third pillar' as a sort of failed first attempt does not do it justice: Throughout the history of the European construction treaty reforms have played an important role as 'enablers' of its further development, and this is even more true in a case like the given one where a whole new policy field has been formally introduced by a treaty reform.

This contribution will analyse and assess the impact of the Maastricht Treaty on the development of the EU JHA domain. In order to better understand the background of the innovations and limitations of the Maastricht 'third pillar' it will start with a look at its precursors and the compromises negotiated in the Maastricht IGC. This will be followed by an analysis of the 'third pillar's gate-opening for JHA cooperation and its rather mixed legacy as a specific governance framework in terms of legal basis and instruments, institutional and decision-making framework and parliamentary and judicial control. The conclusions will then try to do justice to the overall importance of the Maastricht Treaty for the subsequent development of today's AFSJ.

The Precursors of the Maastricht 'Third Pillar'

As masters of the treaties the member states enjoy, in intergovernmental conferences and in principle, unlimited powers of creation. Yet — although Title VI TEU on JHA cooperation was formally a completely new creation within the framework of the treaties — it was not a *creatio ex nihilo*. When the EU heads of state or government agreed during the 1990–1991 IGC to bring JHA cooperation into the new treaty framework cooperation between the member states in this field was already taking place for some time, and in this in no less than three different frameworks:

The longest existing framework at the time was the TREVI cooperation which had been established in 1976 on the basis of an agreement between the EC interior ministers reached in Rome in December 1975.[1] With most member states keen on avoiding any potential 'supranationalisation' of the sovereignty sensitive internal security domain TREVI had come into being as a rather weak *ad hoc* intergovernmental cooperation mechanism providing only for information exchange and coordination meetings at expert and ministerial level on a flexible schedule: it was not based on any formal treaty provisions, not supported by any permanent institution and had initially been focused only on the fight against terrorism. Yet it had been the first ever cooperation mechanism involving the interior ministries and also some of the law enforcement authorities of all EC member states and had been judged to be a useful enough formula to be gradually expanded to other forms of serious cross-border crime, such as drug and arms trafficking, as well as to coordination efforts in matters of police training, techniques and equipment and the comparison of national law enforcement strategies and crime threat assessments (Bonnefoi 1995). At the time of the Maastricht negotiations TREVI therefore covered already much of the substance of the post-Maastricht 'third-pillar' law enforcement cooperation — but still functioned as a loose intergovernmental coordination framework outside of the legal and institutional framework of the EC and without any legal or financial instruments.

The second existing framework was also located outside of the EC Treaty framework, but with a different background and for a different purpose: The big relaunch of the integration process in the 1980s, which started with the successful conclusion of the Fontainebleau European Council in June 1984, had brought the uncompleted objective of free movement to the forefront of European politics. Two special committees set-up at Fontainebleau had submitted in 1985 proposals with major JHA implications, the *Dooge Committee* by proposing the completion of the Internal Market before the end of the decade and the *Adonnino Committee* by stressing the importance of free movement of persons for the creation of a *Europe of the citizens*. The recommendations of both committees had questioned more or less directly the continuation of existing controls on persons at internal borders. Faced with an obvious reluctance of several member states — and in particular the UK — to proceed with the abolition of internal border controls within the EC, France, Germany and the three Benelux countries signed on 14 June 1985 the *Schengen Agreement* outside of the EC Treaty framework which provided not only for a gradual abolition of controls but also a broad range of 'compensatory measures' in the JHA domain to offset any potential internal security and migration management risks. Although essentially driven by the single objective of 'only' abolishing internal border controls the Schengen group had by the time of the Maastricht IGC became by sheer necessity a pioneer of advanced JHA cooperation as the projected 'open border' Schengen system would *de facto* create a single area with common internal security and a migration management challenges. Just before the start of the IGC — in June — the Schengen countries had signed the Convention implementing the Schengen Agreement (CISA) which constituted a much more advanced JHA cooperation framework than the non-agreement based TREVI coordination: In 142 Articles the CISA set out detailed rules on the abolition of controls at internal borders, the crossing of external borders, visas, movements of aliens, the responsibility for the processing of applications for asylum, police cooperation, extradition and other matters of criminal justice cooperation, on narcotic drugs, firearms and ammunition, the Schengen Information System (SIS), transport and movement of goods and the protection of personal data (Schutte 1991). As the Schengen countries had made it clear that their ultimate objective was to eventually incorporate their system into the EC they had obviously a major interest in the Maastricht IGC to create — at the very least — for the first time a legal basis for JHA cooperation within the treaty framework, and the political weight of the group was increasing at the time with Italy having signed up to Schengen just before the IGC started[2] and several other member states readying themselves for doing so as well.[3]

Yet in addition to these two cooperation frameworks outside of the EC Treaty JHA issues had at the beginning of the 1990s also made their appearance on the EC agenda: From 1986 onwards the implementation of the EC internal market programme with its progressive reduction of border checks on transports of goods and liberalisation of other cross-border economic transactions had forced the member states to also look in the context of the internal market for compensatory measures to offset potential internal security risks resulting from the enhanced 'freedoms' of the internal market. The absence of any EC competences in law enforcement matters and continuing fears about a potential 'communitarisation' through the backdoor had kept compensatory law enforcement cooperation firmly within the TREVI framework. However, there were wider JHA issues which had to be dealt with but fell outside of the scope of TREVI such as asylum, immigration and external border controls and the prevention of the smuggling of prohibited goods into and within the 'open' internal market. In the absence, again, of any explicit powers for the EC to deal with the JHA issues involved the member states had set up several intergovernmental coordination groups since 1986, such as the *Ad Hoc Group on Immigration*, the *'Rhodes' Coordinators' Group on Free Movement*, the *Mutual Assistance Group* (GAM) and the *Comité européen de la lutte anti-drogue* (CELAD). At the time the Maastricht IGC started these groups were playing a useful role in identifying JHA challenges in relation with the completion of the internal market and coordinating national compensatory measures, but their undefined position within the orbit but formally outside of the EC institutional framework and the persisting lack of EC legislative action possibilities seriously limited their impact (Cullen, Monar, and Myers 1996, 18–23).

At the end of the 1980s of JHA cooperation between the member states was therefore already quite a crowded one, but also one of extreme fragmentation and complexity. Apart from the inevitable problems of overlap between the different frameworks and groups the effectiveness of this cooperation was severely impaired by the absence of any real common action potential within the existing EC treaty framework. In the months preceding the Maastricht IGC a critical mass of member states emerged which felt that this state of affairs was not any longer adequate to the common challenges in this domain: Not only was the completion of the internal market necessitating some 'hard' compensatory legal measures rather than only loose coordination of national measures, but the dismantling of the former 'iron curtain' borders as a result of the revolutionary transformation in Central and Eastern Europe were seen adding to the already existing challenges in the fields of migration, border management and fight against cross-border crime. Unsurprisingly the Schengen countries formed the core of that critical mass, but within this core it was particularly Germany which appeared as the champion of bringing JHA cooperation into the new treaty reform as — with reunification completed in 1990 — it found itself in charge of an even longer stretch of the newly opened Eastern borders and was also facing the until then unprecedented challenge of over 190,000 asylum applications in a single year which it regarded as a European rather than only a national problem (Bade and Oltmer 2005).

The 'Third Pillar' Compromise in the Maastricht IGC Negotiations

Creating a treaty basis for action in the JHA domain was not among the primary reasons for convoking the 1990–1991 IGC 'on Political Union'[4] and did not dominate its proceedings. The mandate for the IGC, formulated by the Rome European Council of 14/15 December 1990, was exceedingly vague and — providing only for a consideration of 'whether and how activities currently conducted in an intergovernmental framework could be brought into the ambit of the Union' (European Council 1990, 8) — left it even open whether or not the JHA domain should find a place in the new treaty framework. Because of the continuing opposition, in particular of the UK, to the abolition of controls at internal borders, a possible incorporation of the Schengen system had not even made it on the agenda of the IGC. Yet most of the member states' governments regarded the upcoming treaty revision as an opportunity for finally securing at least some form of legal base for common action on JHA issues which should not be missed, although the differences between national positions were significant enough: The governments of the Benelux countries, Italy and Spain — which at the time appeared as the 'maximalists' in terms of ambition for JHA-related treaty reforms[5] — favoured a full 'communitarisation' of the JHA domain. France and Germany shared with the 'maximalists' the objective of creating a comprehensive new legal base for JHA policy-making, but considered a full 'communitarisation' beyond that of asylum and immigration policy (a strong German interest) premature, aiming instead at a solution within a separate and more intergovernmental part of the reformed treaty system. The governments of Denmark, Greece, Ireland and the UK — which at the time appeared as the 'minimalists' in terms of ambition for JHA-related treaty reforms[6] — wanted to leave it at an only brief reference to intergovernmental JHA cooperation in the treaty, with Denmark even indicating that it would be content with cooperation continuing as before outside of the treaty framework.[7]

The position of Denmark, Greece, Ireland and the UK — which shared what can be called a 'minimalist' approach — practically excluded right from the start of the IGC the option of a full 'communitarisation', but left considerable scope for negotiating a compromise on how and to which extent the new JHA dimension would be incorporated. The finding of the eventual compromise was greatly eased by the fact that the first few weeks of the negotiations made it obvious that there would need to be a separate treaty to accommodate foreign policy cooperation which several member states — and in particular the UK — did not wish to see located within the ambit of the 'supranational' EC treaty. With a separate and more 'intergovernmental' treaty thus anyway on the cards using it as harbour also for the new JHA provisions seemed an obvious solution It was then also this option which the Luxembourg presidency — although nationally favouring the 'communitarisation' option — duly chose in its highly influential 'non-paper' of April 1991 which for the first time sketched out the Maastricht 'temple' architecture with its three distinct 'pillars' (Vanhoonacker 1992, 159–60). The fact that the member states favouring a 'communitarisation' then gradually regrouped behind the Luxembourg compromise proposal with its distinct JHA 'pillar' in what was to become the Treaty on European Union (TEU) had much to do with the strong backing of this solution by France and Germany, both of which were perfectly content with this solution which they saw as an intermediate step paving the way to a full or partial 'communitarisation' at a later stage. With their primary objectives of keeping the JHA domain outside of the EC Treaty being, the 'minimalist' group of member states then became more flexible on the substantive provisions of the new 'third pillar' which eventually went significantly beyond the brief references only in the treaty they had initially been aiming at. It was in this context of the 'minimalists' feeling less threatened in their national sovereignty preoccupations by substantive JHA provisions because of the non-community treaty framework that Germany was also able at a relatively late stage of the negotiations to secure the inclusion of the establishment of the European Police Office (Europol) in the new Title VI TEU (Corbett 1993, 49). The 'maximalists' held on longest with their 'communitarisation' objective in the domain of asylum and immigration policy, but could in the end — because of the fierce resistance of the UK and Ireland — only achieve the transfer of visa policy matters to the 'first pillar'[8] Yet after severe criticisms of the intergovernmental solution for the JHA domain from Commission President Jacques Delors and the European Parliament in November 1990 and in exchange for the removal of any treaty reference to a 'federal' orientation of the European Union the British government accepted shortly before the final session of the IGC on 9/10 December that a possible further 'communitarisation' of the domain could be discussed in a new IGC in 1996 (Curti Gialdino 1993, 11 and 295–6).

The Maastricht 'Third Pillar': A Wide Gate Opened — But Without Further Directions

While the 'maximalists' during the 1990/91 IGC had to give way on their 'communitarisation' objective they won the day on the question of creating a broad base for JHA cooperation within the reformed treaty framework: New Article K.1 TEU defined as 'matters of common interest' all of the relevant fields of JHA cooperation from asylum, immigration and external border management over combating drug addiction and fraud on an international scale to judicial cooperation in both civil and criminal matters, customs cooperation and police cooperation. Looking back after 20 years this wide initial opening for treaty based JHA cooperation appears all the more remarkable as its scope went well beyond the at the time still rather fragmentary coverage of the various fields in the different existing intergovernmental groups (de Lobkowicz 2002, 46–7): in the case of asylum and judicial cooperation in civil and criminal matters (Article K.1(1), (6) and (7)) the entire fields were opened up for cooperation without any restrictive definition, and even in the sensitive fields of immigration policy and police cooperation (Articles K.1(3) and (9) — where specific matters instead of the entire field were identified as being of 'common interest' — the new provisions covered the most substantive issues such as family reunion, access to employment and combating unauthorized immigration in the field of immigration and all forms of serious international crime in the field of police cooperation.

The gate to JHA cooperation within the EU framework was thus cast wide open — and at least as important was the fact that Maastricht replaced the fragmented set of different intergovernmental groups in which the member states were already cooperating by a single treaty-based framework. While it is true that the Schengen system had for the time being to continue with its involuntary exile outside of the EC/EU treaties, the TREVI cooperation and the various internal market related coordination mechanisms could now be merged within a single framework. Even the Schengen system was to some extent brought closer to the EU framework as several matters closely related to Schengen, such as external border management, asylum and immigration policy (Article K.(1)-(3)) were now also identified as 'matters of common interest' of the EU which opened up the possibility for the Schengen countries to seek progress on Schengen related issues via EU instruments wherever there was a prospect of all member states agreeing to those and not just those committed to the Schengen abolition of internal border controls. This reduced not only the risk of further differentiation of JHA cooperation between the member states but also facilitated the intended later incorporation of the Schengen system into the EC/EU framework. During the life of the Maastricht 'third pillar' 1993–1999 several EU Council Resolutions and Positions were, for instance, adopted on a range of important principles for asylum procedures and the admission and return of third-country nationals (de Lobkowicz 2002, 76–9) which spared the Schengen countries the need and potential later complications of having to define those separately and outside of the EU framework.

The gate to JHA cooperation was thus not only cast wide open by the Maastricht reforms — but it also had the additional advantage of being a consolidated and — with the exception of Schengen — single gate. The importance of this treaty-based gate-opening for the subsequent evolution of the JHA policy-making domain can hardly be overestimated: the weaknesses of the Maastricht 'third pillar' in terms of governance, to which we will come back below, may have seriously reduced its eventual policy out-put, but there can be no question about its introduction in the TEU formally establishing the new policy domain on a broad and consolidated basis. This gave to JHA cooperation between the member states — which had until then been largely floating in uncertain outer intergovernmental space — a new legitimacy as a formally recognised domain of common EU action. Although the 'communitarisation' option had been rejected (with the exception of visa policy) the Maastricht 'third pillar' also drew some strength and legitimacy from its strong connection with the by then solidly established Community framework (Anderson, den Boer, and Miller 1994, 115-6). This connection consisted not only through the newly established EU being formally founded on the European Communities and the 'third pillar' as all of the new forms of cooperation being qualified as only 'supplementing' them (Article A TEU) and the single institutional framework, which rendered the old Community institutions also responsible for this new policy domain, but also through the possibility for the Council to decide to charging JHA expenditure to the EC budget (Article K.8(2)) and to transfer any of the JHA matters covered by Article K.1(1)-(6), i.e., all JHA matters with the exception of police, customs and judicial cooperation in criminal matters, to the Community 'pillar' by way of the 'passerelle' clause of Article K.9.

The Maastricht 'third pillar' thus created a major *fait accompli* as to the legitimacy and scope of JHA as a domain of Community related EU cooperation. Historians a rightly wary of the famous 'what if' question, but it seems difficult to imagine that the significant substantive progress achieved just a few years later with the introduction of the partially 'communitarised' and politically much more ambitious AFSJ would have been possible without this breakthrough of the domain in the Treaty of Maastricht: The Maastricht 'third pillar' provided the base of initial acceptance and experience with the JHA domain on which the AFSJ could subsequently be built.

Yet, however wide open and consolidated the new gate to JHA cooperation may have been, the member states as masters of the treaties had failed to agree in the Maastricht IGC on any clear directions on where to go beyond the gate. Article K.1 referred rather vaguely to the 'objectives of the Union' and specifically mentioned only the free movement of persons amongst those. This formally limited the political ambition for the 'third pillar' to the provision of compensatory measures in relation with the free movement of persons only, an old objective of the EC Treaty[9] whose reach was weakened by the absence of consensus amongst the member states on whether or not it should include the abolition of controls on persons at internal borders. While opening up the above mentioned wide range of JHA fields for cooperation the Maastricht Treaty gave few indications on what actually should be achieved either overall or in the respective fields individually. Unlike in the subsequent reforms of the treaties of Amsterdam and Lisbon no development of common rules, let alone 'common policies', were provided for, and even in the case of the most concrete of the 'matters of common interest' — the possible establishment of Europol — Article K.1(9) left it open whether it would be anything more than a host for the 'Union-wide system for exchanging information'. The absence of more clearly defined objectives for the new treaty based JHA cooperation reflected both the lack of consensus amongst the member states on what they wanted to achieve in the JHA domain and the desire of many of them not to be constrained by binding treaty objectives in a highly sovereignty sensitive domain. The lack of clearly defined objectives left it to the vagaries of changing national interests of the individual member states and the rotating presidencies to set the political agenda for the JHA domain during the lifetime of the Maastricht 'third pillar'. It also did not encourage the European Commission, which anyway remained in a relatively weak position, to try to drive the agenda forward with ambitious proposals. Unsurprisingly the Reflection Group on the 1996 IGC identified the lack of objectives and of a timetable for achieving them as one of the primary deficiencies of the Maastricht 'third pillar' (Reflection Group 1995, 24). However, while the lack of objectives clearly reduced the EU policy output in the JHA domain in the post-Maastricht period, it may also have had a positive effect on the future AFSJ as in the Treaty of Amsterdam this well identified deficit was then almost over-compensated by a plethora of in part deadline linked objectives reaching even into details of individual policy fields (Monar 1998, 323–5).

Maastricht 'Third Pillar' Governance: A Mixed Legacy

The Treaty of Maastricht did not only open a vast new field for treaty-based JHA cooperation but also defined in a sense a *sui generis* governance framework closely linked to but also in many respects quite distinct from the Community framework. As it partially survived the subsequent Amsterdam Treaty reforms and left traces even in the post-Lisbon AFSJ its main elements merit a closer look.

Legal Basis and Instruments

As indicated above the legal basis chosen for the introduction of the JHA domain — Title VI of the new TEU — formed the centrepiece of the compromise between the 'maximalists' and the 'minimalists' during the 1990–1991 IGC. Although heavily criticised at the time by the European Commission, the European Parliament and clearly not to the liking of the 'maximalists' among the member states it is with hindsight probably fair to say that choosing a legal base in the 'intergovernmental' TEU without the transfer of national powers to the EU institutions in accordance with the Community model was the only politically feasible option at the time for bringing the JHA domain into the treaty framework: The opposition of the British Conservative government to a Community legal base may have been the most consistent and vocal one during the IGC, but the fact that concerns about a potential loss of national sovereignty in the domain of justice and home affairs also played a role in the negative first Danish referendum on the Maastricht Treaty on 2 June 1992 and led to a Danish 'national compromise' formally affirming that the country would participate in JHA cooperation only on an intergovernmental basis[10] (Laursen 1992, 71–3) indicated that with the 'third pillar' solution the limits of the possible in this sovereignty sensitive domain had indeed been reached. The fact that the 'third pillar' survived — although henceforth limited to police and judicial cooperation in criminal matters — the comprehensive Amsterdam Treaty reforms and was finally formally abolished only by the Lisbon Treaty in 2009 clearly shows that the separate intergovernmental legal base responded to some fundamental sovereignty and national control concerns of some member states and not just short-term political interests. In that sense the Maastricht 'third pillar' solution can be regarded as quite successful as it enabled a development of JHA cooperation within the EU treaty framework which would otherwise only have taken place in a loose intergovernmental orbit — or even not at all.

While the Maastricht compromise with its location of the new JHA domain in the TEU allowed the member states to avoid the 'supranational' constraints of the Community legal system, it also forced them to define a specific framework for the new 'cooperation in the fields of justice and home affairs' (Article K TEU). The use of the term 'cooperation' was of some importance as it underlined the fundamental rationale of providing a framework for better interaction between the member states rather than any integration via potential 'common policies'. Article K.1 TEU consequently defined the aforementioned list of 'matters of common interest' which distinguished the 'third pillar' from the 'first (EC) pillar' with its extensive provisions on common measures to be taken. The emphasis on cooperation was also underlined by Article K.3(1) TEU which provided for member states to 'inform and consult one another in the Council with a view to coordinating their action'. But this had arguably already been done extensively in the TREVI context and the other pre-Maastricht intergovernmental groups, so that a crucial question for the potential progress to be achieved on the basis of new Title VI was that of the instruments which could be used for the now treaty based cooperation. In retrospect the set of instruments provided for was clearly one of the weakest elements of the new legal base and the 'third pillar' overall.

With the use of the well established Community legal instruments ruled out by the 'minimalists' during the IGC it was obvious that different instruments had to be defined in conjunction with the new legal base. As this applied also to the CFSP domain the negotiations drifted eventually in a strange sort of 'economies of scale' logic to the decision to introduce for the 'third pillar' largely the same instruments as for the CFSP (de Lobkowicz 2002, 48). As a result Article K.3(2)(a)-(b) provided for the possibility for the Council to adopt 'joint positions' and 'joint actions'. For a domain where potential progress clearly depended more on legislative action than political positions and joint operations (as this was the case for the CFSP) this choice was a most peculiar one indeed. It may be attributed to the fact the negotiations on the Title VI TEU provisions had been conducted by the Foreign ministers and their 'personal representatives' — who were all career diplomats — with no direct involvement of the ministers of interior and justice. Any potential effectiveness of the 'joint positions' and 'joint actions' was further reduced by uncertainties as to the binding legal effects of the two instruments: contrary to the Council's legal service and the other member states Portugal and the UK took the view that 'joint actions' were not automatically binding, and the use of mandatory language in JHA 'joint actions' varied indeed considerably. In the case of 'joint positions' it was never clarified whether they had any legal effect (Peers 2011, 14–5). As a result of these uncertainties only around a quarter of the 127 formal decisions taken by the JHA Council during the post-Maastricht period took the form of 'joint actions' or 'joint positions' (de Lobkowicz 2002, 66) although these had clearly been intended to be the most frequently used ones under Title VI TEU. The member states preferred instead to use an extensive range non-binding texts such as Council 'Resolutions', 'Conclusions' and 'Recommendations' which did little to enhance legal certainty under the 'third pillar' (Peers 2011, 14).

The treaty provided, it is true, for one instrument whose legal effects were beyond doubt — 'conventions' drawn up according to Article K.3 (2)(3) — but these were agreements under public international law which needed to be ratified by each individual member state. The lengthy ratification procedures meant that only 1 of the 10 Conventions adopted by the Council during the lifetime of the Maastricht 'third pillar' — the Europol Convention — actually entered into force before the Treaty of Amsterdam reforms, and even this one only after more than three years.[11]

Looking back it seems fair to say that while the separate TEU legal base for the JHA domain may have been unavoidable at the time the instruments which were connected with it were clearly inadequate to the nature and needs of the new policy field. It took not long for this to become fully apparent: Already in 1995 the Commission concluded in its report on the functioning of the TEU concluded that JHA cooperation was 'ineffectual' also because of the 'inappropriate' instruments (Commission of the European Communities 1995, 6), and a few months later the Reflection Group on the 1996 IGC criticised the Title VI TEU instruments equally as inappropriate as they had been 'copied' from CFSP Title V TEU, pointing out in all due clarity that whereas 'external policy rarely involves laying down laws and requires flexibility of action... matters relating to the security of citizens require legal protection and therefore a legislative framework' (Reflection Group 1995, 24). The lesson about inadequate instruments was clearly learnt: Whereas the Maastricht 'third pillar' survived the Amsterdam Treaty reforms in a leaner form its instruments did not and were replaced by fully binding Council 'decisions' and 'framework decisions' much more appropriate to the legislative needs of the domain (Monar 1998, 326–7).

Institutional Framework and Decision-making

With the entry into force of the Maastricht Treaty on 1 November 1993 all existing JHA cooperation structures between the member states with the obvious exception of those of the Schengen group became part of the 'single institutional framework' of the EU provided for by Article C TEU. This meant, in particular, that all the different TREVI bodies were absorbed by the EU Council framework, with the JHA Council meetings replacing the former TREVI Ministerial Meetings, the TREVI Group of Coordinators becoming the 'Coordinating Committee' provided for by Article K.4[12] and the various TREVI working groups being transformed into Council working groups (Nilsson and Siegel 2010, 54–5). This resulted in both a consolidation of working procedures — the Council's Rules of Procedure became applicable — and more regular meetings at all levels of decision-making. Not to be underestimated is also what may be called the EU 'mainstreaming' effect of the integration of the various intergovernmental groups and cooperation mechanisms in the Council context: regular meetings and negotiations under defined EU procedures and in Brussels rather than — as most often the case before — in the capitals of the countries holding the Presidency became the normal framework of cooperation thereby introducing a certain dose of 'communitarisation' of work procedures through the backdoor as the Council framework and its procedures had been thoroughly shaped by Community practice and negotiating culture. This was not necessarily to everyone's liking: even a few years after the entry into force of the Maastricht Treaty some senior officials from the interior ministries tended still to suffer from a sort of 'TREVI blues',[13] regretting the greater flexibility and informality of cooperation within the loose intergovernmental TREVI framework which was felt to have been lost as a result of the passage to the much more regulated and constraining Community procedures within the Council framework. While it may be difficult to assess the extent of the impact of this 'councilarisation' of intergovernmental JHA cooperation there can be no doubt that the complete familiarisation of the ministries of interior and of justice with Council procedures and negotiation techniques facilitated the rapid expansion of JHA policy-making in the AFSJ context after the entry into force of the Amsterdam Treaty in 1999.

The Maastricht 'third pillar' also opened the way for a new role of the Commission in the JHA domain — although this in the form of a more gradual change. Having been largely limited to the role of a mere (and occasionally even excluded) observer in the context of the pre-Maastricht intergovernmental groups Article K.4(2) TEU established the principle of a 'full association' of the Commission with the new treaty based cooperation framework. More importantly K.3(2) TEU gave the Commission for the first time a formal right of initiative in the domain. Yet ever wary of too much of a 'supranational' influence of the Commission the 'minimalists' had ensured during the IGC that this right of initiative, firstly, was only a shared one with the member states (which could propose Council measures individually) and, secondly, did not apply to the fields of judicial cooperation in criminal matters, customs cooperation and police cooperation. While giving the Commission a place at the table of the Council at all levels of decision-making and some scope for initiatives the Maastricht Treaty was therefore far from assigning the Commission the traditional Community role of a 'motor' of policy-making based on an exclusive of initiative. A former senior Commission official having had the experience of the Maastricht 'third pillar' has described the Commission's post-Maastricht role as that of a 'tolerated partner' (de Lobkowicz 2002, 49), which indicates the institution's slightly ambiguous position as the probably most quintessential Community institution in the still heavily intergovernmental context of Title VI TEU.

The Commission asserted its new position under the 'third pillar' only slowly and with a strong focus on EC related matters. Of its first two formal proposals of January 1994[14] the first one — on a Convention on the crossing of external frontiers — was presented as a necessary complementary measure to the free movement of persons within the EC and the second one — on a regulation determining the third-countries whose nationals must be in possession of a visa when entering the EU — was based on the new Article 100c TEC 'first pillar' legal base. This set in a sense the tone for the lifetime of the Maastricht 'third pillar' with the Commission contributing actively to decision-making in the JHA domain only on issues connected with its core competences in the EC context and carefully avoiding to penetrate into the more sovereignty sensitive fields such as police and judicial cooperation in criminal matters. This can partially be attributed to its still relatively weak position under the treaty — as mentioned before the Commission had not been given a formal right of initiative in these fields — but there are also indications that the Commission did at the time not regard the JHA domain as much of a priority and worthy of investing political capital: under the Delors III Commission the responsibility for the new domain was simply 'annexed' to the portfolio of Commissioner Padraig Flynn who continued to mainly focus on social affair and employment, under the Santer Commission the domain was upgraded to a portfolio in its own right but given to Commissioner Anita Gradin who did not show much of a political ambition for it, and within the Commission services the domain was dealt with by a unit (later directorate) of the Secretariat General rather than being given a Directorate General (DG) of its own. Looking back one is therefore tempted to say that it was the post-Amsterdam period — with the much more active Commissioner Antonio Vitorino and a new dedicated DG from 1999 onwards — rather than the post-Maastricht period which marked the real political breakthrough of the Commission in this domain.

Neither the Commission nor the speed and substance of decision-making under the Title VI TEU were helped by the unanimity requirement in the Council. Article K.3(2) TEU provided for the possibility of majority voting only in the case of 'implementing measures' of Joint Actions (qualified majority) and Conventions (two thirds majority), and even that possibility was used most sparingly by the Council, mainly in respect of funding programmes and technical issues of the implementation of Conventions (Peers 2011, 11). The 'unanimity culture' of the 'third pillar' — a clear reflection of its intergovernmental TREVI background and founding rationale — has remained one of the most lasting elements of its legacy, surviving the Amsterdam Treaty reforms[15] and casting its shadow even over parts of the post-Lisbon AFSJ in which particular sensitive issues of police and judicial cooperation in criminal matters (the fields which formed the now abolished pre-Lisbon 'third pillar') remain under the iron grip of the unanimity requirement.[16]

Parliamentary and Judicial Control

While the Maastricht Treaty gave the Commission at least a 'tolerated' place at the table of decision-making in the Council the European Parliament had to content itself with a vaguely worded obligation for the Presidency to 'consult [it] on the principal aspects of activities' in the new JHA policy-making domain and 'to ensure that [its views] are duly taken into consideration' (Article K.6 TEU). Although this amounted at least to a first formal recognition of the EP in this domain (Gautier 1995, 854–5) it left it entirely to the member states to decide what was to be considered as belonging to the 'principal aspects' and how far their 'consideration' of the Parliament's views should go, and in practice it meant a complete political marginalisation of the Parliament apart from fairly general regular briefings from the Presidency and rather perfunctory responses to parliamentary questions and recommendations which had also been provided for by Article K.6 TEU. The extent of the Council's side-lining of the Parliament reached its peak in 1995–1996 with its refusal to consult the EP on the Draft Europol Convention — an instrument which can clearly be regarded as one of the most 'principal' of the Maastricht 'third pillar' period — and this in spite of two strongly worded Resolutions of the Parliament invoking its rights under Article K.6.[17] Having regard to the potentially highly sensitive implications of JHA cooperation for the rights of individuals — both EU citizens and (in the case of asylum and immigration policy) third-country nationals — this marginalisation of the EP made the Maastricht 'third pillar' clearly lack an adequate basis of democratic legitimacy at EU level and betrayed — once again — its intergovernmental origins which had been entirely outside of the EP's reach. This constituted a legacy which took some time to be overcome, with the EP obtaining formal consultation rights on all legislative AFSJ acts only in 1999, the first co-decision rights with regard to the 'communitarised' AFSJ fields only in 2005 and co-decision or consent rights for nearly all AFSJ matters only in 2009 with the Lisbon Treaty. With hindsight, however, the 'democracy deficit' of the Maastricht 'third pillar' appears somewhat mitigated by the fact that Conventions under Title VI TEU needed to be ratified in any case by all national parliaments — so that there was a strong element of national parliamentary control — and that the overall legislative out-put of the Council during the post-Maastricht was rather limited because of the aforementioned extensive use of non-binding texts.

With the 'minimalists' wary of any potential creeping 'communitarisation' of Title VI TEU via the case-law of the Court of Justice of the European Communities (ECJ) the Maastricht compromise had excluded by virtue of Article L TEU any mandatory jurisdiction of the ECJ in the new policy domain. This created an 'institutional void' as regards both the protection of the rights of individuals at EU level and the ensuring of a uniform interpretation and application of 'third pillar' provisions and measures (Barret 1997, 26–8). Article K.3(2)(c) TEU only provided for a possibility for Conventions to grant the Court jurisdiction to interpret their provisions and to rule on any disputes regarding their application. This not only exempted all other Title VI TEU acts of the Council from judicial control by the ECJ but also led to an initial lack of agreement in the Council to what extent the Court's jurisdiction should be provided for in 'third pillar' Conventions. This was only overcome in 1996, i.e., half-way through the life of the 'third pillar', and necessitated the later addition of several Protocols to already signed Conventions (Peers 2011, 15–6). In a highly unusual criticism of the treaty itself the ECJ expressed in May 1995 its own concerns about an adequate judicial protection of individuals in the domain of JHA cooperation (Court of Justice of the European Communities 1995, 2). In terms of judicial control the Maastricht 'third pillar' served therefore no more as positive model for the later evolution of the AFSJ than in terms of parliamentary control and continued in this respect the intergovernmental cooperation traditions more than changing them. Nevertheless the later acceptance of the Court's jurisdiction in the context of Convention can be regarded as a small step towards the later gradual extension of its mandatory jurisdiction in the context of the AFSJ which was, again, only completed with the Lisbon Treaty reforms in 2009.

Conclusions

Over the distance of two decades the Maastricht 'third pillar' — widely regarded as a failure in the 1990s — appears to justify a more positive, or at least more balanced, judgement:

Its output during its lifetime was certainly limited. It consisted essentially of least common denominator compromises on basic common principles on the status and procedural guarantees of asylum seekers, a (very restrictive) approach to legal immigration for work purposes, jurisdiction and mutual recognition in civil matters, the facilitation of extradition, the fight against organised crime and drug trafficking and the establishment of Europol (de Lobkowicz 2002, 64–87). Most of the texts adopted on these issues were non-binding and most of them were replaced by much more advanced instruments after the Treaty of Amsterdam reforms just a few years later. It is therefore not altogether surprising that shortly before the Amsterdam reforms the 'third pillar' was considered less successful as the 'exiled' Schengen system in which the constraints generated by the abolition of internal border controls forced the participating member states to more substantial legislative and operational progress (Den Boer 1997, 148–9). As a result of both the limited progress in terms of binding legislation and the absence of central command-and-control structures — Europol, for instance, being established with initially only information exchange and analysis and no active coordination functions — the impact of the Maastricht Treaty reforms on national legal frameworks and structures in the JHA fields was very limited. In the years following the entry into force of the Maastricht Treaty — and before the Amsterdam reforms — there was little pressure on the member states to adapt national systems to the new JHA dimension of the EU Treaty and hence little 'Europeanization' of the national JHA policy contexts beyond the need to send more officials, and this more regularly, to Brussels for participation in the meetings of the various Council bodies and to seek mostly vague common intergovernmental positions at the European level. JHA cooperation under the Maastricht Treaty can certainly also not be regarded as a model for high treaty defined ambitions, effective instruments and parliamentary and judicial control. In all these respects it appears more wedded to the TREVI past than to the AFSJ future.

Yet all of this has to be put into the balance with the wide opening of the gate to JHA cooperation within the framework of the EU treaties brought by the Maastricht 'third pillar' as well as its integration of loose intergovernmental cooperation within the more regular and consolidated EU Council framework with full association of the Commission and — in spite of its severe limitations — a first recognition of the need for some sort of an EU parliamentary and judicial control. Although Schengen still remained in its involuntary exile, the Maastricht Treaty brought JHA cooperation decisively within the EU system and laid the foundations on which the AFSJ could be built after the Amsterdam Treaty reforms. Although the effects of the Maastricht JHA provisions on national legislation and structures remained very limited the full institutionalisation of JHA cooperation within the EU institutional and decision-making context brought the national ministries concerned — primarily those of the interior and of justice — in a context of regular meetings, information exchange and coordination efforts of unprecedented intensity. On a limited range of issues the post-Maastricht JHA even managed — in spite of its limitations in terms of objectives, instruments and decision-making procedures — to be pioneering for later developments within the AFSJ context: the entry into force of the Europol Convention in 1998 may be the most obvious example, but it is not the only one: the 1996 EU Convention on Extradition prepared the ground for the revolutionary European Arrest Warrant of 2002 by abolishing for the first time the double criminality requirement as a precondition for extradition[18] and the Joint Action of 21 December 1998 which made participation in a criminal organisation irrespective of other crimes committed a crime as such[19] defined a core principle in the EU's fight against organised crime which has remained important ever since. However serious the weaknesses of the legal framework of the Maastricht 'third pillar' might have been, it therefore clearly provided an important enough consolidated framework and potential for the future AFSJ. Even its inadequacies may have contributed positively to the later reforms of Amsterdam and Lisbon by amply demonstrating that EU JHA policy-making needed clearer objectives, more effective instruments and — for the sake of its legitimacy — better parliamentary and judicial control. In this respect the lessons to be learnt from the Treaty of Maastricht remain as valid as ever.

Notes

1. The name *TREVI* was a reference both to the venue of the ministers' meeting near the famous Trevi fountain and to the participating Dutch minister Fonteijn (Dutch 'fountain'). Only later the term TREVI was reinterpreted as being an acronym for the French *Terrorisme, radicalisme et violence internationale*.

2. On 27 November 1990.
3. Portugal, Spain and Greece did so already in 1992.
4. Which — it should be recalled — ran in parallel to the IGC on Economic and Monetary Union.
5. And will therefore be referred to as 'maximalists' in the following.
6. And will therefore be referred to as 'minimalists' in the following.
7. This is not the place to retrace in detail the positions adopted by each individual government with regard to JHA-related reforms in the Maastricht Treaty as this has already been done convincingly in the existing literature (see the chapters on the individual member states in Laursen and Vanhoonacker 1992 and also Corbett 1993, 48–9).
8. Under Article 100c of the revised EC Treaty.
9. Then Article 8a TEC.
10. Which was formally recognised by the 'Edinburgh Agreement' on 'Denmark and the European Union' adopted by the Edinburgh European Council of 11/12 December 1992 (OJ C 348 of 31/12/1992).
11. The Europol Convention (OJ C 316 of 26/11/1995) was signed by the member states on 26 July 1995 and entered into force on 1 October 1998. However, because of the delayed Protocol on the immunities of Europol staff, which also needed national ratification, Europol became fully operational only on 1 July 1999.
12. Now the 'Article 36 Committee' (CATS) although this former TEU article has not survived the Lisbon Treaty reforms.
13. A telling expression used by Adrian Fortescue, who later became the first Director-General of the Commission's DG Justice and Home Affairs, in an interview with the author in 1997.
14. OJ C 11 of 15 January 1994.
15. Even in the JHA fields of asylum, migration, border controls and judicial cooperation in civil matters which were 'communitarised' by the Treaty of Amsterdam in 1999 qualified majority voting only became applicable in 2005.
16. Matters of criminal procedural law under Article 82(2)(d) TFEU, the extension of the crime fields subject to potential approximation of substantive criminal law under Article 83(1) TFEU, the establishment and potential further extension of the competences of the European Public Prosecutor's Office under Article 86(1) and (4), operational police cooperation under Article 87(3) and the definition of the conditions and limitations under which police authorities may operate in the territory under Article 89 TFEU.
17. EP Resolutions B4-0732/95 of 19 May 1995 (OJ C 151 of 19/06/1995) and A4-0061/96 of 14 March 1996 (OJ C 96 of 01/04/1996).
18. OJ C 313 of 23/10/1996 (Article 8).
19. OJ L 351 of 29/12/1998 (Article 2).

References

Anderson, M., M. den Boer, and G. Miller. 1994. European citizenship and cooperation in justice and home affairs. In *Maastricht and beyond. Bulding the European Union*, ed. A. Duff, J. Pinder and R. Pryce, 104–22. London: Routledge.

Bade, K., and J. Oltmer. 2005. *Flucht und Asyl seit 1990*. Bonn: Bundeszentrale für politische Bildung.

Barret, G. 1997. Cooperation in justice and home affairs in the European Union — an overview and critique. In *Justice cooperation in the European Union*, ed. G. Barret, 3–47. Dublin: Institute of European Affairs.

Bonnefoi, S. 1995. *Europe et sécurité intérieure: Trevi, Union européenne, Schengen*. Paris: Delmas.

Commission of the European Communities. 1995. Report on the operation of the Treaty on European Union, SEC(95) 731 final. Brussels: Commission of the European Communities.

Corbett, R. 1993. *The Treaty of Maastricht. From conception to ratification: a comprehensive reference guide*. Harlow: Longman.

Court of Justice of the European Communities. 1995. *Report of the Court of Justice on certain aspects of the application of the treaty on European Union*. Luxembourg: Court of Justice of the European Communities.

Cullen, D., J. Monar, and P. Myers. 1996. *Cooperation in justice and home affairs. An evaluation of the third pillar*. Brussels: European Interuniversity Press.

Curti Gialdino, C. 1993. *Il Trattato di Maastricht sull'Unione Europea*. Roma: Istituto Poligrafico e Zecca Dello Stato.

Curtin, D., and J. Pouw. 1995. Samenwerking op het gebied van justitie en binnenlandse zaken in de Europese Unie: pre-Maastricht-nostalgie? *SEW Tijschrift voor Europees en Economisch Recht* 43, no. 9: 579–605.

De Lobkowicz, W. 2002. *L'Europe de la sécurité intérieure. Une élaboration par étapes*. Paris: La documentation Française.

Den Boer, M. 1997. Travel notes on a bumpy jorney from Schengen via Maastricht zo Amsterdam. In *The implementation of Schengen. First the widening, now the deepening*, ed. M den Boer, 147–54. Maastricht: European Institute of Public Administration.

European Council. 1990. European Council Rome, 14 and 15 December 1990. Presidency Conclusions. SN 424/1/90. Brussels: Council oft he European Union.

Gautier, Y. 1995. Titre VITUE. In *Traité sur l'Union européenne. Commentaire article par article*, ed. V. Constantinesco, R. Kovar, and D. Simon, 813–59. Paris: Economica.

Laursen, F. 1992. Denmark and the ratification of the Maastricht Treaty. In *The ratification of the Maastricht Treaty*, eds. F. Laursen and S. Vanhoonacker, 61–86. Maastricht: European Institute of Public Administration.

Laursen, F., and S. Vanhoonacker. 1992. *The Intergovernmental Conference on Political Union*. Maastricht: European Institute of Public Administration.

Monar, J. 1996. Der Dritte Pfeiler der Europäischen Union zu Beginn der Regierungskonferenz: Bilanz und Reformbedarf. *Integration* 19, no. 2: 62–70.

Monar, J. 1998. Justice and home affairs in the Treaty of Amsterdam: reform at the price of fragmentation. *European Law Review* 23, no. 4: 320–35.

Nilsson, H., and J. Siegl. 2010. The Council in the Area of Freedom, Security and Justice. In *The institutional dimension of the European Union's Area of Freedom, Security and Justice*, ed. J. Monar, 53–82. Brussels: P.I.E. Peter Lang.

Pauly, A. 1996. *De Schengen à Maastricht: voie royale et course d'obstacles*. Maastricht: European Institute of Public Administration.

Peers, S. 2011. *EU Justice and Home Affairs Law*. Third edition. Oxford: Oxford University Press.

Reflection Group. 1995. Progress report from the Chairman of the Reflection Group on the 1996 Intergovernmental Conference 1995, SN 509/1/95 REV 1 (REFLEX 10). Brussels: Council of the European Union.

Schutte, J. 1991. Schengen: its meaning for the free movement of persons in Europe. *Common Market Law Review* 28, no. 3: 540–70.

Vanhoonacker, S. 1992. Luxembourg and the European Political Union. In *The intergovernmental conference on political union*, eds. F. Laursen and S. Vanhoonacker, 155–62. Maastricht: European Institute of Public Administration.

Twenty Years of Co-decision Since Maastricht: Inter- and Intrainstitutional Implications

ANNE RASMUSSEN

Faculteit Campus Den Haag, Instituut Bestuurskunde, Leiden University, The Netherlands

ABSTRACT One of the most important institutional changes in the history of the EU was the introduction of the co-decision procedure in 1993. This new legislative procedure has transformed the EU system of governance by affecting both the balance of power between the EU institutions and their internal workings. This contribution takes stock of the first 20 years of co-decision by systematically bringing together and reviewing the findings in the existing literature on EU co-decision. Empirical and theoretical work is scrutinized, which examines the interinstitutional balance of power between the institutions, intrainstitutional power shifts within them and the normative implications of the procedure. Based on these findings, an overall assessment of the long-term implications of co-decision for the functioning of the EU is made.

Maastricht introduced the co-decision legislative procedure, which made the European Parliament (EP) a co-legislator to the Council of Ministers (Council). What was originally intended to be a gradual increase in the legislative[1] role of the EP has ended up having much more far reaching consequences than the founding fathers of co-decision ever anticipated. From the beginning, these developments were far from evident. After difficult treaty negotiations a compromise was finally struck between the

---

"The journey of co-decision" seems to continue for me even if I keep saying it is over. During all the years, I have been privileged by the company of several excellent "travel mates", most importantly Adrienne Héritier, Christine Reh, Michael Shackleton, Dimiter Toshkov and Nikoleta Yordanova.

member states about a rather cumbersome procedure, which would only be applied in a limited range of legislative areas (Moravscik 1998; Duff et al. 1994). Not surprisingly, this new procedure did not exactly receive a warm welcome. Observers warned about the high degree of complexity of the new procedure, which allowed the EU to use as many as three readings to reach a legislative deal and allowed for a lot of new institutional features, with which the system had little experience (Earnshaw and Judge 1996; Westlake 1994). Moreover, academics showed how, under certain conditions, the move from the cooperation to the co-decision legislative procedure might not represent a *net gain* but a *net loss* in the influence of the EP. Hence, it would loose its ability to act as a conditional agenda setter in the new institutional set-up (Tsebelis 1994; Tsebelis and Garrett 1997).

In spite of these warnings, co-decision worked surprisingly well. The cumbersome procedure did not result in chaos and stalemate. Very few files ended up not getting resolved between the co-legislators. Thanks to active efforts from the secretariats of the institutions, a series of informal procedures were developed which contributed to the smooth functioning of the procedure. Moreover, despite the warnings from some academics that co-decision put the EP at risk of loosing influence, practitioners generally agreed that co-decision strengthened rather than weakened the legislative role of the EP (Corbett 2000, 2001). Despite all the hesitations co-decision had been met with from some of its founding fathers, the academic community and a range of observers, it proved itself as a success (Shackleton 2000; Raunio and Shackleton 2003).

This did not mean that co-decision was flawless. Even if the procedure was generally believed to strengthen the EP, there was still concern that the procedure did not put the EP on an equal footing with the Council. Moreover, it was only applied in a limited set of topic areas to begin with. Further reforms were needed. The Amsterdam Treaty gave the EP a stronger role in the procedure and each new treaty that followed expanded the scope of the procedure, so that today it is the rule rather than the exception than co-decision applies. Moreover, Amsterdam introduced the institutional invention that the institutions could conclude dossiers as early as the first reading stage, which radically changed the workings of the legislative processes and meant that working methods both within and between the institutions had to be adapted. Even if this development was generally welcomed from the perspective of speeding up legislative matters and increasing efficiency, it was heavily criticized for moving negotiations outside the public realm and privileging certain actors at the expense of others (Raunio and Shackleton 2003; Farrell and Héritier 2004).

No matter whether the final verdict on all of these developments is positive or negative, it is very obvious is that the impact of co-decision is much greater than most people expected in the early days of this procedure. Today, it is clear that this procedure has affected the daily interaction in the EU legislative processes in a radical way. After 20 years of co-decision, it is time to take stock of some of these developments. This will be done in the current contribution by systematically bringing together and reviewing the findings in the existing literature on EU co-decision. After a brief overview of the procedure, we start by reviewing the literature of the practical functioning and institutional development of the procedure. Thereafter, we examine both empirical and theoretical work of how co-decision has affected the interinstitutional balance of power between the institutions and led to intrainstitutional power shifts between actors within these institutions. Finally, we scrutinize work discussing the normative implications of early agreements in the procedure and make an overall assessment of the long-term implications of co-decision for the functioning of the EU system.

The Co-decision Procedure and its Predecessors

In the early days, the EP's involvement in the legislative affairs of the Community was restricted to a right to be consulted in certain legislative areas. This power was not unimportant to the EP, which often successfully managed to use consultation to put pressure on the Council for example by delaying legislative matters (Kardasheva 2009). At the same time, there were limits as to what the EP could achieve with this power (Corbett *et al.* 2007). The Single European Act increased the role of the EP further by introducing the cooperation procedure in a limited set of issue areas. An important factor for the EP's success was that this procedure was introduced together with qualified majority voting in the Council. In practice, the EP could influence whether the Council would be able to use the qualified majority. Hence, if the Council was not unanimous and the European Commission (Commission) supported the EP position, the EP could exert a great deal of influence on the final compromise. In George Tsebelis's words (1994), this gave the EP the opportunity to act as a conditional agenda setter under certain circumstances. In some cases legislation amended by the EP became easier to accept than reject, and in others legislation rejected by the EP could not be overturned by the Council.

Largely as a result of the positive experiences with cooperation, heads of state decided to move matters one step further and introduce the co-decision procedure with the Maastricht Treaty. Originally the procedure applied to 15 legal bases, or approximately one fourth of the legislative texts passed by the EP (Corbett *et al.* 2007). However, each new treaty has expanded the scope of the procedure. Today, co-decision applies to virtually all areas where the Council decides by qualified majority voting, which means that sensitive issues relating to taxation, agricultural policy and justice and home affairs now also fall within this procedure. As a result, it has been renamed 'the ordinary legislative procedure' of the EU.

The Amsterdam Treaty made it possible for the legislators to conclude as early as the first reading, meaning that today agreement can be reached at the first, second or third reading. The legislative process stops at the first reading if the Council accepts the Commission's original proposal with any amendments that the EP might have tabled. The deliberation comes to a conclusion at the second reading if the Council accepts the EP's second reading amendments to its common position, or if the EP has not amended the common position. Finally, a proposal is agreed at the third reading if, after a conciliation committee between an equal number of representatives from the Council and the EP, the compromise text is approved by both legislative bodies. Since the Amsterdam treaty, failure to reach agreement in the conciliation procedure has meant that the proposal falls. Just as in the cooperation procedure, agreement can typically be reached at the different reading stages by a qualified majority of the Council unless it is trying to change matters against the opinion of the EP, in which case it requires unanimity. Moreover, the EP requires a simple majority for adoption at the first and third reading stage and an absolute majority of its members at second reading.

Institutional Functioning

Empirical studies soon emerged which showed how the co-decision procedure in general (Earnshaw and Judge 1995, 1996; Boyron 1996; Foster 1994; Jacobs 1997) and the conciliation processes in particular (Garman and Hilditch 1998), worked in practice. As an example, Shackleton (2000) and Raunio and Shackleton (2003) showed how a closer working relationship had developed between the Council and the EP over the years, including a common understanding — or maybe even a shared culture — concerning how co-decision should be managed in practice. The general conclusion in these studies was that co-decision was working well despite the heavy criticism of the procedure to start with. The EP had used its new power in a responsible and constructive manner, and a set of informal procedures had developed to make sure that the procedure works in practice.

In order to understand the real functioning of co-decision over the years, it is thus necessary to go beyond the formal treaty provisions and also look at agreements between the institutions. Crucial here are the 1993 inter-institutional agreement on the workings of the conciliation committee[1] and the subsequent Joint Declarations from 1999 and 2007 on the practical arrangements for the operation of the co-decision procedure as a whole.[2] These agreements describe the principles behind the procedure, clarify the role of the different institutions at the different reading stages and settle some more practical issues. An important institutional invention in co-decision over the years has been the so-called trialogues involving the EP, the Council and the Commission. Their usage became standard practice before conciliation negotiations under the Spanish Presidency in the second half of 1995. They consist of restricted forums containing representatives from the EP, the Council and the Commission (EP 2000). Today trialogues do not simply take place at the third reading stage, but at all stages of co-decision. At the conciliation stage, some trialogues have a relatively formal character, whereas they tend to be more informal at earlier legislative stages. Especially at the first reading stage, trialogues have played an important role in brokering deals between the institutions. Whereas the 1999 Common declaration between the institutions spoke of the possibility of entering into 'appropriate contacts', the 2007 agreement for the first time directly spoke of trialogues, and also clarified the arrangements for negotiations at the early stages of the procedure.

Farrell and Héritier (2003, 2007) and Hix (2002) have shown how the formal institutional changes that accompanied the introduction of co-decision in the 1993 Maastricht treaty have given rise to the creation of informal institutions that regulate the daily interaction between the key actors, and how these in turn have affected the formal institutional changes to the procedure contained in the 1999 Amsterdam Treaty. In this way, the period between the treaty negotiations has functioned as a laboratory for the testing of new elements. This experiment was successful, and therefore a logical decision was taken to include the informal modifications to formal treaty-level provisions in the subsequent round of treaty negotiations. In substantive terms, the EP successfully expanded its 'legislative rights' in the co-decision procedure through the evolution of informal agreements between the key players that were subsequently formalized in the treaty.

Interinstitutional Implications

In the first years after the introduction of co-decision, there was quite a vivid debate between theorists and practitioners over whether co-decision contributed to strengthening the legislative powers of the EP. In fact, most of the literature was concerned with exactly this issue. Contrary to the conventional view, Tsebelis and his collaborators (Tsebelis 1994, 1996, 1997; Tsebelis and Garrett 1997, 2000; Garrett 1995; Garrett and Tsebelis 2001) argued that the net effect of the co-decision procedure on the influence of the EP was not a positive one, despite its power of absolute veto, because under this procedure it lost the previously-discussed conditional agenda setting power that it had had in the co-operation procedure. That is, it could no longer make proposals which, if accepted by the Commission, were easier for the Council to accept than to modify (only a qualified majority being required for acceptance, but unanimity for modification) (Tsebelis 1994). Other game theorists criticized this conclusion (Scully 1997a,b; Moser 1997; Crombez 1997, 2000).

So did policy practitioners and other academics (Corbett 2000, 2001; Rittberger 2000). One of the reasons for the existence of disagreement among the game theorists themselves was that they interpreted the decision-making procedures differently, and therefore made different assumptions about the decision-making context in their models (Hörl et al. 2005, 593; Selck 2004, 82–4). The essence of this disagreement seems to be that Tsebelis was correct in stating that the EP would have more influence when it acted as a conditional agenda-setter in cooperation than when it possessed an absolute veto in co-decision, although in reality the conditions required for acting as a conditional agenda-setter did not occur very often.[3]

Data from the EP itself shows that in the early days of co-decision its second reading amendments were generally more successful under co-decision than under cooperation. Under the former, 47 per cent were accepted, whereas the figure under cooperation was 21 percent (EP 1997). In fact the adoption rate of second reading EP amendments has been surprisingly high considering that many of them are reinstated unsuccessful amendments from first reading. Hence, Rule 62 of the EP Rules of Procedure restricts the type of amendments that can be tabled at second reading. Tsebelis and his collaborators are somewhat skeptical about this conclusion. They argue that it is necessary to control for the influence of the Commission when comparing the EP success rate at second reading under cooperation and co-decision, because one of the conditions for the EP's conditional agenda setting is that the Commission must be in agreement. When doing so, they did not find that the success rate of parliamentary amendments is higher in the co-decision procedure than in the co-operation procedure. However, Kreppel (2002) based on the same data set showed that EP was more successful in co-decision than in co-operation, even when the impact of the Commission was controlled for. The difference between the two was probably a result of the fact that whereas Tsebelis *et al.* counted anything other than outright rejection as representing success for the EP, in her study Kreppel (2002) only counted as successful amendments that were wholly or mostly adopted.

Over the years, the academic literature went from discussing the relative influence of the EP in different legislative procedures to focusing on the relative distribution of power between the institutions within the co-decision procedure. Just as the EP was initially rather disappointed about cooperation, it also expressed disappointment about co-decision. Even though for the first time the procedure required the EP to agree to a compromise with the Council, it enabled the Council to reinstate its previous position if it did not manage to reach an agreement with the EP in the conciliation committee. This position would become law unless the EP managed to find an absolute majority of its members to overrule the Council within six weeks of confirmation.

In practice, this imbalance was not as serious for the EP as it first seemed. In fact, the Council reconfirmed its previous position only once, shortly after the introduction of co-decision. This occurred on a proposal on voice telephony (COD 1994 437), where disagreements over comitology had prevented agreement from being reached in the conciliation committee. After the Council's reconfirmation, the EP succeeded in finding the necessary absolute majority to overrule it and the act fell (EP 1995). In addition, the EP added a rule to its procedures (Rule 78) whereby it would in future ask the Commission to withdraw its proposal in the case that conciliation negotiations failed. If this did not happen and the Council reconfirmed its text, the rule stated that the EP would automatically propose a motion rejecting the proposal irrespective of whether the Council text was one that it preferred to the status quo or not. It thus declared itself willing to give up short-term policy gains in its fight to achieve long-term institutional gains. Even though this procedure did not have a formal status as it was not subject to third party enforcement by the European Court of Justice, it had an effect in practice (Hix 2005). For example, this became clear in a subsequent case on Transferable Securities (COD 1995 188), where the EP and the Council also failed to reach agreement in the conciliation committee, again due to disagreements on comitology.

Anticipating a subsequent rejection by the EP, the Council decided not to reconfirm its common position on Transferable Securities (EP 1999). These developments acted as a stepping-stone to the removal of the provision in the treaty allowing the Council to reconfirm its common position, when the Amsterdam Treaty was negotiated. Since May 1999, it has been the case that an act automatically falls if no agreement is reached within the conciliation committee between the EP and the Council.

Tsebelis and Garrett argued that whereas the Council's possibility to reinstate its common position in cases where the conciliation committee had failed to reach an agreement in the Maastricht version of co-decision made the Council more powerful than the EP, the removal of this possibility in the Amsterdam Treaty turned the EP and the Council into co-equal legislators in the procedure (2000). On the contrary, a game theoretical study by Napel and Widgren (2003) of the conciliation committee found that even though the Council and the EP are in a symmetrical position in the legislative procedure, the Council is still the dominant legislative body. For example, the Council benefits from being more conservative than the EP and thus less willing to change the existing legislative situation. König (2008) and Hagemann and Hoyland (2010) also question that the EP and the Council are on an equal footing in co-decision. In a supranational preference scenario where the EP has incomplete information, König shows the Council can exploit co-decision to its own advantage. This allows the Council to present a minority rather than its qualified majority position to the EP and thus get a better deal than it is likely to get under consultation with a fully informed Commission. According to Hagemann and Hoyland, the Council's advantage results from its ability to exploit the fact that the EP majority requirement at second reading is more demanding than at first reading. They argue that the absolute majority requirement in the second reading makes it harder for the EP to amend or reject a Council proposal than to accept it and that this gives the Council conditional agenda setting power.

Empirical work has produced mixed findings on the relative strength of the EP and the Council. Numerous policy cases demonstrated EP success in the co-decision procedure. A good example comes from the Working Time Directive for the road transport sector (COD, 1998 319). Here, the EP succeeded in expanding the scope of the directive from drivers employed by freight companies to self-employed drivers, despite heavy opposition from several member states. Corbett *et al.* explicitly comment that, 'there is little question that without co-decision it would have been impossible to overcome such opposition and to reach an agreement with the Council as a whole' (Corbett *et al.* 2007).

Quantitative research on the relative strength of the Council and the EP has produced mixed findings. König *et al.*'s empirical analysis (2007) of 'who wins?' in the conciliation processes shows that the EP won more often than the Council, but that the Council was more successful in disputes that involve multiple issue dimensions. In contrast, Miller's study (1995), conducted shortly after conciliation had entered into force, showed that in 46 per cent of the first 26 cases, the text emerging from the conciliation committee was effectively the same as the Council's common position. In 23 per cent it was closer to the EP position, and in only 31 per cent did it genuinely reflect a joint position between the Council and the EP. Also a recent study by Mariotto and Franchino (2011) of the 175 conciliation committee joint texts since Maastricht show that even if the advantage of the Council has diminished in conciliation, these texts are more similar to the prior positions of the Council than the EP. Moreover, Thomson and Hosli's more general analysis (2006) shows that even if the relative power of the EP to the Council is greater in co-decision than in consultation, it is the Council that is most powerful.

In order to move forward from the debate about the relative influence of the EP, the literature has examined the effect of other factors on variations in the EP's influence, such as enlargement, its internal unity, the costs and benefits of different types of policy, the types of EP amendments proposed and whether the EP rapporteur and the Council presidency come from the same country or party group (Kreppel 2002; Burns 2005; Burns et al. 2012; Mariotto and Franchino 2011; König et al. 2007). Findings from a recent study by Costello and Thomsen (2011) for example show that the choice of EP rapporteur affects the EP's success vis-à-vis the Council. It is in a better position when it is represented by a rapporteur close to the EP median and who comes from a national governing party. Such rapporteurs may have an easier time being taken serious by the Council and also be able to use its party links to the Council to facilitate bargaining.

The role of the Commission has received much less attention. The Commission is the loser in co-decision since its formal powers are reduced in this procedure compared to previous legislative procedures. If files move to the final stage, it can no longer make it harder to the Council to adopt files by requiring it to vote by unanimity (Rasmussen 2007). It still serves as an honest broker in conciliation helping the Council and the EP to reach a deal, but at this stage it also cannot withdraw its legislative proposals anymore (Rasmussen 2007). Scholars acknowledge that it has lost ground (Thomson and Hosli 2006). Some have even gone as far as to conclude that, 'under co-decision the Commission is effectively taken out of the game before the real bargaining over policy begins' (Garrett 1995, 305), and that the Amsterdam version of the co-decision procedure, 'renders the Commission irrelevant' (Crombez 2001, 101). Others have acknowledged the Commission's difficulties in co-decision, but have argued that despite being put in 'a situation of structural disadvantage' by the treaty, the Commission is not irrelevant to the procedure and can still exploit its expertise to informally influence the final deals (Rasmussen 2003; Burns 2004). Moreover, König et al. (2007) show that the likelihood for the Council and the EP of winning in conciliation is higher for an institution if it has the Commission on its side.

Intrainstitutional Implications

A distinct feature of many of the early studies of co-decision was that they regarded the legislative bodies as unitary actors without much concern for internal developments. Although there may be good justifications for doing this, there are also some associated weaknesses. Hence, it is clear today that co-decision has had consequences not only for the power distribution *between* but also *within* the legislative bodies. Different studies have examined the consequences of concluding at different stages of the co-decision procedure for the relative distribution of power between the actors within the institutions.

Most importantly, the effect of early conclusion in co-decision has been examined. Ever since the Amsterdam Treaty introduced the possibility for reconcile deals already at first reading, there has been a clear trend to expand the use of this option. The increasing share of first reading deals exceeded even the expectations of practitioners involved in conduct of the procedure (Shackleton 2000). From the 899 co-decision cases submitted to the fifth and sixth EPs, 53 per cent have been completed at the first reading stage, second reading conclusion took place for a little under a third of all files and third reading conclusion (after the involvement of the conciliation committee) is the exception, accounting for 8 per cent of the files (10 per cent of all files introduced have not been completed by the end of this study). If we distinguish between first reading conclusions which have involved a genuine early agreement and those which have been finalized at first reading because the EP has made null or a trivial number of amendments that the Council has accepted in full, early agreements still account for between 41 per cent and 57 per cent of all co-decision files concluded between 2005 and July 2009[4] (Toshkov and Rasmussen 2012). Formally an early agreement reached at first reading looks exactly like an ordinary first reading where all EP compromises are accepted by the Council. However, the difference is that these EP amendments are not longer *pure EP amendments* but compromises agreed between the EP and the Council in informal negotiations. In this way, the EP amendments are simply *vehicles* for incorporating the compromises into the Commission proposal.

Since Amsterdam, the practices of concluding early have also been expanded by inventing so-called *early second reading agreements*. An early second reading looks like a case where the Council's common position is adopted without being amended by the EP. However, the difference is that the common position is no longer a *pure* Council text but a legislative compromise reached between the EP and the Council. The method was used, for example, to reach agreement on the Multi-annual Financial Framework for all Community Expenditure during the period 2007–2013. Such deals are now also formally recognized in the Joint Declaration between the institutions on the practical arrangements of the co-decision procedure. They are attractive to the EP because it is often easier for it to persuade the Council to incorporate its views before the Council reaches its formal position.

The tendency to conclude deals earlier in the co-decision procedure over time can be interpreted as the cumulative result of several factors (Rasmussen 2011; Reh *et al.* forthcoming). Rasmussen's study of 401 first readings under co-decision in the fifth EP term shows that early conclusion is not primarily a question of the technicality and political salience of the file, as the institutions originally expected it to be. Instead, there is evidence that factors linked to the character of the bargaining context matter. In particular, the tendency to conclude at first reading has increased over the years as the working relationship between the two co-legislators has become closer, and bargaining uncertainty between them has been reduced. Reh *et al.* (forthcoming) confirm and add to these findings in a study of all co-decision files in fifth and sixth term which uses a modified version of the dependent variable that also comprises early second reading agreements, but excludes first readings deals that were not negotiated informally. Their study includes a series of new control variables and indicators measuring the character of the files. Their findings also demonstrate an increased tendency to conclude early over time and the higher the workload of the legislators and indicate that early agreements are not ruled out even when the files are highly politically salient.

Farrell and Héritier (2004) argue that the possibility of reaching these "early agreements" between the legislative bodies at the first reading stage of co-decision has benefited certain actors at the expense of others within the institutions. They argue that the option to conclude early has benefited actors with 'formal negotiating authority', as well as actors from the legislative bodies who possess policy expertise, networking skills, and political support. In the EP, this means that large political groups and the spokesperson on each file (the so-called rapporteurs) have become more powerful at the expense of small political groups and the chairmen of the standing committees. Rasmussen (2011) does not question these findings, but shows that, despite this strengthening of ability of rapporteurs to influence legislative outcomes early in the policy process, the implications for the EP as a whole may not be as serious as first thought. Hence, her analysis demonstrates that these deals are not very likely in exactly the situations where rapporteurs might have an incentive to exploit such a power. The more biased the view of the rapporteur compared to the median member of the EP the less likely are such deals.

In addition to examining how early conclusion has affected the relative distribution of power between the actors within the institutions, scholars have studied what the consequences of concluding at the conciliation stage are for the ability of different actors to affect the legislative deals. Rasmussen (2005) has examined whether actors with a seat in the conciliation have a disproportionate influence on the policy outcomes compared to the average member of their parent bodies. She argues that, rather than being runaway agents, EP conciliation delegates behave as loyal agents of the EP in the conference phase. She also shows that EP conciliation delegates are generally representative of their parent body (Rasmussen 2008) and highly constrained. Their scope for negotiation is explicitly limited to the second reading amendment made to the Council's common position by the EP, and during the conciliation negotiations rapporteurs regularly have to report back to and obtain mandates from their conciliation delegations (Rasmussen 2005; Rasmussen and Shackleton 2005).

Finally, studies have examined intrainstitutional power implication of co-decision by comparing the role of different actors within the EP and the

Council in co-decision and other legislative procedures. Yordanova (2011) has for example shown that there is a systematic difference between co-decision and consultation in who gets allocated rapporteurships. Under codecision, legislators from the centre-right majority coalition and loyal party group members are privileged, whereas policy outliers and experts are given access to consultation reports only. On the Council side, Häge (2011) finds a systematic difference in which actors that take the decisions under co-decision and consultation. He shows that decisions are more likely to reach the ministerial stage under co-decision than consultation even when controlling for the salience of the files. According to him, increased politization of Council decision-making in co-decision can help explain why the likelihood that bureaucrats refer decisions to the ministerial level is higher under co-decision than consultation. Along the same lines, Neuhold and Settembrini (2009) also find increased evidence of politization within the EP in co-decision as opposed to other procedures. Apart from the first reading, they find that co-decision reports are more contested at the committee stage than reports adopted under other procedures.

Early Agreements and Their Normative Implications

A final body of literature on co-decision has dealt with the normative implications of the procedure. This discussion has been closely linked to the increased tendency to conclude earlier in the policy process. Clearly, these developments have been successful from an efficiency point of view because they have enabled the co-legislators to save time and energy by concluding early. Nevertheless, a price may have been paid in terms of democracy (Raunio and Shackleton 2003; Farrell and Héritier 2004; Häge and Kaeding 2007; Héritier and Reh, forthcoming). When early deals are reached, democratic control is not always strong. The co-decision literature emphasizes how the environment of delegation is different at the first reading stage than later in the legislative process (Farrell and Héritier 2003, 2004; Rasmussen and Shackleton 2005). In the beginning of the legislative process, no established institutional position of the EP needs to be defended; there are also no restrictions on the type of amendments that can be introduced to the Commission's proposal. The EP as a whole does have to accept the deals reached with the Council before they can become law just as it does at second and third reading. However, at an early stage the average parliamentarian often does not have a sufficient level of information to assess the actual content of the deals. Moreover, attempts to modify a deal are often not practically feasible as this would reopen the negotiations and waste time and energy.

This means that early deals are often reached among a small subset of legislators, and it can be relatively difficult for the EP as a whole, and the public, to monitor what is going on in these informal trialogues. The EP itself is aware of the democratic challenges involved in reaching early agreements. A paper on internal reform, agreed by its working group at the beginning of 2008, expressed concerns about what it called the 'potential lack of transparency and democratic legitimacy' in early agreements.[5]

The paper also argued that there is 'too much focus on fast-track negotiations at the expense of an open political debate within and between the institutions'.[6] The Commission too is aware of the side effects of early agreements and has recently stated in its internal co-decision guide that first reading conclusion 'should not be pursued indiscriminately for more sensitive dossiers because of their substantial, budgetary, legal or institutional aspects'.[7]

An attempt has been made to avoid some of these problems by letting the Conference of Presidents adopt a set of guidelines for the adoption of first and second reading agreements in November 2004 (EP 2006, 2009; Shackleton and Rasmussen 2005; Héritier and Reh forthcoming). Also the subsequent Joint Declaration from 2006 on the conduct of co-decision between the institutions made reference to how each institution would designate and define the mandate of their representatives in the meetings. Moreover, the guidelines have recently been replaced by a 'Code of Conduct for Negotiating Codecision Files' adopted by the Conference of Presidents on 18 September 2008. According to the EP itself, 'In comparison to the rather vague term "guidelines", its name is intended to underline its more binding nature' (2009, 26). The code also specifies in more detail how negotiations ought to be conducted, for example how the negotiating team of the EP should be monitored and collect mandates and what the role of the relevant EP committee monitoring the key negotiators is. When the EP adopted a revision of its Rules of Procedure on 6 May 2009, a new Rule 70 on 'Interinstitutional negotiations in legislative procedures' was introduced and the code got annexed to its 'Rules'. Finally, the Working Party on Parliamentary Reform introduced a period of 'cooling-off', i.e. 'a period of at least one month between the vote on any legislative report in committee (on first reading) and the vote on it in plenary'. The rule became applicable on 1 January 2008 and its aim was to facilitate time for deliberation within the political groups after conclusion of first readings negotiations with the Council and the resulting vote in the EP plenary (EP 2009).

All of this demonstrates that early agreements are no longer struck in the kind of institution-free environment that existed initially. Nowadays, there are quite elaborate constraints on the key negotiators by requiring them to report back to their committees regularly, collect mandates, etc. It is difficult to generalize how well the guidelines work in practice, because of the very different ways negotiations are conducted in different committee areas, but there is a tendency for a greater number of people to be involved in the EP negotiations than was sometimes the case previously (EP 2006). The success of the guidelines in fulfilling their purpose is indeed mixed (Héritier and Reh forthcoming).

At the same time, a recent study shows that, even if early agreements restrict access of certain actors to decision-making, they *do* allow more time for substantive debate at the first reading stage than similar files reconciled later in the legislative process (Toshkov and Rasmussen 2012). Moreover, there has been a tendency for first readings in co-decision to last longer after the new guidelines have been implemented and research shows that the EP spends more time on its first readings in co-decision compared to other legislative procedures even when we control for the political salience of the files (Toshkov and Rasmussen 2012; Rasmussen and Toshkov 2011). At the same time, the democratic concerns of early agreements go much further than criticizing their speed of course, and successful internal coordination and control of its negotiators will be crucial for the EP to guarantee the democratic control of EU decisions in the future. Recent work by Héritier and Reh (forthcoming) and Obholzer and Reh (2012) indicate dissatisfaction with existing reform efforts to strengthen democratic control of first readings within the EP and new reforms of the code of conduct and the EP's Rules of Procedure are now underway.

Conclusion

The everyday workings of the institutions in the EU legislative processes look remarkably different today than they did before Maastricht. The changes introduced by the co-decision procedure have affected the balance of power between the EU institutions and internal decision-making within these institutions in a fundamental way. After 20 years of co-decision it is clear that this procedure has influenced both the way the institutions cooperate and the role of different actors within each of them.

Despite continued discussion of whether the EP and the Council are on an equal footing in the procedure there is no doubt that this procedure has dramatically changed the role of the EP in the legislative process from what it was before Maastricht. Co-decision has effectively made the EP a co-legislator to the Council in a variety of legislative areas by requiring that the Council and the EP jointly agree on the vast majority of legislative compromises. Moreover, even if the EP and the Council may not have equal power in practice, the EU functions in a bicameral fashion with the EP and the Council acting as co-legislators in this procedure. Whereas the EP had not previously been an institution of much concern for the Council, co-decision was instrumental in establishing a closer relationship between these two bodies. The fact that the Council could no longer ignore the views of the EP and that it could no longer keep interacting with it through the Commission, forced the institutions to be moved closer together and increase coordination.

Co-decision has also resulted in some important changes to the internal lives of the institutions themselves. It has contributed to increased politization and put pressure on the institutions to act efficiently. The institutions have organized their internal work differently and have developed new internal procedures and rules for their daily business. As a result, actors holding different portfolios within their institution have had to play different roles than they used to. Some internal actors have benefited from these chances while others have been put in a more vulnerable position when it comes to influencing the daily state of deliberations with the other co-legislator. The price for the institutions as a whole may have been high since increased efficiency might have come at a cost. Critics have explained how the new working method have gradually moved negotiations to small forums in which average members of the EP and the Council do not participate and whose work they cannot control. At the same time, it remains yet to be seen whether the leading negotiators from the co-legislating actually try to abuse their role in these shielded negotiation forums. Moreover, we still do not know how effectively the procedures set up to monitor and control the daily work of these smaller negotiating forums will end up functioning.

No matter what, it is clear that consequences of introducing co-decision have been far reaching both in inter- and intrainstitutional terms. Moreover, these changes do not only have an effect when the issues at the negotiating table concern co-decision but spill over to the other shares of their daily business. In this way, co-decision has been more than simply a new legislative procedure for the Community by introducing changes that they go far beyond the interaction in the procedure itself. It has acted as a venue for some more fundamental changes in the EU construction and the way it operates as a political system.

Notes

1. OJ C 331, 7.12.1993, p. 1.
2. OJ C 148, 28.5.1999, p. 1 and OJ C 145, 30.6.2007, p. 5.
3. Because the preferences of the key actors are in practice not always distributed in such a way that it is possible for the EP to make a proposal that would make a qualified majority of the Council better off with than any unanimous decision the Council could make. Moreover, even if this were possible, it is not a given that the EP would be able to agree to such a proposal and that the Commission would support it.
4. In order to separate early agreements from the rest of the first reading conclusions Toshkov and Rasmussen (2011) employed automated text analysis on the documents provided by the Legislative Observatory database. More details on the procedure are given in 'Research design and data' section of their article.
5. Despite the fact that early agreements raise democratic challenges for the EP, a recent article has argued that they may also benefit the EP by strengthening its relative influence vis-à-vis the Council. The argument is that because the Council has limited organizational resources it is more willing to give in to the EP to reach a deal early on compared to later on in the policy process (Häge & Kaeding 2007).
6. European Voice 'MEPs quick-deal concerns', vol. 14, no. 2, 17 January 2008.
7. 'Nouvelle version du guide pratique des procedures internes — codécision', SPI(2007)73.

References

Boyron, S. 1996. Maastricht and the codecision procedure: a success story. *International and Comparative Law Quarterly* 45, no. 2: 293–318.

Burns, C. 2005. Who pays? Who Gains? How do costs and benefits shape the policy influence of the European Parliament. *Journal of Common Market Studies* 43, no. 3: 485–505.

Burns, C., N. Carter, and N. Worsfold. 2012. Enlargement and the environment: the changing behaviour of the European Parliament. *Journal of Common Market Studies* 50, no. 1: 54–70.

Corbett, R. 2000. Academic modeling of the codecision procedure: a practitioner's puzzled reaction. *European Union Politics* 1, no. 3: 373–81.

Corbett, R. 2001. A response to a reply to a reaction (I hope someone is still interested!). *European Union Politics* 2, no. 3: 361–6.

Corbett, R., F. Jacobs, and M. Shackleton. 2003. The European Parliament at fifty: a view from the inside. *Journal of Common Market Studies* 41, no. 2: 353–73.

Corbett, R., F. Jacobs, and M. Shackleton. 2007. *The European Parliament*. London: John Harper.

Costello, R., and R. Thomson. 2011. The nexus of bicameralism: rapporteurs' impact on decision outcomes in the European Union. *European Union Politics* 12, no. 3: 337–57.

Crombez, C. 1997. The co-decision procedure in the European Union. *Legislative Studies Quarterly* 22, no. 1: 97–119.

Crombez, C. 2000. Codecision: towards a bicameral European Union. *European Union Politics* 1, no. 3: 363–81.

Crombez, C. 2001. The Treaty of Amsterdam and the co-decision procedure. In *The rules of integration. Institutionalist approaches to the study of Europe*, ed. G. Schneider and M. Aspinwall, 101–22. Manchester: Manchester University Press.

Dimiter Toshkov, and Anne Rasmussen. 2012 Time to Decide: The effect of early agreements on legislative duration in the EU, *European Integration online Papers (EIoP)*, Vol. 16, Article 11 http://eiop.or.at/eiop/texte/2012-011a.htm. (accessed Oct 1 2012)

Duff, A., J. Pinder, and R. Pryce. 1994. *Maastricht and beyond: building the European Union*. London: Routledge.

Earnshaw, D., and D. Judge. 1995. Early days: the European Parliament, co-decision and the European Union legislative policy process post-Maastricht. *Journal of European Public Policy* 24: 624–49.

Earnshaw, D., and D. Judge. 1996. From co-operation to co-decision. The European Parliament's path to legislative power. In *European Union – power and policymaking*, ed. J. Richardson, 96–127. London: Routledge.

EP. 1995. Delegations to the Conciliation Committee: progress report for the second half of 1994.

EP. 1997. Delegations to the Conciliation Committee: progress report, 1 August 1996 to 31 July 1997, PE 223.209.

EP. 1999. Delegations to the Conciliation Committee: Activity Report 1 November 1993–30 April 1999.

EP. 2000. Delegations to the Conciliation Committee: Activity Report 1 May 1999 to 31 July 2000.

EP. 2006. Conciliations and Codecision Activity Report, DV/651053.

EP. 2007. A Guide to how the Parliament co-legislates, DV\684001EN.doc.

Farrell, H., and A. Héritier. 2003. Formal and informal institutions under codecision: continuous constitution-building in Europe. *Governance* 16, no. 4: 577–600.

Farrell, H., and A. Héritier. 2004. Interorganizational negotiation and intraorganizational power in shared decision making: early agreements under codecision and their impact on the European Parliament and Council. *Comparative Political Studies* 37, no. 10: 1184–212.

Farrell, H., and A. Héritier. 2007. Codecision and institutional change. *West European Politics* 30, no. 2: 285–300.

Foster, N.G. 1994. The New Conciliation Committee Under Article 189B EC. *European Law Review* 19, no. 2: 185–94.

Garman, J., and L. Hilditch. 1998. Behind the scenes: an examination of the importance of informal processes at work in conciliation. *Journal of European Public Policy* 5, no. 2: 271–84.

Garrett, G. 1995. From the Luxembourg compromise to codecision: decision making in the European Union. *Electoral Studies* 14, no. 3: 289–308.

Garrett, G., and G. Tsebelis. 2001. Understanding better the EU legislative process. *European Union Politics* 2, no. 3: 353–66.

Hagemann, S., and B. Hoyland. 2010. Bicameral politics in the European Union. *Journal of Common Market Studies* 48, no. 4: 811–33.

Héritier, A., and C. Reh. Forthcoming. Codecision and its discontents: intra-organisational politics and institutional reform in the European Parliament. *West European Politics*.

Hix, S. 2002. Constitutional agenda-setting through discretion in rule interpretation: why the European Parliament won at Amsterdam? *British Journal of Political Science* 32, no. 2: 259–80.

Hix, S. 2005. *The political system of the European Union*. London: Palgrave MacMillan.

Häge, F. 2011. Politicising Council decision-making: the effect of European Parliament empowerment. *West European Politics* 34, no. 1: 18–47.

Häge, F., and M. Kaeding. 2007. Reconsidering the Parliament's legislative influence. formal vs. informal procedures. *Journal of European Integration* 29, no. 3: 341–61.

Hörl, B., A. Warntjen, and A. Wonka. 2005. Built on quicksand? A decade of procedural spatial models on EU legislative decision-making. *Journal of European Public Policy* 12, no. 3: 592–606.

Jacobs, F.B. 1997. Legislative co-decision: a real step forward? Paper presented at the Fifth Biennial Conference of the European Community Studies Association, Seattle, 29 May–1 June.

Kardasheva, R. 2009. The power of delay: the European Parliament's influence in the consultation procedure. *Journal of Common Market Studies* 47, no. 2: 385–409.

König, T. 2008. Why do member states empower the European Parliament. *Journal of European Public Policy* 15, no. 2: 167–88.

König, T., B. Lndberg, S. Lechner, and W. Pohlmeier. 2007. Bicameral conflict resolution in the European Union. An empirical analysis of conciliation committee bargains. *British Journal of Political Science* 37, no. 2: 281–312.

Kreppel, A. 2002. Moving beyond procedure. An empirical analysis of European Parliament legislative influence. *Comparative Political Studies* 35, no. 7: 784–813.

Mariotto, C., and F. Franchino. 2011. Explaining outcomes of Conciliation Committee's negotiations. Paper prepared for the 'Decision-making before and after Lisbon workshop', Leiden University, November 3–4.

Miller, G. 1995. Post-Maastricht legislative procedures: is the Council institutionally challenged? Paper presented at the Fourth Biennial Conference of the European Community Studies Association, Charleston, April.

Moravscik, A. 1998. *The choice for Europe. Social purpose and state power from Messina to Maastricht*. Ithaca, NY: Cornell University Press.

Moser, P. 1997. The European Parliament as a conditional agenda setter: what are the conditions? A critique of Tsebelis (1994). *The American Political Science Review* 90, no. 4: 834–8.

Napel, S., and M. Widgren. 2003. Bargaining and distribution of power in the EU's Conciliation Committee, *CESifo Working Paper No. 1029*.

Neuhold, C., and P. Settembrini. 2009. Achieving consensus through committees: does the European Parliament manage? *Journal of Common Market Studies* 47, no. 1: 127–51.

Obholzer, L., and C. Reh. 2012. How to negotiate under co-decision in the EU. Reforming trilogues and first-reading agreements, *CEPS Policy Brief No. 270*, May.

Rasmussen, A. 2003. The role of the Commission in co-decision: a strategic facilitator operating in a situation of structural disadvantage. *European Integration Online Papers* 7, no. 10, http://eiop.or.at/eiop/texte/2003-010.htm (accessed 1 October 2012).

Rasmussen, A. 2005. EU conciliation delegates — responsible or runaway agents? Principal–agent analysis and the study of delegation. *West European Politics* 28, no. 5: 1015–34.

Rasmussen, A. 2007. Challenging the Commission's right of initiative? Conditions for institutional change and stability. *West European Politics* 30, no. 2: 244–64.

Rasmussen, A. 2008. The EU Conciliation Committee. One or several principals? *European Union Politics* 9, no. 1: 87–113.

Rasmussen, A. 2011. Time choices in bicameral bargaining: evidence from the co-decision legislative procedure of the European Union. *European Union Politics* 12, no. 1: 41–64.

Rasmussen, A., and M. Shackleton. 2005. The scope for action of European Parliament negotiators in the legislative process: lessons of the past and for the future. Paper presented at the Biennial Conference of the European Union Studies Association, Austin, Texas, March 31–April 2.

Rasmussen, A., and D. Toshkov. 2011. The inter-institutional division of power and time allocation within the European Parliament. *West European Politics* 34, no. 1: 71–96.

Raunio, T., and M. Shackleton. 2003. Co-decision since Amsterdam: a laboratory for institutional innovation and change. *Journal of European Public Policy* 10, no. 2: 171–87.

Reh, C., A. Héritier, E. Bressanelli, and C. Koop. Forthcoming. The informal politics of legislation: explaining secluded decision-making in the European Union. *Comparative Political Studies*.

Rittberger, B. 2000. Impatient legislators and new issue-dimensions: a critique of the Garrett–Tsebelis 'standard version' of legislative politics. *Journal of European Public Policy* 7, no. 4: 554–75.

Scully, R.M. 1997a. The European Parliament and the co-decision procedure: a reassessment. *Journal of Legislative Studies* 3, no. 3: 58–73.

Scully, R.M. 1997b. The European Parliament and co-decision: a rejoinder to Tsebelis and Garrett. *Journal of Legislative Studies* 3, no. 3: 93–103.

Selck, T. 2004. The European Parliament's legislative powers reconsidered – assessing the current state of the procedural models literature. *Politics* 24, no. 2: 79–87.

Shackleton, M. 2000. The politics of codecision. *Journal of Common Market Studies* 38, no. 2: 325–42.

Thomson, R., and M. Hosli. 2006. Who has power in the EU? The Commission, Council and Parliament in legislative decision-making. *Journal of Common Market Studies* 44, no. 2: 391–417.

Tsebelis, G. 1994. The power of the European Parliament as a conditional agenda setter. *American Political Science Review* 88, no. 1: 128–42.

Tsebelis, G. 1996. More on the European Parliament as a conditional agenda setter: response to Moser. *American Political Science Review* 90, no. 4: 839–44.

Tsebelis, G. 1997. Maastricht and the democratic deficit. *Aussenwirtschaft* 52, no. 1/2: 29–56.

Tsebelis, G., and G. Garrett. 1997. Agenda setting, vetoes and the European Union's co-decision procedure. *Journal of Legislative Studies* 3, no. 3: 74–92.

Tsebelis, G., and G. Garrett. 2000. Legislative politics in the European Union. *European Union Politics* 1, no. 1: 9–36.

Tsebelis, G., C.B. Jensen, A. Kalandrakis, and A. Kreppel. 2001. Legislative procedures in the European Union: an empirical analysis. *British Journal of Political Science* 31, no. 4: 573–99.

Tsebelis, G., and J. Money. 1997. *Bicameralism*. Cambridge: Cambridge University Press.

Westlake, M. 1994. *A modern guide to the European Parliament*. London: Pinter.

Yordanova, N. 2011. Interinstitutional rules and division of power within the European Parliament: allocation of consultation and co-decision reports. *West European Politics* 34, no. 1: 97–121.

The Maastricht Treaty and the European Council: The History of an Institutional Evolution

WOLFGANG WESSELS

Department of Political Science, University of Cologne, Germany

ABSTRACT Since its creation in 1974 the European Council has turned into the key institution in the institutional architecture of the EU polity. The Maastricht Treaty on the European Union was a history-making product of this body of heads of state or government. For the institutional evolution of the European Council itself the Maastricht Treaty confirmed and reinforced trends starting with the Hague summit in 1969. This article covers the pre-history of the European Council as well as the road from the birth of the European Council in Paris, 1974, to the Maastricht Treaty and the next steps via two treaty revisions and the constitutional convention to the Lisbon Treaty in 2009. This article will not only try to satisfy some historical curiosity, but point out fundamental factors, explaining why Union executive leaders have invested time and energy in the labour-intensive and partly frustrating exercise of the making and working of their club: this key institution helped them to emerge as powerful multi-level players in a multi-institutional architecture.

The Maastricht Treaty was a history-making act of heads of state or government. The agreement of the national leaders opened a new age for European construction and generally for Europe. Before, the fall of the Berlin Wall, leading to the end of German and European division and of the bipolar confrontation between the superpowers, had fundamentally changed Europe's political landscape. After some short but serious hesitations about the future direction of European construction, the highest political representatives of the 'masters of the Treaties' (BVerfG 2009, para. 298) upgraded the political significance of the EU by shaping the highly ambitious Maastricht Treaty. Though formally members of both the European Council and the 'Intergovernmental Conference' (see, for the legal differentiation, de Schoutheete 2012, 44), the heads of state or government of the then 12 EU member states used the European Council to exercise a role as constitutional architect for the Union.

We can highlight a long and differentiated set of items pointing at the relevance of the Maastricht 'Treaty on the European Union'. The High Contracting Parties of the treaty not only baptized this political system as the 'European Union'; they achieved major system-making decisions — especially the creation of the Economic and Monetary Union. It also redesigned the Union's general constitutional framework, with the temple structure based on three pillars.

The respective treaty provisions also formed a revised institutional architecture. Besides extending the powers of the EP by introducing the co-decision procedure, the treaty formulated a set of functions and of institutional features for the European Council. My article will deal with the Maastricht Treaty's contribution to shaping the institutional form of this key institution. I will not deal with all functions exercised by the European Council as constitutional architect in system-making or as ultimate decision maker in policy-making, but rather analyse its formal features along three institutional models, which signal competing conceptions of this key body.

One major point of departure follows a conventional approach. This 'presidency model' starts with the French version of a 'Europe des patries'. The 'summit' at the apex of the Union's institutional pyramid is then the most authoritative sign of the 'con-federal' nature of the European construction (Fontaine 1979, 357). The European Council is per se the supreme authority for Europe, as its members as top national policy-makers are the key actors to 'formulate a consistent set of national preferences', bargain with one another to reach 'substantive agreements' and finally 'choose to delegate and pool sovereignty in international institutions that secure the substantive agreements they have made' (Moravcsik 1998, 20). Irrespective of the legal words of primary law, the European Council is supposed to be the key locus of power in the EU, exercising the prerogatives of ultimate leadership. Such a body of national leaders of sovereign states should not be subject to any legal constraints.

As a clear alternative to the 'presidency model', the 'council model' aims at integrating the political potential of the highest national decision-makers into the 'ordinary' institutional architecture characterized by the Community method. National chief executives then act according to the relevant treaty rules, including the use of qualified majority voting. As one among several possible Council formations, the European Council may take legally binding decisions applicable for all relevant policy domains and modes of governance as regulated by EU treaties. The European Council will be subject to the constitutional checks and balances of the EU system; thus in this model the Court of Justice of the European Union is empowered to review the legal acts of the European Council. In this model the body of the heads of state or government becomes 'communitarised'. Following neo-functionalist logics (see, e.g., Niemann and Schmitter 2009), the Union's heads of state or governments turn into 'agents' of functional spill-over mechanisms. So-called 'necessities' from 'anonymous' structural forces (Hallstein 1969), especially those arising from the 'market' or the 'logics' of the international system, push the chief executives of the day to extend the scope of common policies and improve earlier institutional structures and procedures.

In my fusion model (see Wessels 2005, 2010) the European Council is the driver of a fundamental evolutionary dynamic of the EU system. It incorporates and carries forward both the vertical fusion between levels as well as the horizontal fusion between EU institutions, as it is the central institution in a complex vertical multi-level constellation and in horizontal multi-institutional architecture with a large and differentiated set of modes of governance (Diedrichs *et al.* 2011): each head of state or government has — as multi-level player — a 'double hat': he is active in a set of opportunities and constraints on the European and domestic level. In order to enhance their problem-solving capacity, the members of the European Council turn this institution into a norm entrepreneur, exercising important rule-making functions in an increasing number of policy fields of vital national interest, jointly with other EU institutions. At the same time the highest representatives of the European states protect their respective national influence by at least reinforcing their own institution in the EU architecture.

With our focus on institutional evolution, we run the risk of falling into traps resulting from a sometimes too-narrow look at this unconventional institution. A first bias, and in quite a lot of academic contributions, consists in just enumerating the treaty provisions. As a consequence, one might easily draw faulty conclusions if the 'legal words' are taken to constitute the 'real world'. Such a shortcoming might not only lead to a misleading analysis of this strange *sui generis* institution itself; it might also miss a rare opportunity to explain essential developments in the European Union's evolution in the post-World War II history of Europe. Just to look at the forms — and not at the political functions and major agreements — might block a deeper understanding of the dynamics of the European construction itself, taken up and reinforced by the Maastricht Treaty.

There is a second major trap in analysing and assessing this institution: we might be persuaded too easily by a purely intergovernmental characterisation and explanation of this institution; there is a temptation to reduce the role of the European Council to a presidency model in which national leaders just agree on 'big bargains' at 'critical junctures' or on sovereignty-sensitive domains like foreign and security policy. Such a view underestimates the extensive agenda the European Council pursues in its regular work, and its on-going influence on major domains of policy-making. Thus, keeping the council model and the fusion model as points of reference helps us to reduce these risks.

Pre-history: Roads to the European Council's Creation

For analysing the Maastricht provisions on the European Council we need to look at the history of this key institution. I propose to start with the summit at The Hague in 1969, as this conference was a 'turning point' (see Bitsch and Loth 2009, 110) to 'relaunch the European integration' (Marhold 2009, 24), and thus a milestone for the history of the European construction in general (see Mittag and Wessels 2004). It set a path (Pierson 2000) which influenced not only the agenda of the Maastricht Treaty but is still affecting the Union's agenda.

Points of departure for analysing this event are changes in the historical context — especially the economic and political crises of the late 1960s. One major motivation to convene the summit was the desire to overcome the EC's internal institutional blockages; this interest was reinforced by major pull effects from developments in the international system. Problems in the final years of the Bretton Woods system were creating serious difficulties for European economies. The Soviet invasion of Czechoslovakia in 1968 and the intensification of the Vietnam War had reduced the hope for a detente in the bipolar world with a potential 'third power' role for Europe.

This kind of challenge was also typical for later periods. The leaders of the EC member states were confronted with a strategic choice: should they use the then existing EC merely as one among several technical organisations with restricted functional objectives in clearly delimited domains — similar to a European OECD — or should they upgrade this framework into a comprehensive priority arena for tackling major international economic and political challenges? To formulate it from a more fundamental perspective: was the EC to be extended to be the major arena for pursuing their problem-solving instinct over a broad range of public policies?

The historical context also led to a renaissance of fundamental motivations in France and Germany. The French strategy for the European construction was, in 1969 (as before and later on, including the Euro zone crisis 40 years later), strongly influenced by its assessment of the growing economic power of its neighbour on the other side of the Rhine.

The agreement of the conference, achieved on the first evening of the summit in bilateral talks between the French President Pompidou and the German Chancellor Brandt (Brandt 1978, 321f), paved the way to the next stages up to the Lisbon Treaty and the crises from 2008 onwards. As to 'completion', the heads of state or government agreed 'to lay down a definitive financial arrangement for the common agricultural policy' which included the creation of 'own resources' and 'greater budgetary powers for the European Parliament' (The Hague, December 1969).[1]

'Enlargement' in the direction of the UK was agreed on with a major precondition that 'applicant States accept the Treaties and their political aims [and] the decisions taken since the entry into force of the Treaties' (*ibid.*, point 13). It pre-fixed the third condition of the so-called Copenhagen accession criteria, which the European Council passed in 1993.

As for 'deepening', the conference requested the Council of Ministers to produce a plan 'with a view to the creation of an economic and monetary Union' (*ibid.*, point 8), which then led to the 'Werner Plan' and initiated the process leading eventually to the Economic and Monetary Union. On the matter of political co-operation, the foreign ministers were instructed to 'study the best way of achieving progress in the matter of political unification within the context of enlargement' (*ibid.*, point 15). Thus, the heads of state or government launched the procedure for 'European Political Cooperation' (Allen and Wallace 1982, 24–7) in foreign policies, which became the 'Common Foreign and Security Policy' under the Maastricht Treaty.

For understanding the making of and working of the European Council it is important to note that the summit contributed to framing the perception of national leaders with regards to European construction. In their view, 'those who bear the highest political responsibility in each of the member states' (The Hague, December 1969) stressed 'the irreversible nature of the work accomplished by the Communities… paving the way for a united Europe capable of assuming its responsibilities in the world of tomorrow' (*ibid.*).

Even if we acknowledge some usual summit rhetoric, the top national politicians signalled to themselves and also to their political and administrative machinery that they had earmarked the European construction as a priority arena for a joint exercise of shared responsibility on a broad set of public policies.

However, even with this basic commitment, the national leaders were not able to take any significant steps to reform the institutional architecture, as deeply rooted conflicts about the general direction and the finality of the integration construction were not overcome. This obvious misfit between ambitious political objectives on the one hand and the unreformed set-up of institutional arrangements on the other is also of significance for the later conceptual debate on the European Council in the Maastricht Treaty and beyond.

Given the upgrading of the European level and faced with the weak performance of Community institutions, it's not a surprise that in the following years further *ad hoc* summits were held — in Paris in 1972 and in Copenhagen in 1973. They offered a wide range of experiences and lessons for institution building.

The Paris summit of 1974 then decided to create the European Council (de Schoutheete 2012, 44–6). Its chairperson, the French President Giscard d'Estaing, also coined the label of the new institution: 'the summits are dead, long live the European Council' (Moreau Defarges 1988, 35).

The key for this agreement was a deal to establish an institutionalized summitry and to introduce direct elections to the EP. Thus, this institutional package was balanced between more intergovernmental and more supranational elements: whereas the creation of the European Council was regarded as a 'victory' of intergovernmental strategy, federalists claimed that the commitment to the direct elections of the EP was a major step towards upgrading the EP as the body of representatives legitimized by the 'European people'.

This first significant agreement by the heads of state or government on the institutional architecture set a precedent; also, with later decisions including those for the Maastricht Treaty and up to the Lisbon Treaty, the heads of state or government reached a consensus on institutional issues only by pursuing both the intergovernmental and the supranational direction at the same time.

Shaping the Idée Directrice

In order to analyse the Maastricht formula for the European Council we need to look at the heritage and at the state of the deliberations and disputes about guiding concepts for the institutional model.

The *ad hoc* summits in the 1960s and early 1970s had intensified the debate on why and how regular conferences of the heads of state or government should be installed. The early controversy centred on whether an institutionalized summitry was desirable for the European construction at all. Inevitably, this question was linked to fundamental visions, narratives and theories of European integration. Based on long enduring disputes on the nature of the integration construction, political and academic debates on the overall role of the European Council were dominated by the cleavage between supranational and federal positions on the one hand and intergovernmental and con-federal views on the other. Although quite often those heated controversies may block an analysis of the European Council's real impacts on the institutional architecture, they also help us to understand certain pre-occupations which have come up repeatedly — also in the formulations of the Maastricht Treaty and in later periods of its evolution. Thus, some significant arguments in this apparently perennial war of words can explain major elements in the shaping and making of the respective institutional form for the European Council in the Maastricht Treaty and beyond, e.g., in creating and shaping the permanent presidency for European Council in the Lisbon TEU (Wessels and Traguth 2011). The long shadow of this debate affects the analysis and assessment of the European Council's position in the institutional balance in the EU architecture up to the presence.

The concept of an institutionalized summitry had been launched by de Gaulle, who saw in 'the realities of Europe' the need for a 'regular organised concert of the responsible government' with 'subordinated specialised working organisation' (de Gaulle 1970, 244–5; translation by the author). In his proposals for the summits in 1961, the Fouchet plans, more specific provisions for this body were then formulated. These formulations are an exemplary case for the presidency model. They were rejected especially by the smaller member countries. The provisions of the 1974 Paris Summit on the institutional features of the European Council, the starting point for the articles of the Maastricht Treaty, are more hybrid and in view of the models more ambiguous:

(2) Recognizing the need for an overall approach to the internal problems involved in achieving European unity and the external problems facing Europe, the Heads of Government consider it essential to ensure progress and overall consistency in the activities of the Communities and in the work on political co-operation.

(3) The Heads of Government have therefore decided to meet, accompanied by the Ministers of Foreign Affairs, three times a year and, whenever necessary, in the Council of the Communities and in the context of political co-operation.

> The administrative secretariat will be provided for in an appropriate manner with due regard for existing practices and procedures. (Meetings of the Heads of State or Government 1974)

A closer look shows us that the wording remained vague regarding the political functions the European Council was supposed to take up. In view of 'internal problems involved in achieving European unity' and 'external problems facing Europe', the text defined as a major task 'to ensure progress and overall consistency in the activities of the Communities and in the work on political cooperation'. With the term 'progress', the wording alluded in an ambiguous sense to system-making. These formulations did not delimit the scope of the potential agenda, allowing the members to deliberate about any subjects they considered appropriate for a summit.

The text documented an important concern of heads of state or government — namely to integrate different activities on the European level: in view of 'the need for an overall approach', these formulations stressed the nascent function of the European Council to bridge gaps between several domains of common activities and different modes of governance. Heads of state or government were supposed to 'ensure consistency' between external economic relations run by Community institutions according to the rules of the Rome Treaties and the (diplomatic) political cooperation managed jointly by national foreign ministries. The two 'pillars' of the EU's international actorness were and still are a regular topic when improving the external profile and performance of the EU. The Maastricht Treaty, like the Lisbon TEU, again addressed this issue.

The Paris text on the institutional form is short; it simply enumerates the members of a first and second rank ('accompanied by ministers of foreign affairs'). The provisions to meet as a 'Council of the Communities' indicates a certain, though not clearly defined location within the institutional architecture. This wording widely remained an empty prescription until new formulations in the Maastricht Treaty, but it had an impact on the membership. To meet as the Council meant that the president of the European Commission was a member accepted by the peer group in formal terms as one among equals. As to the frequency of meetings, the formulations prescribed a minimum number and allowed flexibility.

The presidency country, rotating on an equal basis among the member states, was put automatically in charge of the chair.

In view of different institutional models for the European Council, the agreement of the Paris 1974 summit was a typical diplomatic product. One reading might lead to the assessment that provisions are nearest to the council model of institutionalized summitry. Specific concessions on forms and functions of the European Council were granted to those who perceived summitry as a threat to the EC's supranational aspirations. However, it became clear that the founding fathers Giscard d'Estaing and Schmidt expected the meetings to include a full and frank discussion and, if necessary, decisions on all issues required, thus invoking a central feature of the presidency model. Giscard d'Estaing even drew an analogy to traditional 'governmental bodies' (Moreau Defarges 1988, 35).

With historical hindsight the first permanent President of the European Council explained the creation as a compromise:

> ... the European Council itself was the result of a legal and political compromise, between those Member States who wanted a strong executive power, through bringing together the heads of the national executives, and those who were against the new institution as such and who would have preferred a stronger Commission. (van Rompuy 2010, 5)

His additional assessment is near to the fusion model:

> ... this compromise has, in fact, overcome the old distinction between the intergovernmental and the supranational; it has resulted in a synthesis allowing the Union to build both on the strength of the Member-States and the qualities of our common institutions. (*ibid.*)

From Paris to Maastricht

The short Paris text on the European Council quickly proved to be insufficient to define its overall role; some of the founding members soon started to reflect on the optimal mixture of function and form for this institution.

Of high significance for formulating the European Council's future role was the nowadays almost forgotten 'Solemn Declaration' of Stuttgart of 1983. The members of the European Council then agreed on a set of objectives and principles for their own work. For the first time heads of state or government enumerated a differentiated set of major tasks reflecting some of the already practised functions of the European Council in its first years of existence. These formulations had long-lasting effects, as they returned later in the provisions of the Maastricht Treaty and were taken up again in the Lisbon TEU.

The heads of state or government defined the major functions of the European Council as:

- an initiator and agenda-setter;
- a provider of guidelines;
- a forum for deliberation;
- a bridge-builder between different pillars;
- a constitutional architect; and
- an external voice.

In the middle of the 1980s the new generation of members pushed the European Council towards more ambitious agreements. The French President Mitterrand, after a period of hesitation, the German Chancellor Kohl and the Commission President Delors, supported by other members, developed a set of bolder initiatives.

The first such initiative was the agreement on the goal of a 'Europe without frontiers' during the intergovernmental conference on the 'Single European Act'. This treaty amendment also revised legislative procedures by enlarging the scope of rules with a qualified majority voting in the Council and by increasing the rights of the EP.

The Single European Act did not locate the provisions on the European Council among the amendments to the original Treaties establishing the European Communities, but rather placed them in a separate title (Title I, 'Common Provisions'). While the High Contracting Parties thus codified the European Council in primary law for the first time, they allocated a special status to this body outside the Community checks and balances. This formal position outside the EC Treaty was then taken up by the Maastricht Treaty and kept until the revisions of the Lisbon Treaty. The original formulation of the Paris summit which appeared to be near to the council model was given up.

The specific provisions of the SEA on the European Council were limited: Article 2 confirmed the rules of membership with an equal status for the president of the Commission and second rank for ministers of foreign affairs. This first treaty wording did not define any functions for the European Council.

The Maastricht Treaty and its Revisions

The Maastricht Treaty, which entered into force in 1993, created a revised institutional architecture. For the European Council it formulated articles on the major institutional features, which were basically confirmed and partly amended by the Treaty of Amsterdam (1999) and the Treaty of Nice (2003). The relevant articles dealing with the European Council were valid until November 2009. In the following description I will refer to the articles in the version of the Nice Treaty.

The Maastricht Treaty and follow-up revisions extended the legal basis for the activities of the European Council; the number of references in the treaties increased from 13 in the Maastricht Treaty to 27 in the Nice Treaty.

As to legal status, the High Contracting Parties placed the European Council in the treaty chapter on 'common provisions'. Within the so-called temple structure of the EU system the European Council was positioned at the 'roof', as part of the 'single institutional framework' dealing with all three pillars of the Union's policy areas and its different modes of governance. The European Council however was not enumerated in Article 7 of the 'Treaty on the European Community' (TEC), which fixed the list of EC institutions. From this exclusion followed that the activities, agreements and acts of the European Council could not be subject to any judicial review of the legality of its acts by the European Court of Justice (ECJ) (Art. 46 TEU (Nice)). This legal provision implied that the European Council was located outside the EC's institutional architecture with its checks and balances, which is characterized by the fact that each organ has to respect the tasks of the others laid down in the treaty (Louis and Ronse 2005, 185f).

Thus, following the SEA, the Maastricht Treaty confirmed the legal status of the European Council as one of a specific nature. Apparently, the highest political representatives of the Masters of the Treaties preferred to keep their own institution out of too many procedural and legal constraints.

The basic provision (Art. 4 TEU (Nice)) took up earlier formulations about functions and forms:

> The European Council shall provide the Union with the necessary impetus for its development and shall define the general political guidelines thereof.
>
> The European Council shall bring together the Heads of State or Government of the Member States and the President of the Commission. They shall be assisted by the Ministers for Foreign Affairs of the Member States and by a Member of the Commission. The European Council shall meet at least twice a year, under the chairmanship of the Head of State or Government of the Member State which holds the Presidency of the Council.
>
> The European Council shall submit to the European Parliament a report after each of its meetings and a yearly written report on the progress achieved by the Union.

The article repeated formulations of the 1983 Stuttgart Solemn Declaration concerning the set of general tasks; it again underlined the terms 'provide impetus' and 'define general political guidelines'. The implied political functions, however, remain again vague and ambiguous.

The High Contracting Parties also extended the scope of the European Council's activities: beyond this general role assignment the treaty provisions also allocated additional tasks to the European Council. Of specific importance are the articles for a strong role in the second pillar, which the Maastricht Treaty established for the 'Common Foreign and Security Policy' (CFSP). They constitute the European Council as the most authoritative body in this field: the European Council 'shall define the principles of and general guidelines for the common foreign and security policy' (Art. 13 (1) TEU (Nice)) and 'decide on common strategies' (Art. 13 (2) TEU (Nice)); it shall also set the agenda for the Council. Beyond this role in normal policy-making for the second pillar, Article 17 (1) TEU (Nice) gives the European Council a gate-keeper position with respect to treaty-making in this policy domain: it has to take a first decision related to 'the progressive framing of common defence policy, which might lead to a common defence'.

The European Council's function as an ultimate decision-maker and highest instance of appeal is also inserted into this treaty chapter. Thus, in rare cases of qualified majority voting in the Common Foreign and Security Policy (Art. 23 (2) TEU (Nice)), the Council was empowered to refer an item vetoed by one member state 'to the European Council for decision by unanimity' (Art. 23 (2) TEU (Nice)).

Not only in the second pillar but also in the first — the EC pillar — the treaty provisions attributed certain tasks to heads of state or government. Dealing with macroeconomic and social issues, the European Council was empowered to agree on conclusions 'for the broad guidelines of the economic policies of the Member States and of the Community' (Art. 99 (2) TEC) and 'shall each year consider the employment situation in the Community and adopt conclusions thereon' (Art. 128 (1) TEC).

The Maastricht Treaty also introduced a new legal form: for certain delimited EC matters the body of the chief national executives was asked to act as the 'Council in the composition of the Heads of State or Government'. On this legal basis and following long-time practices, national leaders were to exercise electoral functions for top positions in the institutional architecture such as nominating the president of the European Commission (Art. 214 (2) TEC) and the president of the European Central Bank (Art. 112 (2) (b) TEC). In these cases, the body of the heads of state or government was enabled to pass decisions by a qualified majority vote — a feature which is also taken up by the Lisbon TEU.

The Council on this highest political level was also empowered to take essential system-making decisions, e.g., on entering the third step of the European Monetary Union (Art. 121 (4) TEC) and on accessions of new members into the EMU (Art. 121 (4) TEC). As Council the heads of states or government had also to get involved in the suspension of rights of members states in the case of a 'serious and persistent breach' of fundamental values (Art. 7 (2) TEU (Nice)).

When acting as a Council formation, the heads of states or government had to comply with the rules of the EC Treaty; it implied that the European Court of Justice might review the legality of these acts in view of the relevant primary law.

In the provisions for the third pillar, dealing with major items of justice and home affairs, the treaty did not assign any explicit role to the European Council, although the rules allowed it to become active in setting guidelines for problem-solving in these areas of public policies.

Reading these treaty provisions, we can identify considerable similarities to the presidency model — especially with reference to the general provisions and the treaty articles concerning the CFSP. However, in introducing 'the Council in the composition of the Heads of State or Government', the EC Treaty clearly follows the characteristics of the council model.

A further step in the evolution of the written provisions for the European Council but below a treaty amendment was the Seville 2002 agreement on the 'Rules for the organisation of proceedings of the European Council' (Seville, June 2002). After frustrating experiences with shortcomings in its intra-group working — manifested again at the labour-intensive summit in Nice (de Schoutheete 2012, 64) — the members agreed on rules for the 'preparation, conduct and conclusions' (Seville, June 2002) of their meetings. This document was based on a 'Report by the Working Party set up by the Secretary-General of the Council' of March 1999 (Piris and Trumpf 1999).

The Seville formulations served as a major point of departure for the decision on the 'Rules of Procedure for the European Council' (European Council Decision 2009/882/EU), which entered into force together with the Treaty of Lisbon on 1 December 2009.

Via the Constitutional Convention to the Lisbon Treaty

The heads of state or government did not regard the Maastricht Treaty and its two amendments as the final stage of Union's architecture. Especially in view of the challenges originating from the 'Big Bang' enlargement in 2004, the European Council pursued its role as constitutional architect, with the Lisbon Treaty as final product of its intensive work in the constitutional decade from 1999 to 2009. The Lisbon TEU and TFEU, then, constitute a major milestone in the evolution of the legal provisions for the European Council. Most probably the documents will constitute the formal point of reference for some time to come. The heads of state or government themselves have declared: 'The Lisbon Treaty provides the Union with a stable and lasting institutional framework. We expect no change in the foreseeable future' (Presidency Conclusion, December 2007).

The history of the respective articles in the Lisbon Treaty starts immediately with the post-Nice 2000 deliberations. With the Laeken agreement the European Council installed a 'Convention on the Future of Europe', which elaborated a 'Treaty establishing a Constitution for Europe' (Scholl 2006; Magnette and Nicolaidis 2004; Norman 2003). This unusual treaty-shaping body put the reform of the European Council high on its agenda and formulated proposals for the functions and the form of the European Council. Especially, the President of the Convention, Giscard d'Estaing, the mastermind of the making of the European Council in 1974, submitted three decades after his original contribution a far-reaching concept. Of specific importance was the controversial debate about the creation and the functions of a permanent president of the European Council (Traguth and Wessels 2004, 224–35; Norman 2003). After a draft by Giscard d'Estaing and an intensive dispute between large and smaller states the Convention finally agreed on a text based on a Franco–German proposal. The formulations of the Convention were confirmed in the subsequent intergovernmental conference leading to the official signing of the 'Treaty establishing a Constitution for Europe' (see, e.g., Laffan 2006).

The provisions on the European Council also survived the rejection of the Constitutional Treaty by the French and Dutch voters: the following intergovernmental conference drafting a 'Reform Treaty', later called the 'Lisbon Treaty', eliminated certain articles and changed others of the Constitutional Treaty, but member state governments and later the national ratification processes left the articles on the European Council untouched.

After three decades of existence the articles of the Lisbon Treaty mark considerable changes on the basic institutional features compared to the pre-existing legal provisions of the Maastricht and Nice TEU. The High Contracting Parties fully integrated the European Council into the treaty.

Major points of differences are:

- In the 'provisions on the democratic principles' (Title II TEU) the European Council is one of the institution mentioned in the article on 'representative democracy'(Art. 10 (1): 'Member States are represented in the European Council by their Heads of State or Government themselves democratically accountable either to their national parliaments or to their citizens' (Art. 10 (2)TEU). The European Council is then also enumerated in the list of the 'Union's institutions' (Art. 13 TEU).

- In these terms they upgraded the role of the European Council to complete treaty status and with it affected the overall institutional balance of the EU's architecture (Monar 2011). But with these rules the heads of state or government also set more constraints for their institution.
- Provisions of the TEU and TFEU (CEPS *et al.* 2010; Piris 2010, 205–9) then list the major functions and features of its institutional form (see Art. 15 (1) TEU). They took up the wording of the Stuttgart Solemn Declaration and the Maastricht Treaty. Thus, also in view of key areas of EU's activities on 'Union's external action' (Art. 22 TEU) and more specifically in the CFSP pillar (see Art. 26 TEU) the Lisbon TEU confirms and extends the legal empowerments of the European Council.

Whereas provisions on functions of this institution can be seen as a confirmation and as an extension of the Maastricht Treaty and its revisions, I argue that the High Contracting Parties of the Lisbon Treaty have fundamentally changed the institutional form. They inserted the European Council in the list of the 'Union's institutions' (Art. 13 TEU), and installed a permanent President (Art. 15 (5) and (6) TEU).

Even if we might not expect any changes in the treaty provisions for some time to come, the institutional evolution of the European Council has not come to an end. The crisis years have not only increased the use of its functions and extended some of them in a dramatic night session, but they have also affected relevant institutional features: with the creation of the Euro summit and its political and administrative infrastructure in new legal forms (Kunstein and Wessels 2011) heads of state or government have again changed the institutional form of their set-up.

Conclusions: Maastricht and Beyond: Creating Institutional Opportunities for Ambitious Multi-level Players

In an institutional analysis this article argues that the Maastricht Treaty and its two revisions have confirmed and extended earlier trends, whereas the Lisbon TEU has created innovative institutional features.

In terms of political relevance and impact the Maastricht Treaty has fundamentally increased the significance of the EU for European governments: member states have extensively extended the scope of dealing with public policies and differentiated their modes of governance (Diedrichs *et al.* 2011; Héritier and Rhodes 2011). The 'demand' on top national politicians for getting engaged increased, as did their 'supply' — exercising a leadership role in an arena which has become increasingly salient for their own role in domestic and international politics. The political programme of the Maastricht Treaty — especially the EMU — has augmented pressures for stronger cooperation among the 'bosses', which they did not want to leave to the Community's traditional institutional architecture. The European Council could offer institutional opportunities to the heads of state or government to act as multi-level players in a multi-institutional architecture. The national leaders have reinforced their own institution to achieve a leadership role in the EU system. Irrespective of all controversies about the functions and the exact form of the European Council, they created an institution which has served as a significant bridge between the national and EU arenas of their activities.

Regarding the models as points of reference I see several co-evolutions: whereas the Stuttgart Solemn declaration, the SEA and the Maastricht Treaty and its amendments have highlighted features which are characteristic of the presidency model, the council model has regained importance in the Lisbon TEU, though these treaty provisions exclude the European Council from the legislative procedures (Art. 15 (1) TEU). An increasing number of treaty articles in which the European Council has to share powers with other institutions point at trends towards a fusion process. Examples for this reading are the procedures for electing the President of the Commission (Art. 17 (7) TEU) and those for the revision of the treaties (Art. 48 TEU).

In an historical review the Maastricht Treaty had two major effects on the European Council: this act by the heads of state or government extended the policy agenda of their institution and it confirmed and extended fundamental institutional features.

Acknowledgements

This contribution is based on Wolfgang Wessels, *The European Council* (Palgrave, 2013). I thank Birte Windheuser for her support.

Note

1. This refers to the respective communiqué/conclusions of the heads of state or government/the European Council.

References

Allen, D., and W. Wallace. 1982. European political cooperation: the historical and contemporary background. In *European political cooperation: towards a foreign policy for Western Europe?*, eds. D. Allen, R. Rummel, and W. Wessels, 21–32. London: Butterworth.

Bitsch, M.-T., and W. Loth. 2009. European institutions and political integration. In *Experiencing Europe: 50 years of European construction 1957–2007*, ed. W. Loth, Baden-Baden: Nomos Verlagsgesellschaft.

Brandt, W. 1978. *Begegnungen und Einsichten: die Jahre 1960–1975*. Munich: Droemersche Verlaganstalt Th. Knaur.

de Gaulle, C. 1970. Discours et Messages. Avec le Renouveau. 1958–1962 (Plon).

de Schoutheete, P. 2012. The European Council. In *The institutions of the European Union*, ed. J. Peterson and M. Shackleton, 3rd ed., 43–67. Oxford: Oxford University Press.

Diedrichs, U., W. Reiners, and W. Wessels. 2011. The dynamics of change in EU governance. In *The dynamics of change in EU governance*, eds. U. Diedrichs, and W. Reiners, and W. Wessels, 1–20. Cheltenham: Edward Elgar.

Fontaine, P. 1979. Le rôle de Jean Monnet dans la genèse du Conseil européen. *Revue du Marché commun* 229: 357–65.

Hallstein, W. 1969. *Der unvollendete Bundesstaat. Europäische Erfahrungen und Erkenntnisse*. Düsseldorf: Econ Verlag.

Héritier, A., and M. Rhodes. 2011. *New modes of governance in Europe: governing in the shadow of hierarchy*. Houndsmills: Palgrave Macmillian.

Kunstein, T., and W. Wessels. 2011. Die Europäische Union in der Währungskrise: Eckdaten und Schlüsselentscheidungen. *Integration* 34, no. 4: 308–22.

Laffan, B. 2006. Getting to a European Constitution. From Fischer to the IGC. In *The making of a European Constitution. Dynamics and limits of the convention experience*, ed. S. Puntscher-Riekmann and W. Wessels, 69–89. Wiesbaden: VS Verlag für Sozialwissenschaften.

Louis, J.V., and T. Ronse. 2005. *L'ordre juridique de l'Union européenne*. Basel: Helbing and Lichtenhahn.

Magnette, P., and K. Nicolaidis. 2004. The European Convention: bargaining in the shadow of rhetoric. *West European Politics* 27, no. 3: 381–406.

Marhold, H. 2009. How to tell the history of European integration in the 1970s: a survey of the literature and some proposals. *L'Europe en formation* 50, no. 353/354: 13–38.

Monar, J. 2011. The European Union's institutional balance of power after the Treaty of Lisbon. In *The European Union after the Treaty of Lisbon: visions of leading policy-makers, academics and journalists*, ed. European Commission, 60–89. Luxembourg: Publications Office of the European Union.

Moravcsik, A. 1998. *The choice for Europe: social purpose and state power from Messina to Maastricht*. Ithaca, NY: Cornell University Press.

Moreau Defarges, P. 1988. Twelve years of European Council history (1974–1986): the crystallizing forum. In *The European Council 1974–1986: evaluation and prospects*, eds. J.-M. Hohscheit and W. Wolfgang, 35–60. Maastricht: European Institute of Public Administration.

Niemann, A., and P. Schmitter. 2009. Neofunctionalism. In *European integration theory*, eds. A. Wiener and T. Diez, 2nd, 45–66. Oxford: Oxford University Press.

Norman, P. 2003. *The accidental constitution. The story of the European Convention*. Brussels: EuroComment.

Pierson, P. 2000. Increasing returns, path dependence, and the study of politics. *The American Political Science Review* 94, no. 2: 251–67.

Piris, J.-C. 2010. *The Lisbon Treaty: a legal and political analysis*. Cambridge: Cambridge University Press.

Piris, J.-C., and J. Trumpf. 1999. Operation of the Council with an enlarged Union in prospect. Report of the working party set up by the Secretary-General of the Council. Brussels.

Scholl, B. 2006. The impact of constitutional traditions on the EU-reform discourse in Austria, France, Germany and the UK. In *The making of a European Constitution. Dynamics and limits of the convention experience*, ed. S. Puntscher-Riekmann and W. Wessels, 175–99. Wiesbaden: VS Verlag für Sozialwissenschaften.

Traguth, T., and W. Wessels. 2004. The Constituional Treaty within a fusion trend? In *The political dynamics of the constitutional reform*, ed. A. Michalski. Clingendael Institute: Den Haag.

van Rompuy, H. 2010. Speech by the President of the European Council, Mr Herman van Rompuy pronounced today at the 'Klausurtagung' of the CSU-Landesgruppe Wildbad Kreuth, Germany, January 7th, 2010, http://www.consilium.europa.eu/uedocs/cms_data/docs/pressdata/en/ec/112174.pdf (accessed 9 January 2012).

Wessels, W. 2005. The Constitutional Treaty: three readings from a fusion perspective. *Journal of Common Market Studies* 43, Annual, Review, 11–36.

Wessels, W. 2010. The European Council. Beyond the traditional view towards a fusion. In C *Chemins d'Europe. Mélanges en l'honneur de Jean Paul Jacqué*, ed. J.G. Cohen, 75–164, Paris: Dalloz.

Wessels, W., and T. Traguth. 2011. Der hauptamtliche Präsident des. Europäischen Rates: 'Herr' oder 'Diener' im Haus Europa? *Integration* 11, no. 4: 297–311.

Official Documents

BVerfG (German Federal Constitutional Court): 2 BvE 2/08, 30/6/2009, para. 1–42, http://www.bverfg.de/entscheidungen/es20090630_2bve000208en.html (accessed 10 October 2012).

European Council. 2002. Presidency conclusions, Seville, 21–22 June.

European Council. 2007. Presidency conclusions, Brussels, 14 December.

European Council. 2009. European Council Decision adopting its Rules of Procedure (2009/882/EU), 1 December.

Meeting of the Heads of State or Government. 1969. Communiqué, The Hague, 1–2 December.

Meetings of the Heads of State or Government. 1974. Communiqué, Paris, 9–10 December.

The Maastricht Treaty at Twenty: A Greco-European Tragedy?

JAMES A. CAPORASO & MIN-HYUNG KIM

Department of Political Science, University of Washington, Seattle, Washington, USA;
Department of Political Science, Illinois Wesleyan University, Bloomington, Illinois, USA

ABSTRACT   Since 2010, the financial crisis has raged across Europe, taking down governments of several members of the euro-zone in the process. Despite strong pressure for reform, and many meetings of heads of state, the problems are far from over. The crisis has been widely represented as a sovereign debt fiasco and a failure of fiscal policy by five peripheral member states (Greece, Portugal, Spain, Italy, and Ireland). However, the real causes of the predicament of the euro-zone are more complex. A satisfactory understanding of the crisis is only possible if we distinguish among four phases: background factors, including structural flaws in the original design of the Maastricht Treaty; capital flows and fiscal deficits; dynamics of divergence, especially regarding competitiveness; and the crisis dynamics. In this contribution we identify three sets of factors — i.e., market spillovers and policy externalities, insufficient information related to the management of risk, and perverse incentives related to the configuration of rules and institutions — that may lead to inefficient international outcomes in the environment of structural interdependence and full capital mobility, address how policy coordination can improve the results, explain how the euro-zone crisis developed, and explore a number of possible solutions.

Introduction

For the better part of the first decade of the twenty-first century, Greece enjoyed a powerful boom in its economy. This housing and consumption boom was fueled by high levels of borrowing at low rates of interest set by the European Central Bank (ECB). Investments did take place of course, but they were concentrated in housing, construction, and infrastructure improvements (Manolopoulos 2011, 25). By 2008 the boom had all but run its course and in the following year, the recession hit. Up until then, high levels of growth, along with government-doctored data on debt, had masked the true nature of the crisis. In the October of 2009, Prime Minister Papandreou reported the true level of Greek government debt at around 13 per cent of GDP, more than twice as high as previously thought. In January 2010 the European Union (EU) officially revised upwards Greek debt figures.

The Greek crisis brought dramatically into focus a complex set of issues centering on Greece and other members of the euro-zone who were thought to be in similar trouble. Initial analysis hastily placed Greece, Portugal, Italy, Ireland, and Spain in the same category, resulting in the unfortunate acronym of PIIGS.[1] The category reified the distinction between hard-working Northern Europeans and profligate Southerners. However, the category is conceptually misleading for it groups together countries that are very different in terms of etiology of the crisis. As Marzinotto, Pisani-Ferry and Sapir point out (2010), the Greek crisis is for the most part due to highly questionable fiscal policies along with weak state capacity in the area of tax collection. Existing EU policies and instruments, centering on enforcement of the Stability and Growth Pact (SGP), could have been used to bring Greece into compliance with the norms of the euro-area. Spain and Ireland are different cases altogether. Their difficulties result less from fiscal mismanagement and more from high volumes of capital crossing state lines, leading to credit-fueled booms in housing, tourism, and construction. Public debt was not the problem, especially in Spain, where as late as 2007 there was a budget surplus. But once the bubble burst, the perverse cycle of debt deflation dynamics kicked in, resulting in high levels of unemployment, weaker revenues, and high government debt. Public debt was not exogenous. Rather it was 'unsustainable debt accumulation in the *private* sectors of many euro-zone countries' (DeGrauwe 2011, 1) that was the main driver of the process.

We argue that the narrative of fiscal irresponsibility resonates with government leaders and even more with their restless publics. It would be more difficult for leaders to frame the problem as one associated with the free movement of capital, since this is one of the four fundamental freedoms of the EU, and an integral part of the single European market. Nothing could be more central to the European project than the completion of the market for capital. An important part of our story about the origins of the crisis, and responses to it, has to do with the tension which exists between the region-wide capital market and 17 national-level regulatory and fiscal systems. In the rest of our contribution, we set out our theoretical framework, describe the Maastricht Treaty and its flaws insofar as monetary integration is concerned, develop the theme that there is an unsustainable disjunction between the international market for capital on the one hand and the decentralized system of financial governance on the other, explore several scenarios of possible outcomes, and press our argument that we are likely to see both more centralized practices of coordination and more intrusive surveillance of national budgetary, fiscal, and macro-economic policies in the years ahead. We think developments so far provide support, albeit limited, for the argument that tighter coordination is required, along with a more credible commitment to backstop 'national' financial losses by EU institutions. Financial resources are part of the story but so are institutions.

Theoretical Approach

The framework employed in this piece is based on theories of international economic cooperation and coordination.[2] In choosing this framework, we bypass a major axis of theoretical debate on European integration — functionalism and intergovernmentalism. There are two main reasons for this choice. The first is that we see both state and private actors, at both national and regional levels, as crucial components of the process of monetary integration. There is an obvious endogeneity problem in the sense that the two sets of actors are both important and mutually determining of one another. We see little gain in arguing for the importance of private actors (functional forces), supranational actors such as the Commission, or state actors, a mainstay of intergovernmental analysis. The second reason is that we are less interested in the issue of state sovereignty versus supranational autonomy and more in whether states and private actors (particularly banks in our case) succeed or fail with regard to fashioning policies to meet the challenges of the current financial crisis. Of course, various attempts to solve the crisis may be located at different places on the sovereignty-supranationalism continuum. When the current financial crisis finally plays out — and we expect this to take a long time — analysts will no doubt assess the consequences for European integration, but such is not our goal in this piece.

Our working assumption agrees with that of Andre Sapir (2011). Sapir argues, convincingly we think, that the Maastricht Treaty did not create a political infrastructure to go along with monetary union. There was no real transfer of competence from the member states to the EU, there was 'no significant EU budget, no integrated financial supervision, no strong political counterpart to the central bank nor any provision for crisis resolution' (Sapir 2011, 6). In short, we have what Tommaso Padoa-Schioppa called 'a currency without a state' (cited in Sapir 2011, 8). As a result, we can examine the financial crisis from the standpoint of the member states attempting to find solutions in an environment where there are private social forces (banks, investors, protesters), governments, and international institutions such as the ECB, the Commission, the European Council, and the International Monetary Fund (IMF).

In what follows, we provide a brief working definition of cooperation and identify three factors relevant to its presence or absence. These factors are present in greater or lesser degree in all international situations, i.e., they are variables, but we think they tilt toward the high end of the spectrum in the setting of the euro-area where the 17 member states display unusually high levels of what Richard Cooper calls 'structural interdependence' (Cooper 1986, 292), meaning that the economies in question are open with respect to one another and that events in one country affect events (and perhaps policies and institutions) in the other member states. Such a situation of structural interdependence can be mutually beneficial of course but the links among countries can work both ways, i.e., they can act as transmission belts for conveying both positive and negative effects. Further, positive effects might only be realized if cooperation occurs and negative effects dampened or eliminated under the same conditions. In short, high levels of structural interdependence open the doors to a systematic analysis of cooperative behavior.[3]

We follow Keohane (1984) by defining cooperation as mutual adjustment of the policy of country A to take into account the preferences and outcomes for country B (1984, 51). Keohane argues that cooperative behavior as mutual adjustment is perfectly consistent with self-interest. It merely requires a situation where one actor cannot achieve its goals without the actions of another, perhaps several other, actors. Cooperation is unnecessary if autonomous actions also benefit others (pure market exchange) and impossible if interests are in perfect conflict, so that when A does well, B does poorly. The space for cooperative behavior lies between these two extremes and is most prominent in mixed conflict–cooperative incentive structures, such as the prisoners' dilemma, chicken, or battle of the sexes.

We argue that the conditions under which cooperative behavior can be mutually beneficial are extensive. Jeffry Frieden (2009a, b) makes the general case for cooperation when he points out that countries routinely pursue policies that are harmful to others, such as unilateral exchange rate policies, protectionist tariffs, and domestic anti-inflation programs based on uncoordinated interest rate hikes. In the language of economics, these policy actions create negative externalities. If these policies brought extensive gain to the initiating country, they would not be theoretically problematic but they often inflict damage on others without necessarily improving the position of the country undertaking the action. Better outcomes might be available for both countries with coordinated policies.

We identify three sets of factors that may lead to inefficient outcomes where coordination can improve the results. They are market spillovers and policy externalities, insufficient information related to the management of risk, and perverse incentives related to the configuration of rules and institutions. While these categories are well-known in economic theory, we say a brief word about each one, since we draw freely on developments within these categories to describe and explain how the financial crisis developed, where it is likely to go from here, and what the possible solutions are.

Market Spillovers and Policy Externalities

The ideal of market exchange involves transacting agents who internalize all costs and benefits. Third parties are not affected, either positively or negatively. Yet, in the real world market spillovers are pervasive and the higher the level of interdependence among countries, the greater these spillovers are likely to be. There is no one for one relationship between the level of economic exchange and the occurrence of spillovers since the specification of property rights is also variable across countries. Two countries with well specified property rights will not experience as many spillovers, given a constant level of economic exchange, as two countries with weakly specified rights.[4] Market spillovers occur when private agents conduct business, such as setting up a plant subsidiary across borders, which in turn gives rise to an externality, e.g., pollution. Policy externalities occur when a government policy, such as trade or monetary policy, leads to uncompensated costs to or benefits from another country.

As mentioned, these spillovers can be positive or negative. In the mid-1970s, the rate of growth of the German economy was considered important for all European countries, and Germany was referred to as the 'locomotive economy'. So a fiscal or monetary stimulus by the German government created benign external effects for others in the EU (and elsewhere), even if these effects were purely pecuniary (Buiter and Marston 1985, 1–2). The reason these policy externalities become of interest for cooperation theory is that they can provide the wrong incentives. Uncoordinated action may lead to 'too much harm' inflicted on others (negative externalities) just as it may lead to 'not enough good'. Countries that want their own economy to grow but not spend the resources (taxes, domestic spending) may wait it out and let other, perhaps larger, countries go first. This may lead to the underutilization of fiscal tools, a condition most likely to result among small open economies. The case for controlling negative spillovers is more obvious. A tariff by A may harm the exports of B who may then retaliate and impose its own tariff. A vicious spiral results in which the countries in question do worse than they would under cooperation.

Risk and Moral Hazard

We use the term risk to fit in with established usage: systemic risk, risky assets, risky loans, etc. However, our meaning is much closer to uncertainty in that we are interested in situations without known probability distributions. We follow Cooper who defines risk as 'the possibility of an unforeseen development that influences our welfare'[5] (Cooper 1986, 23). If risky ventures lead to successes or failures where costs and benefits are fully internalized, then risk would not present a problem. That this does not always happen is seen with the risk-taking behavior of economic and political units that are too big to fail. If a bank leverages its assets so as to increase its loans, it presents a problem for society at large. How should society deal with a bank that is 'too big to fail?' Anti-trust laws may deal only with industry structure that leads to uncompetitive behavior. But an industry (such as financial services) can be competitive and yet experience failures that create systemic risk (i.e., the failure of one may lead to failure of the system). In such an event, government will likely bail out the bank (s) so as to prevent damage to the economy as a whole but in bailing out the bank(s), it creates moral hazard. As Keohane puts it, if banks, in effect, 'have automatic insurance against disastrous consequences of risky but (in the short-run at least) profitable loans', they 'have incentives to follow risk-seeking rather than risk-averse behavior' (Keohane 1984, 96).

Perverse Incentives and Institutions

Institutions may facilitate cooperation and help governments and private actors overcome market failures. Consider the general case for institutions. Two agents transact (or wish to transact) to effect an economic exchange. The exchange can go awry, or fail to take place, due to a lack of trust, insufficient information, asymmetric information, fear, or perception of weak enforcement of the bargain. A bank panic, or run on the bank, is a classic case of macro-economic failure based on fear (the fear of being left without recourse to funds, because others have made withdrawals). The international system is particularly prone to panics since regulatory systems, even in the euro-area, are governed by the 'home country' principle while the financial system is itself heavily regionalized. It is sometimes thought that the Economic and Monetary Union (EMU) is immune from this problem, since levels of integration are quite high, but this is not the case. As Gros and Alcidi point out, within the euro-area, 'the usual assumption that public debt is risk-free does not hold' because no individual country has access to the printing press (Gros and Alcidi 2011, 1).

Of course, institutions are no magic cure. As we write this piece, the euro crisis is drawing on a wealth of institutions: the EU, the Commission, the European Council, the Directorate General for Economic and Monetary Affairs, the ECB, the Euro-Group, the IMF, and the G-20, just to name the most obvious actors. Even if an institutional 'cure' were foreseen, it might not be forthcoming, since not all problems have institutional solutions. The problem may be preferences (what do the relevant actors want?), resources, or even technology (designing the right mix of resources, rules, and strategies). Conceding these limits, however, institutions can provide better information (including the goals of other actors), better enforcement (better oversight, appropriate sanctions), and improved guarantees of what will happen if there are market failures at the international level. While most of the discussion regarding the financial crisis has to do with 'finding the right policy', the 'right policy' may be to provide the 'right institution'. We discuss this further in the next section on the development of the financial crisis.

The Maastricht Treaty, a Transnational Greek Tragedy

The Treaty on European Union (TEU), better known as the Maastricht Treaty, was agreed in December 1991 and came into effect in November 1993. The TEU took the unprecedented step toward monetary integration by setting a detailed timetable for the transition to EMU. The economic case for EMU was that it was necessary in order to reap the full benefits of the single market. A common currency and a European central bank would reduce transaction costs, manage uncertainty, and rationalize the financial as well as the trade side of the European regional economy.

In preparation for EMU, the Treaty established a number of convergence criteria[6] in the belief that high levels of economic homogeneity were needed to make the monetary union work. Contemporary critiques of EMU based on *ex post* knowledge that countries did not in fact sufficiently converge miss this important point, namely, that the Treaty did recognize that economic homogeneity, particularly with regard to inflation rates, budget deficits, and accumulated public debt, was highly desirable.

Nonetheless, the Maastricht Treaty had many flaws, and in some respects the euro-zone crisis was heralded by the structural flaws inherent in the Treaty. A tragedy, in the original sense, is a story in which someone comes to a bad end as a result of an inherent character flaw or a mistaken course of action. There is an air of inevitability about a tragedy which makes it only partly appropriate for our purposes. Not all problems of the euro are due to the faulty institutional design of the TEU. Some dynamics, e.g., the development of differential wage costs across countries, had their own sources and were not the inevitable outgrowth of the Treaty. The rest of this section is organized in such a way as to reflect a 'loose determinism' in the movement from the TEU to the present crisis. The organization is as follows: background factors, including structural flaws in the original design of the TEU; capital flows and fiscal deficits; dynamics of divergence, especially regarding competitiveness; and the crisis dynamics themselves.

Structural Flaws of the TEU and Stability and Growth Pact (SGP)

One feature of the TEU that proved to be problematic was that it provided for a common currency without a common governance structure or uniform banking regulations. Since the TEU left many rules of fiscal policy unsettled, the SPG adopted by the European Council in Amsterdam in June 1997 further spelled out the Maastricht fiscal criteria for joining Stage III of EMU. Most importantly, the pact specified the operationalization of the excessive deficit procedure (EDP) — i.e., how to penalize non-compliant countries running excessive deficits, which required an *ex-ante* agreement on fiscal discipline to prevent fiscal misbehavior of member states after the introduction of the euro (Frieden, Gros, and Jones 1998). The strict interpretation of the EDP was deemed necessary to enhance the credibility and the legal independence of the ECB.

As a centerpiece of EMU, however, the SGP had several shortcomings. First, the SGP had a bias toward price stability, and as a result, exerted pressure on governments to shift the domestic policy mix toward fighting inflation at the expense of growth strategies. Second, the SPG had weak enforceability (i.e., there was no way to legally enforce sanctions), especially to large members such as Germany and France. For instance, when France and Germany exceeded the 3 per cent budget deficit limit in 2003, they were not penalized. This not only provoked the SGP crisis but also 'raised questions about the credibility and long-term viability of EMU'

(Dinan 2010, 403). Third, the reform of the SGP in 2005 sought to clarify the TEU's EDP by adding some flexibility in assessing the euro-zone members' deficit situation for special circumstances and to impose common rules on national fiscal policy-making. Nonetheless, it did not take advantage of the period of high economic growth to rein in members' spending (Hoebner 2011, 3).

Fiscal Deficits, Capital Flows, and Market Spillovers

The second problem of the Maastricht Treaty is that it overly focused on fiscal irresponsibility to the exclusion of other potential problems, such as those arising from loosely regulated capital flows. The main concern was that states not run up large annual deficits and that they avoid high levels of debt to GDP. There were compelling reasons for this. Given the disjuncture between the independent fiscal policies of member states and the centralized monetary policy set by the ECB, common fiscal rules specified by the SGP were deemed essential for the proper functioning of currency union. This was particularly important not only because high deficits could produce higher interest rates and inflation but because 'once in EMU incentives to pursue budgetary retrenchment [might] weaken substantially as an equivalently powerful penalty — expulsion from the euro-zone — is not foreseen by the [Maastricht] Treaty' (Buti, Franco, and Ongena 1998, 87). To put it bluntly, the signatory states were concerned that once members had qualified for entry into monetary union, they would backslide into fiscally less responsible habits.

However, except for Greece, the debt problems in the euro-zone were caused by the unsustainable debt accumulation in the private rather than the public sector. As De Grauwe (2011) points out, from 1999 to 2007, the level of bank and household debt in many euro-zone countries dramatically increased whereas the government sector experienced decline of debt from 72 per cent to 68 per cent of GDP. In fact, Ireland and Spain experienced declines in their government debt ratios prior to the crisis but struggled with government debt once the crisis began. The Maastricht Treaty did not anticipate private sector accumulation of debt. This is surprising, to some degree, since one goal of EMU was to free up capital flows from the capital surplus countries to capital scarce countries. As Eichengreen argues:

> Households borrowed from local banks, which in turn borrowed from banks elsewhere in Europe. In other words, banks in the problem countries 'funded' their loans not only by accepting deposits from residents but also by borrowing on the interbank market. As a result, massive amounts of capital flowed from France, Germany, and the other core countries to Ireland and southern Europe. (Eichengreen 2011, 91)

Once these private imbalances existed, even the governments of budget surplus countries such as Ireland and Spain had to take over huge private (mostly bank) debt, allowing their own government debt to rise to unsustainable levels.

The macroeconomic imbalances in uneven capital flows across countries created further imbalances in the trade sector, specifically in the current account balance. While we have not traced the complete causal chain, there is clearly a correlation between the growth of credit in the peripheral countries and balance of trade deficits. As Wolff (2011, 1–3) demonstrates, countries which received a strong dose of credit growth — Greece, Portugal, and Spain in particular — were also countries with the highest deficits in their current accounts as a share of GDP. By contrast, Germany, Austria, the Netherlands and Finland had low credit booms and surpluses in their external current accounts.[7] Italy, who received a modest external credit boost, experienced a near balance in its trade account while Ireland had the unexpected combination of high credit with a near balance. Ireland constitutes an anomaly.

The problems caused by these capital flows did not restrict themselves to GIIPS. Because of the high level of economic interdependence among euro-zone countries, market spillovers were pervasive. All countries in the euro-zone have high exposure to the problems of other member states. Below is a table on the degree of trade openness based on the amount of trade within the EU-17 (Table 1).

We can see from this table that levels of trade (import) dependence on other members of the euro-zone are quite high. They range from a low of 23 per cent in Ireland in 2010 to a high of 68 per cent in Portugal. With import levels this high, there is a greater possibility of transmission of economic disturbances among countries in the euro-zone.

Data on financial interdependence is even more relevant to our concerns. In a study done for the ECB, Castren and Kavonius (2009) constructed a network model based on bilateral financial linkages and found that there was a growing co-variation of risk among the actors in the system, in that 'bilateral financial account linkages have grown markedly, with the banking sector constituting a key part of the euro area financial system' (2009, 6). Shocks generated in one part of the system generally spread quickly to other parts of the system, even when there were no explicit defaults. The threat of default seemed to be sufficient to trigger a response, especially in cases where banks or firms were highly leveraged (2009, 6).

Table 1. Degree of Openness to EU-17 (import shares)

	2007	2008	2009	2010
Greece	48	45	47	42
Ireland	26	26	23	23
Italy	47	44	46	44
Portugal	66	63	69	68
Spain	50	46	47	na

Source: United Nations Commodity Trade Statistics Database, Data accessed multiple times in October 2011. Available at http://comtrade.un.org/db/default.aspx. Note: Figures represent the share of imports from other EU-17 trade partners.

In back of this growing financial interdependence lay the steady growth of cross-border banking activity since the Single European Act came into existence. After the liberalization of capital movements in the early 1990s, integration of banking activities (mergers and acquisitions) across borders increased. As Sapir notes, these changes led to a consolidation of banking activities at the international level, with the result that 'by 2007 European banks were significantly more internationalized than banks in the US, Japan, or China and this resulted primarily from their internationalization within Europe' (Sapir 2011, 2).

In summary, by the year 2000, Europe was highly integrated in both trade and financial services. These two modes of integration served as conduits for the transmission of international disturbances, as well as benefits. When the financial crisis hit Greece in 2009, the chances that contagion could be avoided were small. Once the full dimensions of the Greek crisis were known by early 2010,[8] the markets immediately feared similar problems in other troubled economies of Spain, Italy, Ireland, and Portugal.

The Dynamics of Divergence

During the 1990s, candidate countries for EMU were subject to the rigors of the convergence criteria. These chiefly had to do with controlling inflation and government debt. After introduction of the euro in 1999 the hope was that the economically weaker member states would increase the competitiveness of their economies, since devaluation would no longer be available to adjust to trade deficits. Without the devaluation tool, the weaker member states would be forced to absorb competitive pressures through their domestic labor markets and production structures, i.e., through wage and price controls. Thus, GIIPS countries would be provided an opportunity to converge not just fiscally but also in terms of the efficiency of domestic production.

We now know, however, that wage and competitiveness differentials between Europe's core and periphery increased further in the first decade of the euro. However, this was not due to productivity differences among euro countries, as we can see from the graph below (Figure 1).

From this graph we see that three countries experienced negative or zero growth in labor productivity during this period, but one of the countries was Germany. Spain's figures for 2010 are exactly the same as for 1998 (107.8) while Italy showed downward movement from 120.7 to 101.4 (a drop of 19.3 points). What seems clear is that the competitiveness gap between Germany and the GIIPS countries did not come from a productivity gap from 1998 through the first decade of the twenty-first century. If the competitiveness gap were due to productivity differences, we would expect to see substantial increases in Germany's productivity figures and at least relative decreases for the other countries. The relationship between Germany's productivity movement and changes in the GIIPS countries is small and it goes in the wrong direction.

Instead of productivity, it appears that wage differences may be a bigger source of concern. As Darvas, Pisani-Ferry, and Sapir argue, 'nominal wages

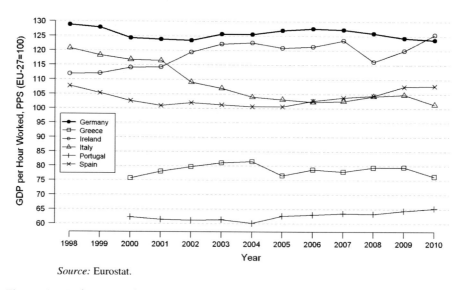

Source: Eurostat.

Figure 1. Labour productivity per hour worked relative to EU-27 (EU-27 = 100)

have... grown beyond what is justified by productivity gains, resulting in prices growing too fast relative to the rest of the euro area' (2011, 2). Nominal wage increases translate into higher prices which in turn imply goods that are less competitive in world markets. This growing loss of competitiveness for the GIIPS countries, along with the implications for the balance of trade, soon became a major part of the developing euro-crisis. Below we provide a figure showing the growing differences in unit labor costs among key countries in relation to costs in Germany (Figure 2).

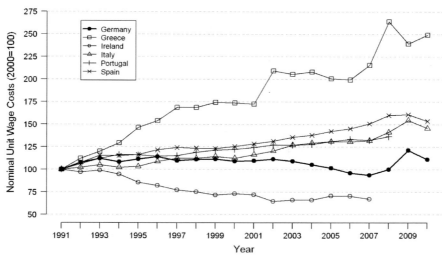

Source: European Commission Economic and Financial Affairs.

Figure 2. Nominal unit wage costs, manufacturing industry (1991 = 100)

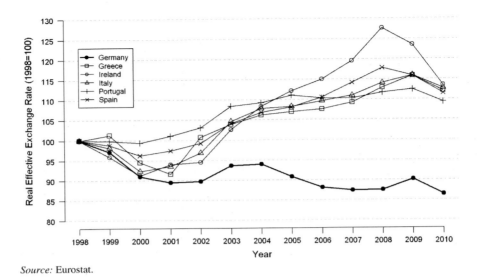

Source: Eurostat.

Figure 3. Real effective exchange rate (1998 = 100)

We can see from this graph that wage costs for Greece increase most rapidly from 1991 to 2010, followed by Spain, Italy, and Portugal. Germany's rate of wage growth is quite modest and increases very little over the 20-year period in question. Ireland's rate of wage growth is the slowest, which runs against expectations that high wage growth translates into being non-competitive in relation to others but here we suspect that more dramatic wage growth for Ireland occurred in the non-manufacturing sector.[9] The important point is that there is a substantial divergence between the growth of wages in Greece, Spain, Italy, and Portugal on the one hand, and Germany on the other.

The growing divergence of wages is likely to have an effect on relative prices of traded goods between countries. We can see from the graph below (Real Effective Exchange Rates) (Figure 3) that the effective exchange rates between Germany and the five GIIPS countries diverge significantly from 1998 to 2010, peaking between 2007 and 2009. Real effective exchange rates are essentially measures of relative prices among countries. They attempt to get at the costs and prices of goods as they are traded in international markets. The term 'exchange rate' may be misleading since all countries in the euro-zone are by definition sharing the same currency. However, prices of traded goods can vary as a result of country-specific inflation, differential wage increases, varying tax rates, or relative price movements in any productive factor. What we clearly see in this figure is that the prices of German goods, those traded on international markets, go up much more slowly than the prices of goods produced in Portugal, Spain, Italy, Ireland, and Greece, giving an advantage to traded German goods. But does the divergence in effective exchange rates lead to growing gaps in the balance of trade?

Unfortunately, we do not have direct data on the trade patterns of Germany and the GIIPS countries. However, we do have data on the net

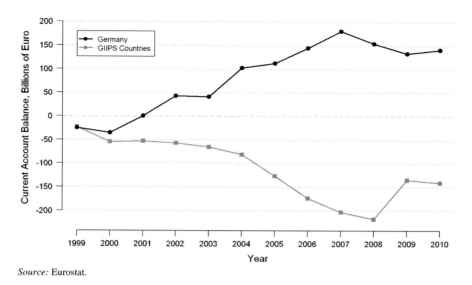

Figure 4. Current account transactions, Germany and GIIPS

balance of trade for Germany, Portugal, Spain, Italy, Ireland, and Greece. If we add together the deficits of the five GIIPS countries and plot them against the figures for Germany, we get the following (Figure 4). There is clearly a negative relationship between Germany's trade position and the aggregate position of the GIIPS countries at the global level. If we had better data on bilateral trade, we could test this relationship more precisely.

This interpretation is strengthened by the work of Marzinotto, Pisani-Ferry, and Sapir (2010). First, Marzinotto and her coauthors convincingly show that labor costs have increased for the GIIPS countries relative to the euro area as a whole. The costs relative to Germany are likely to be even more pronounced. If labor costs of Spain are indexed to those of the euro area so as to equate them to 100 in 1998, and if we observe movements of these costs over time, we find that by 2007 relative wage costs in manufacturing have shot up to 118.3 per cent. Along with this, employment in construction increased to over 13 per cent and the current account balance rose to minus 10 per cent of GDP. This finding supports the next link in a causal chain, namely, a strong relationship between real effective exchange rates, the loss of competitiveness and a negative balance of trade (Figure 5).

There seems little dispute of a basic point about competitiveness, namely that those countries whose real exchange rates have increased relative to others in the euro area, do worse in terms of export performance. Germany and Austria, the two countries whose relative exchange rates have gone down, also have the highest (Germany) and the third highest (Austria) improvements in their exports.[10] And the focus on real exchange rates correctly predicts four out of five of the GIIPS countries in terms of their balance of trade profile. All four (Italy, Spain, Greece, and Portugal) have negative export growth relative to the euro average and all four have weak competitiveness scores, reflected in worsening relative exchange rates, in relation to the euro average. The exception is Ireland, which has an

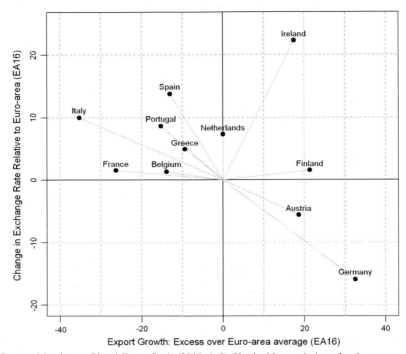

Source: Marzinotto, Pisani-Ferry, Sapir (2010, 1–8). Used with permission of authors.

Figure 5. Real effective exchange rates and export performance

unfavorable relative exchange rate but is above the average in terms of export performance. While this is not the place to assess in detail the Irish exception, one hypothesis is that Ireland experienced most of its wage growth in the service sector and that there are weak mechanisms to transmit wage increases to the tradable sector. Spain, for example, has labor market institutions that transmit increases from one sector to another while perhaps Ireland does not, though admittedly, this analysis is far from conclusive.

The Crisis Dynamics

Our argument so far has been that the Treaty itself, along with the capital liberalization directive, provided the permissive conditions for capital movements across countries. This in turn led to excessive borrowing by GIIPS countries, which then stimulated consumption and increased domestic demand for labor, leading to higher wages not justified by productivity increases, and thus led to declining competitiveness in the peripheral countries (Alcidi 2010). It is now clear that the euro area has moved into a full-fledged crisis, both a banking crisis and a sovereign debt crisis. Part of the reason has been irresponsible fiscal behavior, part unregulated capital flows, and part the crystallization of problems resulting from wage increases untied to productivity improvements. The crisis dynamics include recognition of heavy indebtedness, the rising and in some cases prohibitive costs of borrowing, the construction of various bailout schemes to allow countries to meet payment obligations, and increasing financial panic reflected in the flight to safety. The euro countries, led by Germany and France, are struggling to find a way out that accomplishes two sometimes contradictory objectives, first to save the countries most in danger and second to encourage a restructuring of those same countries' economies, including their labor markets, firms, banking institutions, and even infrastructure. The second goal is a worthy one, and necessary to put the troubled economies on a sound economic footing, but the time frame needed to accomplish this objective may be much longer than required for saving the patient. In general, it has been Merkel and Germany who want to see deep changes in the organization of economic activities and fiscal policies first, as a precondition for aid, and it has been Sarkozy and France who would like to see greater commitment to save countries on the edge of default, and attend later to the restructuring issues. As a recent article in the *Economist* put it, among recommendations for saving the euro, two different diagnoses often collide: 'one emphasises conditions as the only way to confidence. The other emphasises a confidence achievable only with unconditional support' (*Economist*, 17–23 September 2011, 75).

In tackling the financial crisis in the euro area, the EU acted to define a common approach for preventing a meltdown of European financial markets and adopted several initial measures. They include, among others, the agreement (with the IMF) on 2 May 2010 of a 100 billion-euro bailout package to rescue Greece, the decision on 9 May 2010 to create the European Financial Stability Facility (EFSF) that will safeguard financial stability of the euro area with a lending capacity of 440 billion euros, the provision (with the IMF) on 28 November 2010 of a 85 billion euro-bailout to the Irish Republic, the decision on 21 March 2011 to create the European Stability Mechanism (ESM) as a permanent bailout fund with a lending capacity of 500 billion euro and signing of that treaty in July 2011 (the revised treaty was signed again on 2 February 2012), the approval on 16 May 2011 of Portugal's 78 billion euro-bailout by finance ministers (and the IMF), and the ECB's announcement (which was triggered by the growing concern that the sovereign crisis may spread to the larger economies such as Italy and Spain) on 7 August 2011 that it will buy Italian and Spanish government bonds to bring down their borrowing costs.

However, these initial measures did not calm markets. Bond yields (between Germany and the troubled countries) continued to widen, suggesting investor fears that the crisis would not be easily resolved. In an effort to stem the escalation of the financial crisis in the euro-zone, therefore, much bolder and more comprehensive measures have been taken. On 26 October 2011 a package deal was adopted that dealt with Greek debt, preventing contagion, and recapitalizing banks. The package deal included such provisions as leveraging EFSF to boost its firepower to one trillion euros, forcing private investors to accept a 50 per cent haircut on Greek bonds, and pushing European banks to raise 106 billion euros in new capital. After the resignation of Greek (George Papandreou) and Italian (Silvio Berlusconi) Prime Ministers for their mishandling of the government debt crises in November, leaders of the euro-zone countries at an EU

Council summit on 9 December 2011 agreed to sign an intergovernmental treaty that aims to create a new fiscal union for Europe, which will mandate more centralized EU control over national budgets (i.e., a greater role for the Commission in drafting national budgets) and automatic sanctions for countries that fail to meet the deficit and debt reduction targets.[11] On 13 December 2011, the so-called Six Pack (the amended SGP, composed of five regulations and one directive proposed by the Commission and approved by all 27 member states and the Parliament in October 2011) entered into force with a new set of rules for fiscal and economic surveillance. Aiming at safeguarding financial stability, restoring confidence, and preventing future crises, the Six Pack contained the comprehensive reinforcement of economic governance in the euro-zone and in the EU and allowed stronger action when the budgetary execution of a member state deviates significantly — e.g., financial sanctions can be imposed by the Council on the basis of a Commission recommendation to member states currently in EDP who do not take adequate action to correct their excessive deficit, unless a qualified majority of member states vote against it (this is the so-called 'reverse qualified majority' voting procedure, which makes the enforcement of rules more automatic and credible).[12] On 2 March 2012 a total of 25 EU member states (Britain and the Czech Republic decided to opt out) signed the Fiscal Treaty (i.e., the Treaty on Stability, Coordination and Governance in the EMU, or TSCG) of which the content was endorsed at the last European Council meeting in January. Its main objective was to strengthen fiscal discipline and introduce stricter surveillance within the euro area by establishing a balanced budget rule (e.g., the annual structural government deficit should not exceed 0.5 per cent of GDP at market prices). The Treaty required the balanced budget rule to be incorporated into the member states' national legal system, preferably at a constitutional level, within one year of its entry into force.[13] It also empowered the European Court of Justice (ECJ) to impose sanctions (e.g., a penalty of up to 0.1 per cent of GDP, payable to the ESM in the case of euro area members) on countries running excessive deficits.

The ongoing crisis is not likely to be resolved soon. The large overhang of debt in both the private and public sectors will take a long time to extinguish. In addition, there are still large political disagreements that run along two axes: long-term and short-term fixes, represented in the German–French positions, and national vs. supranational control over the outcomes. To this point, there has been almost no actual delegation of authority to the European level, and it is not necessarily the case that those countries which want the strongest response in substantive terms also favor the strongest delegation of power to the European level. France, for example, would like to see quick and decisive action to salvage the troubled economies but is very reluctant to delegate powers to Brussels (the Commission, the ECJ, the European Parliament [EP]) to oversee the process by which budgets are brought into conformity with European standards. Likewise, Germany has so far firmly refused to accept ECB's large-scale intervention in the sovereign bond market (e.g., the ECB as lender of last resort) as well as radical increases of EU rescue funds.

Conclusion

The discussion of the flaws of the Maastricht Treaty and the development of the financial crisis in the euro-zone reveal the inconsistency between financial integration, financial stability, and national financial supervision autonomy, which is the so-called *financial trilemma* (Sapir 2011, 5). It illustrates the trade-off between financial integration and national financial autonomy. As for EMU, it suggests that coordination failure is highly likely in the euro-zone where financial markets have increasingly been integrated but their supervisory powers (regulatory oversight) remain in the hands of the home country (i.e., the home country principle). In this sense, the euro-zone's financial crisis was somehow foreseeable, since as the financial trilemma states, the desire to keep financial/fiscal authority at the national level is incompatible with the objectives of having capital mobility and financial stability all at the same time.

The euro-crisis is far from resolved and its outcome is unknown at this point. The euro could collapse and the EU might revert to a single market. While this is a low probability outcome in our opinion, it is one that is being discussed as a serious possibility. That it is unlikely does not mean it is unthinkable. An alternative outcome is that the stresses and strains of the North-South division might lead to a much smaller euro-zone with a northern tier including Germany, the Netherlands, Austria and Finland and a southern tier of Greece, Portugal, Spain, Ireland[14] and Italy. The most likely alternative to continuation of the euro-zone as presently constituted is for Greece to negotiate an orderly exit. Clearly, Greece is insolvent and cannot service its debts without substantial write-downs and external aid. According to one calculation, the primary budget surplus (i.e., the surplus net of interest) that is needed 'to reduce debt ratios to 60% of GDP by 2034 is 8.4% of GDP'. This, in turn, would require Greece to use at least one-third of its tax revenue for interest payments, a prohibitive sum by any calculation (Darvis, Pisani-Ferry, and Sapir 2011, 3). Greece is not in the position of an emerging market economy which has just experienced a cyclical downturn. It is deeply in debt and it will take years, and painful reforms, to correct the situation.

Much more likely are outcomes that will be costly but that will involve some combination of debt relief, emergency bailout funds, and buffering the crisis to prevent as much contagion as possible. All of this will be costly and does not guarantee protection against the spread of the crisis to other countries. Not all countries have a high degree of exposure to the debt of the worst off member states but that may be less relevant than the fear that has been kindled by the outbreak of the crisis in Greece, Ireland, and Portugal. The panic aspects of financial crises are as poorly understood as the euphoric (mania) parts. Objective facts, e.g., that the Greek economy constitutes a tiny part of the euro area are less important than the financial interdependencies involved and in any case may be trumped by less rational forces of financial crises.

One thing is clear. The costs of a breakup of the euro-zone would be large. One study, done by Union Banque de Suisse (UBS) estimates that the costs for a peripheral country could be 40–50 per cent of GDP while the costs for a core country could run as high as 20–25 per cent (*Economist*, 17 September 2011, 12). Costs would be measured not just in terms of the efficiency losses associated with having to change currencies in international transactions. Also to be considered are the difficulties evaluating the value of property held by nationals of other countries, including the assets of multinational corporations, and the inevitable legal issues that would arise over who owns (and owes) whom what. Rich and strong-currency countries would not escape. One of the first effects of the fallout would be that Germany's new Deutschemark would be substantially revalued, in line with devaluation in the periphery, thus eliminating the huge advantage Germany obtained by locking their currency to those of other, less competitive economies. It is not clear to what extent the German public understands the multiple sources of the advantages brought to them by the euro. Hard work, discipline, and self-abnegation are narratives easily absorbed by the German public. A competitive advantage — inherently zero-sum — partly won by domestically induced wage restraints in Germany, is harder to fit with this dominant narrative. Yet these structural imbalances within Europe are part of the complete story.

Thus, we think the most likely outcome is for the euro to continue, with a substantial increase in the so-called bailout fund (the EFSF, soon to become the ESM). The countries most in trouble will receive bailouts to allow them to pay their bills, and the stronger members will require serious domestic reforms as a condition for these funds: reforms in domestic spending, retirement age, size of the government sector, and tax collection capacity. Many of these domestic reforms require time — one does not increase tax capacity in a day — and some of the problems are temporally pressing (paying bonds at maturity), so there will have to be a combination of payouts and insistence on reforms.

The most important reforms in the euro-zone are likely to include more centralized fiscal powers, stricter debt limits and deficit limits. Some, maybe even most, of these demands are not new and are currently part of the Maastricht rules and the rules of the SGP. What is required and desired by some (particularly Germany) is that these rules have teeth. Thus, we are likely to see more centralized monitoring of national budgets by European institutions such as the European Commission, the EP, and the ECJ. Supervisory power will shift to these institutions because the member states will want to insulate themselves from the everyday pressures to give in to exceptions and the desire to please special constituencies. It is not clear if this strategy will work. It may be vulnerable to the same institutional flaws contained in the Maastricht Treaty. Leaders will be engaged in a delicate question of institutional design. The drafters want to make sure that they have control over the outcomes at the same time that they place the functioning of institutions beyond their control. There is a fundamental tension in the design of institutions, how to craft an institution that executes the preferences of its designers even after they are removed from the institution's day to day operation.

Finally, our theoretical framework highlights why three key sets of factors — i.e., market spillovers and policy externalities, risk and moral hazard, and perverse incentives associated with the configuration of rules and institutions — can produce inefficient outcomes in the environment of structural interdependence (not just between countries but also between banks and sovereigns) and full capital mobility and how international policy coordination can improve the results. This policy coordination is important for the euro-zone countries since the loss of competitiveness of GIIPS vis-à-vis core countries in the single currency area (in particular, Germany) not only underpins the structural problems of the euro-zone crisis but also suggests a possible long-term solution to it. In fact, since joining EMU GIIPS's competitiveness vis-à-vis Germany has declined, as its current account deficits and substantial appreciation of real effective exchange rates illustrate. Austerity measures — e.g., cuts in government spending, reforms in pension system, tax hikes — that have been the main focus of European leaders in tackling the euro-zone's financial crisis may be necessary in the long run, but they hurt growth and make it harder for the crisis-hit countries to meet deficit and debt targets, forcing those countries to implement more austerity measures, which further hit growth and trigger recession, ultimately causing what George Soros calls a 'deflationary debt spiral' (cited in Schuman 2012). In particular, given the growing joblessness in southern Europe,[15] the sole emphasis on austerity measures that have a negative impact on unemployment does not seem to help GIIPS to exit the crisis, at least in the short run. Therefore, we argue that while structural reforms through budgetary austerity in most troubled economies are desirable and the signing of the fiscal compact is a positive step towards a long term solution to saving the euro, policy coordination of euro-zone countries should be geared towards implementing measures in stimulating GIIPS's growth, increasing its job creation, and improving its competitiveness and productivity.[16]

Notes

1. We use the acronym GIIPS.
2. For example, see Robert O. Keohane's *After hegemony* (1984) for a seminal treatment of the role of cooperation in international relations theory. For theories of coordination, see Richard N. Cooper, *The economics of interdependence* (1968) and *Economic policy in an interdependent world* (1986). In this piece, we use the terms cooperation and coordination interchangeably. The first term is prominent in political science; the second in economics.
3. We hasten to add an important qualification, namely that cooperative behavior may not be necessary for the realization of gains. It is possible, though we think unlikely, that unilateral action leads to Pareto superior outcomes. It is also possible, and much more likely, that unilateral action can maximize the welfare of a powerful country while harming the welfare of a weaker country. This result may be stable but it is not Pareto superior.
4. For example, trade among countries with well developed pollution and patent laws will not experience the same level of externalities as two countries with weak pollution and patent laws.
5. Cooper quickly acknowledges that this definition differs from our notion of risk in games of chance, where the probability distributions are known, even if the particular event is not.
6. Article 121 of the TEU specifies the five convergence criteria. First, the inflation rate of participating countries of Stage III must be within 1.5 per cent of the average of the three EU countries with the lowest inflation. Second, the long-term interest rates should be no more than 2 per cent of the three countries with the lowest interest rates. Third, the national currency's exchange rate would have to be kept within the normal fluctuation margin of ERM II (plus or minus 15 per cent) of the EMS. Fourth, the national budget deficit must be lower than 3 per cent of GDP. Fifth, the national debt must not exceed 60 per cent of GDP.

7. See Figure 3, 'Credit growth to the private sector and average current account levels', in Wolff (2011, 3).
8. The Socialist Party won general elections in October of 2009. Soon after that, Papandreou admitted that Greek debt was substantially higher than reported earlier. In January 2010, the EU revised upward estimates of Greek debt from 3.7 per cent of GDP to 12.7 per cent.
9. For example, if one looks at nominal compensation per employee relative to a sample of 15 other EU countries, Ireland score is very high. However, we readily admit to being puzzled by the Irish case.
10. Austria's performance is just behind Finland's by a small margin but Finland is slightly behind Austria in terms of the competitiveness indicator. See Marzinotto, Pisani-Ferry, and Sapir (2010, 7).
11. The major provisions of the new fiscal compact for the single currency area included: Euro-zone members should keep their annual structural deficits below 0.5 per cent of GDP and their overall deficits below 3 per cent of GDP; states that exceed deficit limits would be subject to automatic penalties although they could be overridden by a qualified majority voting; Euro-zone members would be obliged to submit their budgets to the European Commission for approval; While the existing EFSF will remain active until mid-2013, the ESM, the euro-zone's permanent bailout fund, will enter into force in July 2012. The two funds will have a combined funding capacity of up to 500 billion euros; Euro-zone and other EU states will provide up to 200 billion euros in the form of bilateral loans to IMF to help it tackle the crisis.
12. The new rules of the Six Pack were first applied to Hungary on 11 January 2012. Concluding that Hungary had not made sufficient progress towards a timely and sustainable correction of its excessive deficit, the Commission proposed to the Council to move to the next stage of the EDP and recommended that the Council decide that no effective action had been taken to bring the deficit below 3 per cent of GDP in a sustainable manner.
13. The TSCG will enter into force once it is ratified by at least 12 euro area member states. Its target date is 1 January 2013. Since it is not a regular revision of the EU Treaty, the so-called 'repatriation clause' commits the EU to take steps to incorporate its substance into Union law five years after its entry into force.
14. Ireland is of course not a 'southern' country but it is generally included among the countries on Europe's periphery.
15. According to the Eurostat (the EU's statistics office) news release on 2 July 2012, euro-zone unemployment has risen to its highest level (11.1 per cent in May 2012) since the euro was introduced. The seasonally adjusted unemployment rates for GIIPS and Germany in May 2012 are as follows: Greece (21.9 per cent in March 2012), Ireland (14.6 per cent), Portugal (15.2 per cent), Spain (24.6 per cent), Italy (10.1 per cent), and Germany (5.6 per cent).
16. In this regard, the decision on 29 June 2012 at the European Council meeting on a 'Compact for Growth and Jobs' is a welcome progress, since it indicates European leaders' recognition that persistent low growth and macroeconomic imbalances, along with the sovereign debt crisis, are slowing down economic recovery and creating risks for the stability of EMU, Nonetheless, more resolute actions and practical measures need to be taken to boost the crisis-hit countries' growth and employment and to strengthen their competitiveness.

References

Alcidi, C. 2010. Competitiveness: treat the illness, not the symptoms. The Center for European Policy Studies, Commentary, 1–2, www.ceps.eu (accessed 21 December 2011).

Buiter, W., and R.C. Marston. 1985. Introduction. In *International economic policy coordination*, eds. W. Buiter and R.C. Marston, 1–7. Cambridge: Cambridge University Press.

Buti, M., D. Franco, and H. Ongena. 1998. Fiscal discipline and flexibility in EMU: the implementation of the stability and growth pact. *Oxford Review of Economic Policy* 14, no. 3: 81–97.

Castren, O., and I.K. Kavonius. 2009. Balance sheet interlinkages and macro-financial risk analysis in the euro area. *Working Paper Series*, no. 1124: 1–48, European Central Bank, Frankfurt, Germany.

Cooper, R.N. 1968. *The economics of interdependence*. New York: Council on Foreign Relations.

Cooper, R.N. 1986. *Economic policy in an interdependent world: essays in world economics*. Cambridge, MA: MIT Press.

Darvas, Z., J. Pisani-Ferry, and A. Sapir. 2011. A comprehensive approach to the euro-area debt crisis. *Bruegel Policy Brief* 2, February: 1–8.

De Grauwe, P. 2011. Balanced budget fundamentalism. The Center for European Policy Studies, Commentary, September, www.ceps.eu (accessed 10 October 2011).

Dinan, D. 2010. *Ever closer union: an introduction to European integration.* Boulder, CO: Lynne Rienner.

Eichengreen, B. 2011. The euro's never-ending crisis. *Current History,* March: 91–6.

Frieden, J.A. 2009a. Global governance of monetary relations: rationale and feasibility. *Economics: The Open-Access, Open-Assessment E-Journal* 3, March: 1–13.

Frieden, J.A. 2009b. Avoiding the worst: international economic cooperation and domestic olitics. *Vox* February: 1–6, http://www.voxeu.org/index (accessed 31 March 2011).

Frieden, J., D. Gros, and E. Jones. 1998. *The new political economy of EMU.* Oxford: Rowman and Littlefield.

Gros, D. 2010. Europe's competitiveness obsession. The Center for European Policy Studies, Commentary, www.ceps.eu (accessed 5 September 2011).

Gros, D., and C. Alcidi. 2011. Adjustment difficulties and debt overhands in the eurozone periphery. *The Center for European, Policy Studies* 347, May: 1–27.

Hoebner, K. 2011. Does the euro still have a future? *EU Centre Policy Brief,* no. 2, May, EU Center in Singapore.

Keohane, R.O. 1984. *After hegemony: cooperation and discord in the world political economy.* Princeton, NJ: Princeton University Press.

Manolopoulos, J. 2011. *Greece's 'odious' debt: the looting of the Hellenic republic by the euro, the political elite and the investment community.* London and New York: Anthem Press.

Marzinotto, B., J. Pisani-Ferry, and A. Sapir. 2010. Two crises, two responses. *Bruegel Policy Brief* 1, March: 1–8.

Marzinotto, B., A. Sapir, and G.B. Wolff. 2011. What kind of fiscal union? *Bruegel Policy Brief* 6, November: 1–8.

Sapir, A. 2011. Europe after the crisis: less or more role for nation states in money and finance? *Oxford Review of Economic Policy* Vol. 27, No. 4, pp. 608–19.

Schuman, M. 2012. Why the latest euro zone debt-crisis agreement shows how Europe just doesn't get it. *Time,* 31 January, http://business.time.com/2012/01/31/why-the-latest-euro-zone-debt-crisis-agreement-shows-how-europe-just-doesnt-get-it/ (accessed 1 February 2012).

The Economist. 2011. How to save the euro. *The Economist* 400, no. 8751 (17 September): 11–12.

The Economist. 2011. Proligacy is not the problem. *The Economist* 400, no. 8751 (17–23 September): 74–5.

Wolff, G. 2011. The euro area's macroeconomic balancing act. *Bruegel Policy Contribution* 5, May: 1–10.

'Maastricht Plus': Managing the Logic of Inherent Imperfections

KENNETH DYSON

School of European Languages, Translation, and Politics, Cardiff University, Cardiff, Wales, UK

ABSTRACT   Seen from the perspective of the interconnected excessive imbalances, banking, and sovereign debt crises that beset the Euro Area from 2007, the central inadequacy of the Maastricht Treaty was the failure to address the problem of the inherent imperfections of *any* provisions for crisis prevention and management in Economic and Monetary Union. The inadequacy stemmed from a cluster of naïve assumptions: about state capacity to comply with Treaty-based rules to prevent crises; about the tractability of economic and political cultures; about the adequacy of moral hazard as a design principle for monetary union; and about putting in place monetary union without economic, fiscal, banking, and political union. Consequently, managing crises of sovereign and bank creditworthiness had not been a problem on the Maastricht agenda. Subsequent failures to be prepared to manage compound crises were compounded by the complacency induced by the 'political economy of good times' into which the Euro Area was launched. EMU posed questions about the dominant teleological assumption underpinning the Maastricht Treaty. It risked exposing not just the limits of Europeanization but also serving as a catalyst for 'de-Europeanization'.

Introduction

I was unable to imagine at the time [1990–1991] that the Treaty would not be honoured... It was clear that an optimal currency area must endure shocks. By that, I imagined oil price shocks... whatever. But not that suddenly there are states which are actually insolvent. We had put in place every provision so that it would not arise... It was naïve not to have thought of such an eventuality. I have to accept that... (Helmut Schlesinger, 2012, interview in Capital, 19 April; translation by author)

After the commitment to complete Economic and Monetary Union (EMU) in the Maastricht Treaty, the European Union (EU) devoted its energies to complex, serial additions and refinements to its crisis prevention mechanisms (Dyson and Quaglia 2010). Only once the financial and economic crisis evolved from 2007 did it begin to address the need for more ambitious and comprehensive crisis prevention mechanisms and — in a more guarded, hesitant manner — for crisis management mechanisms. The first two phases of the crisis had their epicenters outside the Euro Area in the US sub-prime mortgage market and in the collapse of Lehman Brothers. However, from 2009 the Euro Area found itself at the centre of the storm. External pressure to act — from other EU member states, the US, the IMF, and inside G-20 — assumed a new significance. In responding, the Euro Area was constrained by the monetary constitution of the Maastricht Treaty, by the resolute defence of its principles by Germany and the few other Euro Area creditor powers, and by German strategic interest in both limiting her liabilities and ensuring the balance between any increase in liabilities and enhanced EU and Euro Area control, involving the ceding of sovereign rights.

The history of the design of the Maastricht Treaty as a monetary constitution — and later patterns of adjustment — reflected creditor state power, above all that of Germany, over framing and agenda-setting (Dyson and Featherstone 1999). Germany assigned to itself a special responsibility as the 'economic motor' and the 'stability anchor' of the Euro Area. The Bundesbank continued to claim that it was the guardian of its 'stability culture' (Weidmann 2012). Creditor state power took the form of setting standards of appropriateness and the parameters of reform trajectories in European economic governance (Dyson 2008). There was a strict separation of fiscal and monetary responsibilities. Monetary policy shifted to the Euro Area level; fiscal policy remained with member states, subject to compliance with rules on excessive deficits (Article 104c). The European Central Bank (ECB) was strictly independent and narrowly focused on its responsibility to deliver price stability. Article 104 ruled out quantitative easing in the form of the ECB buying sovereign bonds in the primary market. As the crisis evolved, ECB and Bundesbank thinking were similar. Either member states must comply with the Maastricht Treaty provisions or they must cede fiscal sovereignty to the Euro Area level in a banking, fiscal, and economic union. Emerging evidence of a large-scale 'transfer union', much of it through the unexpected route of the ECB's non-standard monetary policy instruments, led to the diminishing credibility of German belief that Article 104b provided a 'no-bail-out' guarantee. Consequently, German negotiators shifted emphasis to the principle of balance between liability and control in designing banking, fiscal, and economic union. From autumn 2011 German framing, agenda-setting, and veto power began to be devoted to this principle.

The Maastricht Treaty, Excessive Imbalances, and Sovereign Creditworthiness

Ever since the negotiation of the Maastricht Treaty in 1991, scholarly literature has broadly agreed that the institutional arrangements and policy instruments of the new economic constitution were inadequate for a sustainable monetary union (cf. Dyson 2000). It lacked the necessary capacity for crisis prevention and crisis management. This problem mattered because of the heterogeneity of the Euro Area, which increased as its size grew from 11 to 17, its core-periphery attributes, and its lack of approximation to an Optimal Currency Area (OCA). There was broad agreement that EMU was a 'work in progress', especially with respect to its economic and political foundations.

German negotiators had pursued the principle of 'parallelism' in EMU and political union in the Maastricht negotiations. However, as earlier in the Werner negotiations of 1970–1971, France and other leading member states were unwilling to cede core fiscal and economic competences and build strong supranational EU political institutions for this purpose. The French notion of 'economic government' was more focused on delimiting the independence of the ECB in favour of the intergovernmental European Council. The notion made no headway in the face of resolute German promotion of the principle of central bank independence as the core design principle for EMU. It also lacked any clear detailed proposals as the basis for Treaty negotiation (Dyson and Featherstone 1999). In consequence, Germany accepted that monetary union would serve as a catalyst for broader economic and deeper political union in later treaties. However, neo-Classical and neo-Keynesian economists disagreed about the sources of the inadequacies of the Maastricht constitution and thus about appropriate reforms to create economic and political union (cf. Issing 2008; Wolf 2011). In the period 1991–2007 the failure to make substantial parallel progress with political union was disappointing for German negotiators.

The Maastricht Treaty reflected and helped induce two key sources of complacency; about excessive imbalances and about sovereign creditworthiness. Two factors played a role in this neglect: the belief of debtor states that currency union would provide a shield against these traditional vulnerabilities; and the dominance of the treaty negotiating process by the overriding political strategy to 'bind-in' the EU central banks. In consequence, the Treaty focused on the monetary constitution of a currency union.

Complacency about excessive imbalances was increased by a contingent symmetry in benign outcomes during the first decade of the euro. Before the post-2007 crisis, fiscal imbalances were modest, whereas current account imbalances were huge. The consequence was large-scale capital outflows, above all from Germany, the Netherlands, Belgium, and Finland to Portugal, Greece, Spain, and Ireland. As long as the debtor states could continue to attract these capital inflows, the Euro Area created a 'win–win' situation. Surplus states had underpinned the growth of debtor states, which in turn provided expanded export markets for the surplus states. However, with the crisis these capital flows dried up, with deeply damaging effects on private-sector balances and fiscal deficits of debtor states. Creditor states responded by insisting on tough fiscal consolidation and comprehensive structural reforms in the debtor states to reduce fiscal deficits, bring down public debt, and restore competitiveness. This combination destroyed the symmetry that had till then existed within the Euro Area. Adjustment to the crisis was not just asymmetric but visibly so, heightening intra-EU tensions and risking isolation of the creditor states which were much fewer in number than debtor states.

Complacency was also induced by two beliefs that kept sovereign creditworthiness off the Maastricht agenda and conditioned later attitudes to reform. Firstly, the Maastricht economic constitution had been negotiated against the background of the 1980s, when sovereign debt crises, defaults, and restructurings had been confined to emerging market economies. There was an unarticulated assumption that debt defaults and restructuring were neither necessary nor desirable in advanced market economies like those of the EU. The Maastricht negotiations were not framed in terms of how to manage a crisis of state insolvency, let alone of acute and contagious banking and state liquidity problems. Secondly, attitudes to reform of Maastricht were dominated by the belief that a new age of global macro-economic non-inflationary, continuous economic expansion had dawned. It provided time for serial, incremental adjustments to institutional arrangements and policy instruments. Thinking about EMU was framed and constrained by the global 'political economy of good times' (Dyson 2009b).

This widespread complacency was reinforced by the legacy of optimism from the European single market programme of the 1980s. It helped reinforce the teleological assumption that European integration was a self-reinforcing mechanism. EMU was part of a dominant narrative of European 'union', supported by arguments from historical institutionalism literature and neo-functionalism (Dyson 2012). 'Differentiation' was part of this narrative, related to British and Danish treaty opt-outs from monetary union and the logic of the Maastricht convergence criteria for Euro Area entry (Dyson and Sepos 2010). However, 'disunion' was relegated to the margins or silence.

During and after the Maastricht Treaty, the scenario for dealing with the supreme emergency of banking and state insolvency remained off the agenda. The assumption was that the Maastricht convergence criteria, the excessive deficit procedure (EDP), the Stability and Growth Pact (SGP), and the various instruments of 'soft' economic policy coordination would ensure that existential problems of sovereign creditworthiness would not arise to place in imminent danger the very coherence, integrity, and existence of the Euro Area.

The Maastricht economic constitution rested on faith in the principle of European solidarity based on effort by member state to comply with rules that safeguarded sound money and finances. This faith reflected German power in the negotiations, notably expressed in hostility to 'bail-outs' of governments as conducive to moral hazard. Solidarity based on collective financial insurance was seen as the route to a 'transfer union' that would perpetuate irresponsible fiscal and financial policies. Hence in the Maastricht negotiations there had been no discussion of a European monetary fund, Euro-bonds, a European debt management agency, a European financial supervision authority, common deposit guarantees, or the way in which the non-conventional monetary policy operations of the ECB might result in a 'lender of last resort' for European banks. None of these proposals figured in the French government draft treaty on EMU in January 1991 (Dyson and Quaglia 2010, 456–61). The European Commission limited itself to proposing a Community financial assistance mechanism (Dyson and Quaglia 2010, 451–6). The negotiating positions of the leading negotiators of the Maastricht Treaty were framed and constrained by the strategy of 'binding-in' the German Bundesbank to the final outcome (Dyson and Featherstone 1999). Though the Bundesbank subsequently lost monetary policy authority, and though the post-2007 crisis put it on the defensive, this strategy retained significance as essential to retain the support of German political elites and public that the 'euro was as stable as the D-Mark' had been.

From Maastricht to 'Maastricht Plus': Matching Theory and Evolving Practice

After 20 years the Maastricht Treaty remained fundamentally intact as the 'constitution' of European macro-economic governance. Despite many subsequent 'add-ons', like the Lisbon process to raise growth potential and the Luxembourg process to promote employment, reforms were framed and constrained by dominant Bundesbank defence of the separation of fiscal and monetary policies, with fiscal rules designed to support stability-oriented monetary policy, and by German insistence, adopted by the ECB, that sustainable growth depended on fiscal consolidation and structural reforms to goods, services, financial, and labour markets. Keynesian ideas of the collective management of aggregate demand had no impact on reforms. The subsequent Amsterdam, Nice, and Lisbon treaties did not alter the core principles and provisions of the Maastricht Treaty (cf. Dyson and Quaglia 2010).

From the outset the ECB used the 'logic of sound money and finance' to strengthen and mobilize coalitions of support for long-term, 'stability-oriented' policies, consistent with the German Bundesbank notion of a European 'stability culture'. This logic was used in various ways to pursue a quiet revolution in European economic governance towards a 'stability culture':

- To protect the new ECB from interference by member state governments at a time when it had to give absolute priority to establishing its market reputation and credibility in fighting inflation and to reassuring anxious German public opinion.
- To establish and disseminate norms by which electorates and markets could assess the performance of member state governments, notably in fiscal deficits and public debt.
- To open up space for the more active pursuit of structural reforms to capital, labour, product, and service markets by EU institutions and by member state governments, thus reinforcing the single market agenda and reducing the costs of disinflation.
- To strengthen discipline on member state government fiscal policies, again reducing the costs of disinflation.

- To centralize power inside the Eurosystem and to upgrade the authority of the European Commission and the Statistical Office of the European Communities (Eurostat) in ensuring member state integrity and compliance.

The ECB sought to ensure that the logic of sound money and finance, as enshrined in the Maastricht Treaty, became the central reference point and source of legitimacy for those operating within the evolving institutional framework of European economic governance. This logic framed ideas about how economic policy coordination should be designed and how economic growth and job creation should be pursued; formed new common ground between the ECB and the Commission, based on shared self-interests in strengthening economic policy and fiscal policy surveillance; and differentiated European macro-economic governance as distinctive from US and British practices (Dyson 2000; Stark 2011).

The logic of sound money and finance had its epicenter in the German Bundesbank. Nevertheless, its coalition of support included influential domestic reformers, often technocrats, across a range of member states. They sought to use EMU as a rationale for greater fiscal discipline and speedier and more comprehensive structural reforms to open up markets and make them more competitive. However, the unfolding post-2007 financial and economic crisis revealed the past and present limits of this quiet revolution. Even before the crisis it was clear that domestic state capacity to comply was highly variable; domestic political and economic cultures were often intractable; and the limits of Europeanization and domestic ownership of stability culture all too obvious. Some state structures, notably in Southern Europe, opened up opportunities for systemic 'rent-seeking' behaviour.

The Amsterdam, Nice, and Lisbon treaties, along with the Treaty Establishing the European Stability Mechanism (ESM) and the Treaty on Stability, Coordination and Governance in EMU in 2012, sought to make up for deficiencies in the Maastricht Treaty. They did so in ways that sought to satisfy the Bundesbank and ECB that the Maastricht 'monetary constitution' remained fully intact. However, these treaties did little to upgrade the powers of the Commission in macro-economic policy coordination. The Lisbon Treaty (2008) went furthest in empowering the Commission to address a warning to a member state in breach of the BEPGs which formed the basis for mutual economic surveillance. Otherwise it made no substantial changes to the provisions for economic policy coordination. Economic policy coordination was not incorporated in the list of shared EU and member state competences in Article 4 TFEU, unlike the internal market, economic and social cohesion, environment, and energy. Equally, it was not categorized as a 'supportive' competence (Article 6). This unclear definition of economic policy coordination in Article 5 was the result of a messy compromise in the European Convention between advocates of 'shared' and 'supportive' competence. The result was a major mismatch between the authority of the Commission and that of the ECB.

From 1999 German negotiators and the ECB were acutely alert for signs of erosion of the core stability principles of the Maastricht monetary constitution. They were in line with German domestic public opinion, which strongly supported the values of 'stability culture'. Sensitivity was most acute in the Bundesbank, which assigned itself a special role as the guardian of Euro Area 'stability culture'. The post-2007 crisis heightened sensitivity. However, Bundesbank complaints about loss of direction in policy evolution, and 'hollowing out' of Maastricht, predated the crisis. The pivotal event was the crisis of the SGP in 2003. This crisis reflected the lower level of commitment of the Social Democrat (SPD)-led German federal government of Chancellor Gerhard Schröder to the values of 'stability culture' than its centre-right equivalents had been at the time of the negotiations of the Maastricht Treaty and the SGP. Faced with the threat of Germany becoming subject to the EDP, Schröder and his Finance Minster Hans Eichel criticized the 'mechanistic nature' of the SGP. They advocated higher priority to fiscal flexibility to encourage growth and jobs over rigid adherence to economic principles of Ordo-liberal economics (Heipertz and Verdun 2009). SPD and Green politicians were more attracted to 'new Keynesian' economic ideas, which they sought to enshrine in the revised SGP of 2005 with its provisions for more exceptions and discretion (Dyson and Quaglia 2010). ECB officials, and above all the Bundesbank, condemned German behaviour and the SGP reform for fatally weakening the commitment to stability-oriented policies (Issing 2008, 2012). Under SPD finance ministers from 1998 to 2009 'stability culture' was demoted in German federal government discourse.

By autumn 2011 the Bundesbank had persuaded the German federal government that the process of drift away from the Maastricht principles of sound money and finance must be reversed by a radical move to Treaty-based fiscal union, 'Maastricht Plus' (Weidmann 2012). This treaty would enshrine the principle that the assumption of liability must be matched by stronger controls over member states and require the stability-oriented principle of structural fiscal balance to be anchored in member state constitutions, thus opening new avenues of legal redress. Following the loss of federal office of the SPD in 2009 (it had retained the Federal Finance Ministry during the Grand Coalition of 2005–2009), the centre-right government of Angela Merkel restored the 'stability culture' discourse that had originally underpinned the logic of sound money and finance. The evolution of the crisis into one of excessive imbalances and sovereign debts highlighted Germany as the dominant creditor power of the Euro Area. A reinvigorated logic of sound money and finance was signaled in its policy agenda of tough conditionality for collective financial assistance, the 'last-resort' and the non-subsidized interest rate nature of this assistance, new micro-intervention in fiscal policies and structural economic reforms of states in debt distress, and giving treaty form to fiscal discipline and greater automaticity in the EDP. The logic was also used to strengthen the independence of the ECB from mounting political pressures for its more active fiscal role in sovereign bond markets.

The evolving post-2007 crisis confronted the Maastricht 'constitution' with two challenges to its coherence and integrity. First, the ECB chose to resort to unconventional monetary policy instruments to ensure adequate liquidity for the banking system once the inter-bank market dried up and banks could no longer rely on wholesale funding. By 2012 unlimited three-year liquidity was made available to banks. However, huge expansion of the longer-term refinancing operation (LTFO) raised three issues. In particular, German Ordo-liberals worried whether it was being used to prop up insolvent banks in place of governments using fiscal policy to bail out these banks; whether it was leading *de facto* to a transfer union under the auspices of the Eurosystem, reflected in TARGET2 payment system imbalances and the liabilities accumulated by the Bundesbank; and whether it was an indirect form of quantitative easing by stealth, inducing a 'carry trade' in which liquidity from the ECB was being used by national banks to purchase the sovereign bonds of their governments. Commitments to early exit from these unconventional measures lost credibility as the sovereign debt crisis confronted banks with further losses. Nevertheless, the ECB stuck to its script: the measures were temporary; they were consistent with the bank-based nature of the Euro Area financial system; and, in seeking to ensure the efficient transmission of its monetary policy, they were consistent with the conduct of a monetary policy focused on a strict stability-oriented monetary policy.

Assessments of the theory and practice of the Maastricht constitution are in shaped, in part, by the economic theories to which one subscribes; in part, by where one stands on European solidarity and on the sovereignty/integration spectrums; and, in part, by changing perspectives of time. Neo-classical and new Keynesian economies offer different diagnoses and prescriptions. The former stress moral hazard and the solidarity of effort from debtors; the latter argue for collective insurance and mutual adjustment by creditors and debtors. Broadly, centre-left politicians are broadly more favourable to a Europe of solidarity based on collective sharing of adjustment costs.

Federalists and inter-governmentalists have contrasting views about institutional design. The former seek to strengthen supra-national institutions like the European Commission and the European Parliament; the latter seek to privilege the role of the European Council.

Time also mattered. Maastricht at 3, 10, or 15 looked very different to Maastricht at 20. At three, Maastricht was mired in economic 'bad times'. Following the ERM crises of 1992 1993 the prospects for EMU looked very bleak. At 10 and at 15, Maastricht seemed a more robust project, one gradually evolving to address challenges of accelerating growth and employment, and above all delivering the core Treaty objective of price stability, locking in medium-term inflation expectations consistent with this objective. From the mid-1990s to 2007 the reputation of Maastricht could ride on the coattails of sustained global economic expansion without inflation. It inhabited a global political economy of good times (Dyson 2009b). However, at 20 the Maastricht monetary constitution faced the biggest global financial and economic crisis since the 1930s, one that exposed its weaknesses in sharp relief. It looked less like an engine for spreading prosperity than an engine of contagion as interconnected banking and sovereign debt problems spilled across borders. Maastricht seemed to offer mutual pain through locking in deflation rather than mutual gain.

The Potemkin-like Character of Crisis Prevention and Management

As Euro Area and EU deficiencies in crisis prevention and crisis management were progressively laid bare, complacency gave way to a new mood of apprehension, fear, and panic. The BEPGs and mutual surveillance of economic policies under Article 103 had manifestly failed to identify, and act to correct, excessive imbalances in current accounts and competitiveness. The Lisbon process to promote structural economic reforms had not matched up to its aspiration of creating the most advanced knowledge-based economy in the world. The SGP, which regulated the EDP of the Maastricht Treaty, had not identified the scale of domestic fiscal policy risks and indulged Member States that breached its provisions. The central problem in all these failings of crisis prevention mechanisms was a process of 'sinners voting on sinners'. Member states practiced collusion in defence of their sovereign prerogatives, undermining the credibility of the European Commission in economic and fiscal policy surveillance and monitoring. Their governments hesitated to make meaningful and detailed commitments and evaded the implications of commitments. In consequence, economic policy and fiscal policy coordination processes developed an incestuous character of 'Brussels talking to Brussels'. Crisis prevention and management arrangements took on a Potemkin-like character. They appeared like elaborate stage sets: their intricate and impressive facades bore little relation to the contents.

In the first place, the convergence criteria of the Maastricht Treaty proved inadequate as an instrument for ensuring the sustainability of the Euro Area and insulating it from crises. Member states proved adept at manipulating fiscal data, despite the best efforts of the Statistical Office of the European Communities (Eurostat) to check figures and rule on various domestic fiscal innovations (Savage 2005). Assessment periods for establishing adequate convergence in fiscal deficits, public debt, exchange rates, and long-term interest rates proved too short. Moreover, the requirement in Article 109 j (1) to 'take account' of competitiveness trends in the form of unit labour cost developments and current account imbalances lacked the same precision as the nominal fiscal and monetary criteria in the Treaty protocol. Risk from excessive imbalances was neglected. There was also no requirement to take a long and hard look at domestic fiscal governance, including domestic debt rules, and whether they supported long-term convergence. The Greek crisis was to expose all these deficiencies. Greek fiscal data were heavily massaged to secure euro entry; its convergence was ephemeral; it had acute competitiveness problems; and it had too weak a core executive to ensure compliance with external commitments. Contingent outcomes on a narrow range of measurable macro-economic indicators were given priority over more difficult qualitative assessments of state capacity. Precision triumphed over relevance to long-term sustainability.

With the post-2007 financial and economic crisis the European Commission and the European Council responded to the mounting evidence that the design of the Euro Area was fundamentally flawed by successive rounds of institutional and policy reforms. However, by 2012 each round of strengthening crisis prevention and management mechanisms had fallen short of the 'quantum leap' in European economic governance for which the European Commission and the ECB had called. More fundamentally, none of these three bodies, least of all the ECB, identified the key legal and political gap in the Maastricht Treaty and the urgent need to fill it. The Euro Area lacked a capacity to deal with existential crisis in the form of the supreme emergency exemption from its stability-oriented policy paradigm of sound money and finances. The creation of the European Financial Stability Facility (EFSF) as a temporary collective financial assistance mechanism in 2010, and its permanent successor the ESM in 2012, did not address this need.

Crisis Prevention

Crisis prevention was strengthened in five main areas. Firstly, the gap in the Maastricht Treaty provisions on financial stability was addressed. The Treaty had given the ECB a role in 'promoting' financial stability. However, banking and financial market regulation was viewed as falling under the principle of subsidiarity, consistent with the variety and complexity of financial systems and the advantages of tailoring regulation to different conditions. Following the De Larosière Report in 2008, the ECB expanded its role into macro-prudential supervision with the creation of the new European Systemic Risk Board (ESRB). In addition, European-level institutional arrangements and policy instruments in banking, insurance and securities market regulation were strengthened. However, the new authorities lacked substantial staff resources, for instance for bank stress tests. They were also denied the power to pre-commit member state governments to fiscal support of troubled cross-nationally active banks. In June 2012 the European Council took the decision in principle that the ECB should form the nucleus of a new Euro Area banking supervision authority, presiding over a forthcoming banking union.

Secondly, as part of the so-called 'Six Pack' legislation, macro-economic policy surveillance was reinforced. The main innovation was the Excessive Imbalance Procedure (EIP), opening up a new field of action for the European Commission. It rested on a scoreboard, comprising a set of indicators (like current accounts, unit labour costs, and housing and property markets) that would serve as an alert mechanism and form the basis for national action plans to correct imbalances. Unlike the BEPGs, the EIP was backed by 'reverse qualified majority voting' (member states had to build a qualified majority to block the Commission) and by the threat of fines for non-compliance. In the view of the Commission, its main weakness was the lack of clear thresholds to determine excessive imbalances and to trigger automatic corrective action and fines. In the view of the European Central Bank (2011), the weaknesses of the EIP included the sheer complexity of the indicators and their potential for diverting the weight of corrective action from deficit states to surplus states. The ECB feared that it could evolve into a symmetrical adjustment mechanism, with negative consequences for moral hazard and for competitiveness. It reflected the fears of German negotiators, who had been keen to avoid this outcome despite considerable pressure from the European Parliament for more symmetrical adjustment.

Thirdly, successive rounds of substantial reforms to the SGP were made in the 'Six Pack' legislation, in subsequent Commission proposals, and in the Treaty on Stability, Coordination and Governance in the Euro Area of 2012. All bore the strong imprint of German influence. After what had been seen by the ECB and the Bundesbank as retrogressive reforms of the SGP in 2005, the new reforms were designed to strengthen its credibility as a fiscal crisis prevention mechanism by hardening its disciplinary character. They were a price other member states had to pay for German willingness to strengthen crisis management through taking on big liabilities in the new EFSF. German negotiators sought to focus reforms around more effective long-term crisis prevention mechanisms based on tougher, more binding fiscal rules and quasi-automaticity in moving towards sanctions. The focus was shifted to annual public debt reduction targets and public expenditure benchmarks. The position of the Commission in the EDP was strengthened by a new reverse qualified majority voting system: earlier the Commission had had to find a qualified majority to support its recommendations. New, earlier stage and graduated financial sanctions were introduced. Finally, the new so-called 'fiscal compact' treaty was designed to add extra legal authority to fiscal discipline. Member states of the Euro Area were required to introduce 'debt brakes' into their constitutions to strengthen domestic commitment to the fiscal discipline objectives of the SGP.

Fourthly, crisis prevention was to be strengthened by reinforcing the competitiveness agenda with the new Euro Plus Pact. This Pact included the 17 Euro Area member states and those other member states (another six) who opted to participate (23 out of 27). It was the outcome of a Franco–German initiative designed to expand the role of the European Council and of the Heads of State and Government of the Euro Area in economic policy surveillance. Wage and labour market reforms were accorded a central role. In order to protect its own role, the European Commission focused on incorporation of Euro Plus Pact commitments into the national reform programmes (NRPs) that were the outcome of the annual Economic Semester.

The broad umbrella framework for reinforced economic governance in crisis prevention was the European Commission's Europe 2020 programme and the Economic Semester, during which the attempt was made to integrate the various mechanisms. This new temporal synchronization was designed to allow the Euro Area member states to have an earlier view of each other's budgetary assumptions and thus be in a better position to address inconsistencies.

Despite the shift in emphasis to excessive imbalances and to financial stability, crisis prevention mechanisms continued on the Ordo–liberal trajectory of fiscal discipline and structural reforms as preconditions for sustainable growth. German negotiators kept three issues off the agenda of reform or vetoed them: aggregate demand management; Eurobonds and collective debt redemption; and a central role for the ECB in supporting sovereign debt, for instance through quantitative easing. The missing element remained new Keynesian crisis prevention through collective burden sharing. Consequently, the Euro Area faced Keynesian critiques of the heightened, mutually destructive risk of a debt-deflation spiral consequent on one-sided austerity.

Crisis Management

Crisis management mechanisms were even more neglected in the Maastricht Treaty than crisis prevention mechanisms. This neglect stemmed, in part, from the assumption that the quality of, and the commitment to, the latter would obviate the need for the former. It also originated in the principled objection that crisis management mechanisms would act as an incentive to moral hazard. However, there was a failure to recognize implementation problems stemming from the inherent limitations of preventative policy instruments, the problems of matching often 'soft' policy instruments to ambitious and complex goals, and the short-term myopia and 'time inconsistency' problems induced by domestic electoral calendars (cf. Hood 1984; Dyson 2009a). Compliance problems that arise from the incentives of states to engage in creative financial manipulation were underestimated. Not least, neglect of excessive imbalances and of the implications of monetary union for cross-national banking led to under-appreciation of systemic vulnerability to contagious, interrelated banking and sovereign debt crises, making it impossible to contain them within state borders. The Euro Area had not insured adequately against these multiple risks in implementation and from systemic failure.

The second error was that, once events forced recognition of the need for crisis management mechanisms, they were designed to deal with liquidity rather than solvency problems. The EFSF and ESM were created to enable states to buy time to make fundamental domestic economic and fiscal reforms. However, though such mechanisms were necessary, they were not sufficient for addressing threats of state insolvency to monetary union as a whole, especially where the states, like Italy and Spain, were systemically significant. The situation was different in the case of the Euro Area banking system. The ECB made bold and active use of its monetary policy operations to inject large-scale liquidity into Euro Area banks. One- year and later three-year unlimited injections of liquidity enabled banks to buy time for recapitalization, for absorbing losses on their holdings of sovereign bonds of distressed Euro Area member states, and for coping with new EU bank stress tests by the European Banking Authority. These crisis management operations served to tackle both bank liquidity problems and prevent them becoming solvency problems. However, by 2012 bank recapitalization and resolution problems remained unresolved at the Euro Area level. Banking union was in its infancy.

The third error was in the timing and the sequencing of crisis management mechanisms. EU commitment to private-sector involvement in sovereign debt restructuring and to undertake bank stress tests preceded the establishment of strong and resilient collective financial assistance mechanisms. As the ECB predicted, the consequence was to spread alarm in financial markets and to deepen crisis management problems. Moreover, delay in agreeing the EFSF between December 2009 and May

2010, followed by procrastination in increasing its firepower and its instruments, added to investor alarm and increased the eventual costs of bailouts. Member state governments not only did too little, too late; they also mismanaged the temporality of crisis management reforms (cf. Dyson 2009a).

The other new crisis management mechanism was the 'Troika' arrangement for Euro Area member states in receipt of support from the EFSF: initially Greece, later Ireland and Portugal. Detailed, on-the-spot compliance was monitored by a team in each national capital, comprising ECB, European Commission, and International Monetary Fund (IMF) staff. Their reports were distinct from the normal EU mutual surveillance procedure and based on IMF debt sustainability analysis. They informed European Council decisions about whether to release further tranches of financial support or to insist on further fiscal and economic reforms as conditions. The novelty stemmed in part from the depth of intervention into state sovereignty and in part from the role of the IMF. It was seen as strengthening the element of tough conditionality based on IMF track record in dealing with sovereign debt crises. However, it also demonstrated the lack of capacity of the Euro Area for autonomous crisis management.

For states in sovereign debt crisis, the ECB emphasized correction of excessive imbalances by fiscal devaluation through tax reforms, shifting the burden to consumption and property, plus by structural reforms to boost competitiveness. This approach was credible in a collective framework of macro-economic expansion so that export- and investment-led growth was attainable. However, its value as a crisis management instrument was more questionable in a macro-economic framework of collective simultaneous deleverage in public and private sectors. It risked a vicious circle of debt-deflation, locking in problems of sovereign creditworthiness, and worsening challenges of crisis management.

Necessity Knows No Rules: Supreme Emergency

The problems of putting in place effective crisis prevention and management mechanisms highlighted the fundamental gap in the Maastricht Treaty, one which derived from the creation of monetary union without a sheltering political umbrella of democratic legitimacy. EMU illustrated two problems in legal and political thinking about the EU. Firstly, the Euro Area operated in the context of a growing mismatch between the mounting complexity and opacity, and the increasing speed, of financial markets and the capacity for bold, comprehensive, and rapid collective action of its member states. Secondly, the creation of the Euro Area reinforced the potential for cross-national, contagious and interrelated Euro Area sovereign debt and banking crises, making the core vulnerable to the periphery. European-level political arrangements were ill-suited to the need for bold, rapid and joined-up action in the face of acute market vulnerabilities.

For good reasons of European history, legitimacy and consent, EU lawyers placed prime weight on honouring Maastricht Treaty commitments. Their core is provided by the principle of stability-oriented policies, founded on the so-called 'no bail-out' clause, no privileged access of governments to the central bank, and the strict separation of fiscal and monetary policies. Abridgement of these commitments invites not just serious loss of mutual trust amongst member states and market credibility but also legal redress.

In the case of the Euro Area, however, there is central tension between conceptual and logical analysis of crisis capacity and its historically and institutionally specific character. After the disaster of the Nazi seizure of power in 1933, German lawyers retained a particularly deep aversion to endowing public authorities with emergency powers. Like Germany itself, the EU is seen as, above all, a polity based on law. Hence German thinking on what the EU and its institutions can and should do in crisis management is profoundly constrained by respect for primary rules and formal legal arguments, grounded in painful experience. Such thinking is les prevalent in Anglo–American jurisprudence, which places more emphasis on the open texture of rules and on 'rule-scepticism' (cf. Hart 1961).

All polities face the basic existential question of whether there are limits on what they can do, and how (Rawls 1999, 98–99). This question arises when they are faced by clear and imminent danger to their integrity and survival and to the understandings that were at the heart of their constitution making process, like — in the case of the EU — irreversibility and solidarity. It can be argued that the Euro Area is a matter of existential national interest for its member states. They are politically committed to 'making the euro work', to ensuring its survival as 'irrevocable', and to doing 'what has to be done' so that banking collapses and disorderly sovereign defaults do not trigger the collapse of the Euro Area and place the survival of the wider EU, including the single market, at risk. This kind of argument involves a commitment to 'consequentialism': that the costs of not acting in this way would be too awful to contemplate. In legal theory, it finds expression in the notion of establishing legal validity by reference to sources outside specific constitutional or treaty provisions (Hart 1961, 93).

Different justifications for acting outside normal bounds can be found in the Hobbesian argument for a sovereign power with the authority to avert social and political disorder; in Benthamite arguments based on utilitarian calculus, hospitable to 'consequentialism'; in Hegelian arguments about the overriding ethical value of community over calculus; or in Hart's argument in favour of a 'rule of recognition' that derives the legal validity of action from general characteristics of the composite set of rules on which a polity is based. However formulated, the argument remains the same: the Euro Area requires the ultimate capacity to act when the danger to it is 'close and serious' and its very existence is threatened. The key parallel is 'just war' theory. According to Michael Walzer (1992, 254), supreme emergency places a polity under 'the rule of necessity (and necessity knows no rules)'. Walzer's analysis suggests the potential existentially significant costs in rigid formal compliance with principle-based treaty law.

However, acceptance of the overriding requirement for the right to act in supreme emergency raises a series of acute difficulties. It is open to creative construction and abuse in the service of institutional interests; it poses difficult questions of EU-level institutional and instrument design, especially risks of compromising the ECB; and, above all, it highlights the problems of legitimacy and consent at the heart of the EU and the Euro Area, especially its political feasibility in the case of the major creditor states like Germany (on which Dyson 2013). As Chancellor Angela Merkel (2012) emphasized, German power was not unlimited. Excessive liabilities threatened loss of its role as 'stability anchor' and of its own sovereign creditworthiness and that of the Euro Area as a whole.

Capacity to act in supreme emergency requires enhancement of supra-national executive discretion. In the specific historical and institutional context of the Euro Area, it is fraught with enormous legitimacy and consent difficulties, attendant risks of judicial review, and potential polarization of public and elite opinion across creditor states, notably Germany. However, the fundamental question remains: 'what ultimate claim to legitimacy can the EU and Euro Area make in the absence of a capacity to act in supreme emergency?' Making that claim in the absence of a federal state structure, founded on independent democratic legitimacy, is inherently problematic and potentially insuperable. Failure to make the claim exposes the Euro Area to the cruel forces of imperfect states and imperfect financial markets and to the grim necessity that follows.

Limited Liability and Collective Insurance Against the Imperfections of Markets and States: The Achilles Heel of the Euro

Once crisis befell the Euro Area, the inherent tension between limited liability and collective insurance in its design was revealed. The Maastricht Treaty had made no substantial provisions for collective insurance of the member states against each other's and against market imperfections. Insurance depended on individual member state compliance with stability-oriented rules. Article 103a on Community financial assistance for a member state 'in difficulties or… seriously threatened with severe difficulties caused by exceptional occurrences beyond its control' required the Council to act unanimously. Creditor states, led by Germany, were unwilling to go down the route of a 'transfer union' because they mistrusted other key member states and feared immersion in a currency union of moral hazard: the Euro Area as 'Italy writ large'. The Euro Area crises made transparent systemic problems of state capacity, especially in Southern Europe. These problems led to further diminution of trust and heightened fears that the creditworthiness of states like Germany could be undermined. As the German Federal President asked: 'Who rescues the rescuer?' (Wulff 2011). Additionally, debtor states, led by France, were unwilling to cede sovereignty to the EU in fiscal and economic policies, least of all on the terms set by Germany, namely strict controls on fiscal discipline: the Euro Area as 'Germany writ large'. In consequence, the Euro Area lacked a supra-national political framework of legitimacy and consent that would support collective insurance, other than on a very modest scale. Inducements to complacency in the period 1991–2007 exacerbated the scale of the crisis for the Euro Area.

The limits of Europeanization and risks from 'de-Europeanization' were highlighted once intertwined sovereign debt and banking crises threatened to spread to the core of the Euro Area. Problems of domestic political management in creditor states intensified. Their domestic options, and external negotiating leeway, narrowed. This process was demonstrated in Dutch and Finnish elections in 2011–2012 and cast a shadow over impending German federal elections in 2013. The logic of a 'transfer union' was a difficult sell to their taxpayers, for whom European solidarity was a matter of effort to comply with rules of sustainable public finances. Ominously, as the crisis intensified, attitudes of hostility to moral hazard became invested with emotional content and ripe for populist mobilization. Crisis was an unpropitious time for coaxing creditor state publics to accept further Europeanization. Similarly, the domestic options, and external negotiating leeway, of debtor states narrowed. Once sovereign debt crisis set in, elections led to loss of power by incumbent parties, as in Greece and Ireland, and to prospects of major systemic change in party systems. The French Presidential elections of May 2012, and prospective Italian elections in 2013, highlighted further the limits of Europeanization. In the cases of Greece and Italy there were risks of 'de-Europeanization' either as domestic demands became inconsistent with continued Euro Area membership or as exit came onto the political agenda.

The problem in resisting a 'transfer union' seemed to reside in the much fewer number of creditor states than debtor states. By 2012 there were only three triple-A-rated Euro Area member states out of 17. Germany appeared to face isolation. However, this disadvantage of numbers was outweighed by the greater incentive for creditor states to coordinate. Collective action was more difficult for debtor states, which had an incentive to differentiate themselves from each other in their efforts to sustain creditworthiness. Creditor state policy narratives were also more closely aligned with the major international financial institutions like the IMF, as well as with the ECB (though less with the US). Hence the idea of fiscal union became coterminous with institutionalized fiscal discipline at the Euro Area and national levels through treaty and domestic constitutional reforms. Fiscal union was not envisaged as the provision of collective insurance against supreme events that might jeopardize the integrity and survival of the Euro Area. There was no symmetrical definition of 'good' and 'bad' creditor states, to complement that of 'good' and 'bad' debtor states, no notion of reciprocal adjustment. Creditor states were more concerned with disciplining errant debtors than the collective good of insurance for the Euro Area.

The Achilles heel of the creditor state narrative is the inherent imperfections of financial markets and of states both in safeguarding the collective good of financial stability and in promoting sustainable growth. Financial markets are characterized by pro-cyclical, 'herd-like' behaviour. Their superior capacity to enforce discipline is undermined by their inherent volatility, fueled by alternating phases of greed and fear. Corrections tend to be enforced late and dramatically, in ways that can inflict punitive damage on real economies and on public sectors and their beneficiaries. Similarly, however carefully refined, EU and state crisis prevention and management capacities remain limited. Politicians are experts in exploiting exemptions, the ambiguities that are offered by complex goals, and fiscal and accounting devices. They are also disposed to be indulgent to the short-term preferences of voters, unwilling to reign in asset- price and credit booms or to enforce tax increases or public spending cuts to reign in fiscal deficits.

Given the incentives to complacency, and the inherent imperfections of financial markets and states, the long-term sustainability of the Euro Area depends on more than crisis prevention measures to enhance fiscal discipline and promote structural reforms. It also requires more than standard crisis management arrangements that are consistent with stability-oriented policies, including lender of last resort to banks. One option is to recognize that some member states lack state capacity to comply and to put in place mechanisms for euro exit. Solidarity of collective insurance requires trust. Alternatively, the Euro Area requires the capacity to provide ultimate collective insurance against existential threat. Ultimately, its creditor states must define the public good as not just the limitation of their liabilities but also underwriting the Euro Area as a whole. The stakes mount as the crisis intensifies and spreads contagiously towards the core of the Euro Area and as banks are caught up in sovereign debt problems.

Both options remain highly problematic. Euro exit is associated with enormous contractual complexities, capital flight problems, and high risks of disorderly defaults. Capacity of the Euro Area to act in supreme emergency exemption is a double test. Firstly, it poses the question of whether EMU is producing a 'new' Europe to replace conventional patterns of creditor-debtor state diplomacy. Traditionally, sovereign debt crises bred mutual misunderstandings and suspicion, poisoned relationships, polarized opinions, and induced resort to coercive statecraft (Dyson forthcoming). A 'new Europe' requires a quantum leap in trust-building, which is more difficult to achieve as crisis deepens. Secondly, creation of a supra-national capacity to act in supreme emergency tests the inner dynamics of European integration. It places in question both the market-integrating effects of the euro and the role of the Franco–German motor in EMU.

The negotiation of the Maastricht Treaty, the first decade of the Euro Area, and the protracted crisis management after 2007 illustrated the strengths and the limits of endogenous preference formation within the EU. The complex, 'repeated-game' negotiating environment of the EU and, above all, the Euro Area, the lessons drawn from past experiences, and the mounting stakes in European integration fostered adaptive preferences in creditor-debtor state diplomacy. However, the 'red lines' of creditor states around liability test the limits of endogenous preference formation. What risk are creditor states prepared to tolerate to safeguard the euro? How much pain can debtor states bear, and for how long? The answers are primarily political.

References

Dyson, K. 2000. *The politics of the Euro-zone: stability or breakdown?* Oxford: Oxford University Press.
Dyson, K. 2008. The first decade: credibility, identity, and institutional 'fuzziness'. In *The Euro at 10: Europeanization, convergence, and power*, ed. K. Dyson, 1–34. Oxford: Oxford University Press.
Dyson, K. 2009a. The evolving timescapes of European economic governance: contesting and using time. *Journal of European Public Policy* 16, no. 2: 286–306.

Dyson, K. 2009b. Fifty years of economic and monetary union: a hard and thorny journey. In *Reflections on European integration: 50 years of the Treaty of Rome*, eds. D. Phinnemore and A. Warleigh-Lack, 143–71. Houndmills: Palgrave Macmillan.

Dyson, K. 2012. Economic and monetary disunion? In *European disunion*, ed. J. Hayward and R. Wurzel, Houndmills: Palgrave Macmillan.

Dyson, K. 2013. Sworn to grim necessity? Imperfections of European economic governance, normative political theory, and supreme emergency. *Journal of European Integration* 35, no. 3.

Dyson, K. Forthcoming. *States, debt, and power: saints and sinners in European history and integration*. Oxford: Oxford University Press.

Dyson, K., and K. Featherstone. 1999. *The road to Maastricht: negotiating economic and monetary union*. Oxford: Oxford University Press.

Dyson, K., and L. Quaglia. 2010. *European macro-economic governance: commentary and documents, Volume II – policies*. Oxford: Oxford University Press.

Dyson, K., and A. Sepos. 2010. *Which Europe? The politics of differentiated integration*. Houndmills: Palgrave Macmillan.

European Central Bank. 2011. Stronger EU economic governance framework comes into force. *Monthly Bulletin*, December: 98–100.

Hart, H.L.A. 1961. *The concept of law*. Oxford: Clarendon Press.

Heipertz, M., and A. Verdun. 2010. *Ruling Europe: the politics of the stability and growth pact*. Cambridge: Cambridge University Press.

Hood, C. 1984. *The tools of government*. London: Macmillan.

Issing, O. 2008. *The birth of the euro*. Cambridge: Cambridge University Press.

Issing, O. 2012. Die Währungsunion auf dem Weg zur Fiskalunion? *Frankfurter Allgemeine Zeitung*, 6 January, p.

Merkel, A. 2012. Regierungserklärung vor dem Deutschen Bundestag zum Europäischen Rat am 28/29 Juni 2012, Berlin, 27 June.

Rawls, J. 1999. *The law of peoples*. Cambridge, MA: Harvard University Press.

Savage, J. 2005. *Making the EMU: the politics of budgetary surveillance and the enforcement of Maastricht*. Oxford: Oxford University Press.

Stark, J. 2011. Ich konnte mich nicht mehr durchsetzen. *Börsen-Zeitung*, 31 December.

Waever, O. 1995. Securitization and desecuritization. In *On security*, ed. R. Lipschutz, 46–86 New York: Columbia University Press.

Walzer, M. 1992. *Just and unjust wars*. New York: Basic Books.

Weidmann, J. 2012. Wir müssen klare Kante Zeigen, *Der Tagesspiegel*, 2 January.

Wolf, M. 2011. Creditors can huff but they need debtors. *Financial, Times*, 1 November, p. 14.

Wulff, C. 2011. Wer rettet die Retter? *ZDF heute journal*, 24 August.

Post-Maastricht Civil Society and Participatory Democracy

BEATE KOHLER-KOCH

Mannheimer Zentrum für Europäische Sozialforschung (MZES), Mannheim University, Mannheim, Germany

ABSTRACT   The Treaty of Maastricht and even more so the sceptical public response to the further deepening of European integration triggered a new approach to civil society. This contribution explores why the concept of civil society became so prominent in Brussels and why such high expectations were placed in the democratic strengthening of Europe by involving civil society in EU governance and by starting a civil dialogue. The main part of the contribution presents the findings of an empirical investigation demonstrating and explaining how much aspirations differ from reality. At the end of the contribution the democratic potential of civil dialogue is compared with expectations regarding the European Citizens' Initiative.

With the signing of the Maastricht Treaty the idea of European citizenship gained official recognition and the link to civil society came into focus. Whereas European citizenship for a long time mainly attracted academic interest (Bellamy and Warleigh 2005, 3), civil society experienced a remarkable career. Associations claiming to represent Europe's civil society flocked to Brussels; EU institutions became committed to involve civil society in governance, and finally, civil society was seen as a beacon of hope for reducing the democratic deficit by advancing participatory democracy.

The first section of this contribution explains why civil society became so prominent and highlights the factors that influenced success but also made it difficult to achieve democratic legitimacy The second section supplies, in a short-hand fashion, the criteria to assess the democratic value which the involvement of civil society in EU governance may bring about. The following two sections present findings of an in-depth empirical research project which support a critical evaluation of the democratic potential of organized civil society. The contribution is concluded with a summary and an outlook as to whether the Citizens' Initiative rather than civil dialogue may improve prospects for democracy.

The Europeanization of Civil Society

The rise of civil society[1] in the post-Maastricht era can be attributed to strong push-and-pull factors. First, the deepening of European integration provided strong incentives not to leave the shaping of Europe to economic interests. From the very beginning it was obvious that the transition from a common market to an economic and monetary union and especially the ambitious project of a single currency would cut deep into people's lives. Furthermore, the Maastricht Treaty also expanded the Community's competence in fields of general interest such as social policy, environment and consumer protection and added new ones such as public health, education, culture and youth. European policies were to affect Europe's citizens more broadly and the gradual transformation of the Economic Community into a Union with responsibilities in foreign policy and security and in justice and home affairs gave it a more political profile. In addition, the creation of European citizenship was meant to enhance an ever-closer union, foster European identity, and bring citizens into direct relation with EU institutions. It granted Europe's citizens new rights, including the right to petition the European Parliament and to submit complaints to the European Ombudsman.

Consequently, public interest groups increasingly took an interest in EU affairs. This is most visible in the growth of EU-level associations which do not represent the business world or trade unions or professional groups. The majority of non-governmental organisations (NGOs) that claim to represent civil society in Brussels are quite young.[2] Even though several organisations, especially in the field of environment and consumer protection, originate from earlier times, more than half of the European NGOs were established after the late 1980s and only about a third were founded in the last decade. Also, the formation of networks and platforms, which bring together the public interest associations operating in a specific policy field, is a very recent phenomenon.

At first sight, the late and uneven growth of EU-level NGOs seems to reflect the shift of competence from the national to the EU level. It suggests that public interest groups turned to Brussels in order to guard against losing political influence. However, when we take a close look not just at the founding dates but at the founding history of European associations, a different pattern becomes apparent and we can discern the formative influence of EU institutions, above all of the European Commission. It had always been the policy of the Commission to further strengthen European integration by close cooperation with interest groups, and over and again it even took an active part in helping organisations to establish a unified European representation.[3] But at the time of negotiating the Maastricht Treaty, public interest groups still had to take a back seat. A prime example is that charitable associations had to fight hard and only with the strong support of some national governments succeeded to be officially recognized by the EU as relevant cooperation partners in the field of social welfare.[4] Only later, in the post-Maastricht era, the Commission became a major driving force for attracting NGOs to Brussels. One reason is that public interest groups are a formidable alliance partner when it comes to consolidating or even expanding EU jurisdiction in new policy fields. A telling example is the subsequent development of EU–NGO cooperation in the field of social policy. With the appointment of a new Commissioner the managing Directorate–General intensified cooperation with social policy NGOs to overcome the reluctance of some member states to transfer socio-political responsibilities to the supranational level. Pursuant to the Green Paper on European Social Policy (COM (93) 551, November 1993) the Commission established a European Social Policy Forum with representatives of social NGOs. It was conceived as 'a continuous process whereby suggested approaches to policy issues are fed into the main strands of national and international policy-making'.[5] To make it a success, the Commission encouraged the relevant organisations to set up a 'European Platform of NGOs in the social sector' to present coordinated positions. With further encouragement and EU funding it became institutionalized as the 'Social Platform', a confederation of around 40 European non-governmental organisations, federations and networks, which up to today is the privileged partner in the relevant 'civil dialogue'. The very same pattern was repeated with the extension of EU competence in the fields of public health, culture, and of life-long learning (Kohler-Koch and Buth 2013).

Another reason for the upgrading of NGOs was the alarming indifference and in some countries the outright rejection of further integration, which became manifest in the failure and near-failure of the Maastricht Referendum in Denmark and France. In order to stop the slow erosion of the permissive consensus spurred by growing EU-critical attitudes of political parties (Conti and Memoli 2012) and a slowly spreading Eurosceptic discourse in the mass media (de Wilde and Trenz 2012), member state governments and EU institutions focused on bringing the Union closer to its citizens and looked for means to ensure that the Union functioned with greater efficiency and legitimacy.[6] Whereas piecemeal reforms of existing institutions were on the agenda of the European Council, the Commission set out to review its system of governance, including its relationship with social groups. It started to streamline its consultation practice and in doing so moved from 'An Open and Structured Dialogue Between the Commission and Special Interest Groups' (93/C 63/02) to 'Building a Stronger Partnership' with non-governmental organisations (KOM (2000) 11), and finally to 'Involving Civil Society' (Commission 2001) and engaging in 'Interactive Policy Making' (C (2001) 1014). The change in terminology reflects a shift in perspectives concerning the objectives of consultations and in respect to the role attributed to NGOs. Whereas in the past EU–society interaction had mostly been an issue-oriented exchange with economic interest groups and the social partners to improve the effectiveness of EU policies, the new approach to consultations aimed at broad public acceptance and, consequently, included groups representing general interests and introduced more participatory principles, procedures and instruments (Kohler-Koch and Finke 2007). The Commission pledged a commitment to transparency, openness, participation and accountability; it sponsored a 'civil dialogue' in several policy fields and expanded funding to help the so-called weak interests to get organized at the EU-level. New instruments such as online consultations were developed to lower the threshold of access to EU policy-making. All these activities were meant to serve the input and output legitimacy of the EU. Inclusive participation was supposed to channel the concerns of stakeholders directly into the policy-making process and to ensure better law-making by adding their expert knowledge. Participation increasingly gained a normative dimension which exceeded the promise of proficient consultations and good governance. It opened up the horizon to a democratic European future. This new approach then materialized with the insertion of the 'Principle of Participatory Democracy' in the Draft Constitutional Treaty and later in the Treaty of Lisbon.

How did this turn, from political expediency to grand democratic aspirations, come about?[7] It was the wider political context which altered the frame of reference used to view EU–society relations. The peaceful dismantling of authoritarian rule in eastern Europe, the final triumph over the Apartheid regime in South Africa, and the return to democracy in Latin America have all caught the attention of intellectuals in Western Europe. Despite glaring dissimilarities in context conditions, civil society became seen as a universal remedy to crises in political legitimacy. The concurrent global activities of non-governmental organizations anchored the image of civil society as a successful force in the fight for democracy and the protection of civil rights. Their commitment to human rights, environmental protection and social justice ensured public appreciation. Not just civil society organisations but civil society in general ranked highly in political discourse. It equates to committed, dedicated citizens who take a stand for political rights and the common good. It has become the epitome for political emancipation, and the strengthening of civil society is habitually considered as a means of securing political and social self-determination. Thus the concept of civil society is loaded with positive normative connotations.

The positive public perception was spurred not least by academia. Civil society became a popular subject in social science research, which presented more often than not a very sympathetic view (Greven 2000, 4) irrespective of whether they dealt with local citizens' initiatives or the campaigns of global NGOs. In addition, political theory took up the basic issues of democracy anew and linked it to the unsolved problem of EU democracy. Habermas' (1996) discourse–theoretical approach especially found wide acceptance, with its strong emphasis on civil society as key promoter of public discourse and thus crucial supporter of deliberative democracy. Deliberative democracy theory became the preferred reference in intellectual efforts to overcome the European democratic deficit.[8] Thus, civil society achieved a theoretically substantiated importance.

In short, civil society was very much en vogue, which means that every recourse back to civil society found favourable support. It did not irritate supporters that the concepts varied strongly. Rather, they shared a diffused understanding of civil society, which helped foster consensus on the benefits of strengthening civil society in the EU context. It reconciled two images that — from an analytical point of view — are quite different. One image embodies civil society as the active citizenship constituting the politically dynamic constituency of the Union. It is the nucleus of the emergent political community of the Union and, as such, it is attractive to the European integrationists since it holds the promise to be the breeding ground for a European demos. There is a link to 'organised civil society' insofar as civil society organisations form and transform civil society through discourse and interaction in the public sphere.

Commonly the focus on organized civil society is coupled with quite a different image of civil society. A rather broad concept suggesting an ideal-type civil society defines it as 'a dynamic non-governmental system of inter-connected socio-economic institutions' (Keane 2003, 8). In the European context, most scholars prefer a more narrow understanding, confining the relevant institutions to non-governmental organisations that are committed to a public purpose.[9] They are expected to extend democracy by empowering citizens to become active participants in political life; they are 'schools of democracy' and foster social capital. Their commitment is said to compensate for the deficiencies of representative democracies as they give societal interests a voice and convey the demands and concerns of the grassroots to the far-off decision-makers in Brussels. Organised civil society is also attractive as a partner in governance. It is expected not just to voice the diversity of interests and views but also to bring the knowledge and down-to-earth experience of citizens into the policy-making process. Hence, as demonstrated above, civil society organisations are invited to give advice and to participate formally and actively in the collective decision-making process in order to improve the quality of EU governance.

A common feature of these concepts is that they attribute civil society a decisive role in the democratic future of the Union, but they differ considerably as to how this may be achieved. Judging from their self-presentation on the internet or in annual reports, NGOs do not seem to be irritated by these multifunctional expectations. But in personal conversations they readily admit that they are faced with contradicting demands. They see their mission to be the seeds for an emerging transnational civil society in Europe. But they concede that it is an ambitious goal, and it is unclear how such a far-reaching objective can be accomplished. For them the most pressing task is to exert political influence to achieve their thematic priorities. Because they see themselves as advocates of general interest objectives working for minority rights and solidarity, the potentially conflicting objectives of interest representation and promoting participatory democracy are deemed compatible. This argument was put forward particularly clearly at the time when NGOs lobbied for civil dialogue to be included in the Constitutional Treaty. In their statements they established a specific and direct association between civil dialogue, consultations of NGOs and the concept of participatory democracy. Nicolas Beger, at the time coordinator of the Civil Society Contact Group (CSCG), the coalition of the large EU–NGO confederations and networks, put it in one sentence: 'This participation is called civil dialogue — or as I prefer participatory democracy'.[10] However, when faced with the manifold restrictions in the normal process of daily work the same NGOs have reservations concerning the compatibility of efficient lobbying and promoting participatory democracy.

Assessing the Democratic Value of Civil Society Participation

It would be naïve to assume that the dialogue of EU institutions with civil society as such could render the EU more democratic. Organised civil society is no substitute for the sovereign people. The claim of the rights and value based NGOs[11] — that they work towards the common good and not for the sake of specific interests — does not turn them into a legitimate representative of the citizenry. When we talk about organized civil society operating at EU-level there is nothing in the nature of these associations which makes them inherently democratic. Rather, the way they operate may contribute to make the EU more democratic. Three functional contributions stand out as serving best the democratic legitimacy of the EU: they can function as intermediaries in political representation; they may stimulate the development of a EU-wide public sphere; they may advance deliberation in a way that brings EU governance in line with the interests of the people. As is well-known, normative theories of democracy differ in what they consider to be the most essential elements of democracy, and accordingly they attribute different roles to civil society. Even if it is cutting corners in a way that does not live up to the high standards of political theory, we looked for criteria that are shared by all.[12] The first set of criteria relate to democratic participation roughly following Robert A. Dahl (1998). Accordingly, NGOs may bring added value to EU democracy when their involvement makes representation more equal and effective and furthers the enlightened judgment of citizens. The model of civil society organisations as transmission belts depicts best how they are supposed to function. In a bottom-up process they feed citizens' preferences into the policy-making process and in a top-down process they inform the public about issues on the political agenda, about the stakes involved and possible alternatives. The democratic quality varies with the responsiveness of the individual organisations to the preferences of their membership or supporters, respectively, and the representativeness of all civil society organisations together. Thus, empirical research has to investigate first, the composition of the interest group system in total testing whether or not it is reflecting the full range of societal interests and, secondly, whether the internal organization of the associations live up to democratic standards. Further, in order to ascertain if representation is also likely to have an unbiased impact on output, it is important to examine access opportunities, de facto participation in consultations and in cooperative governance, and the characteristics of exchange relations which may yield influence.

The signalling of given preferences is at the heart of a rational choice model, which defines representation as 'a relation between interests and outcomes' (Manin, Przeworski, and Stokes 1999: 8). In a more reflective understanding of democratic representation, civil society organisations are the active promoter of democratic participation and will formation. An important but still modest contribution would be that NGOs inform and teach members, followers and also the wider public by drawing attention to the EU's political agenda, by providing issue-specific information, and by highlighting conflicts and inconsistencies. In this way they give EU policies publicity, which is essential for democratic participation. Only when citizens are confronted in their daily life with what is going on in Brussels, may they develop an interest. As a further step, NGOs may take a leading role in stimulating public debates by taking sides and mobilizing public contestation. This more pro-active engagement fits well with a new reading of representation: good democratic representation is not mirroring a given constellation of preferences in society but is a dynamic process of interaction between representatives and the represented (Thaa 2008). Some authors (Göhler 1992; Young 1997) have challenged the idea that a political constituency is preceding its representation and argue that a constituency only comes to existence in the process of representation. At best it is a continuous exchange, a 'communicative current between civil and political society' (Urbinati 2006, 24). This kind of interaction does not necessarily meet the high standards of public discourse set by Jürgen Habermas (Habermas 2006). As a rule it is not the driver of public deliberation and it does not aim at exerting influence by 'communicative power' but rather by putting political pressure on decision-makers. A second school of thought underscores the positive effect of civil society by looking at the internal processes of EU governance. They suggest a 'democratizing effect' of NGOs because they bring stakeholder experience to the fore and when contesting official proposals they enforce a continued process of deliberation (Sabel and Zeitlin 2010). In general it is assumed that NGO participation will upgrade the discursive quality of negotiations because as weak actors they have to rely on the power of the better argument.

Evaluating the Democratic Role of Civil Society

Reality Test

In a large empirical research project[13] we investigated the participatory turn in EU governance and the democratic potential of civil society involvement. We addressed three key questions:

(1) Did institutional and administrative reforms create a civil society friendly environment, enabling participatory democratic governance to come true?
(2) Do NGOs under the given institutional and organizational constraints manage to reconcile the contradictory demands of effective lobbying and boosting democratic participation?
(3) Will the dialogue with civil society render the Union more democratic or is the EU system as such incompatible with active democratic participation?

The Participatory Turn in EU Governance

We focused on the Commission because NGOs consider it to be the most promising access point for effective participation. Does the consultation regime of the Commission aim at enhancing civil society participation for the sake of gaining democratic legitimacy and is it organized in a way to provide open and inclusive access to EU decision-making? Did it manage to redress biased representation? Do the procedures allow for authentic and differentiated input? Do they secure rational deliberation and accountability so that participation will (probably) have an impact on output?

A benevolent reading of EU documents and Commission statements support the interpretation that involving civil society was meant to further both democratic input and output legitimacy. Norms, rules and new instruments such as online consultations made the EU more accessible. The more frequent use of conferences and other events targeted at a broad audience made consultations more inclusive. By providing extensive information both on substance and procedures the Commission helped low budget groups to monitor the decision-making process and to step in when necessary. More General-Directorates opened a civil dialogue and invited civil society organisations to sit on committees and advisory groups. The NGO umbrella organisations and platforms became privileged partners in negotiations on governance issues and future policy trends whereas national peak organisations mostly outnumber EU federations in the issue specific committees.

The Commission's new consultation regime has definitely lowered the threshold of access. In addition, the Commission with the backing of the European Parliament has actively supported the formation of EU-wide public interest associations. All these reforms have turned to the benefit of NGOs. Their presence in Brussels, their involvement in EU consultations, and their voice in the concert of interest groups have noticeably increased. But did it also enhance the democratic quality of EU governance in terms of redressing biased representation?

Despite noteworthy efforts to become more open, inclusive and participatory, equal representation has not been achieved. In policy fields such as employment and social affairs, consumer protection and public health,[14] representations of the business world do not any longer outnumber public interest groups, but they command more financial resources and are better staffed. Consequently they, too, make extensive use of the new instruments and on most issues are more present than relevant NGOs. Even more pronounced is the distortion in territorial representation: NGOs residing in countries in the North-Western tier of Europe are over-represented in online-consultations and also in civil dialogue meetings as compared to NGOs from Southern and Eastern countries.

The quantitative analysis conveys a first impression concerning the state of democratic participation. The presence in numbers is a proxy and not a reliable indicator for what Robert A. Dahl (1998) called 'effective participation'. Effective civil society participation which is consistent with the principle of democratic legitimacy means that civil society should have a voice that is heard and considered, even though the politically legitimate institutions may decide differently. Here the consultation strategy of the EU is faced with a dilemma: instruments well suited for broad public participation such as large conferences and online consultations with multiple-choice questionnaires give participants hardly any influence on substance.

More effective are advisory groups and online consultations that allow for well-argued comments. However, it takes time and expert knowledge to deliver and, consequently, the performance of stakeholder groups varies with available resources and, as it is well known, these are not distributed evenly despite public EU funding of NGOs. A real obstacle to effective representation is the lack of accountability (Kohler-Koch 2010). The Commission is autonomous and mainly interested to gain support in its negotiating with the Council and the European Parliament. The Commission is not legally obliged to explain and justify its position and does not have to face consequences. NGOs may take recourse to 'naming and shaming', but this is already in principle a soft instrument to sanction unwanted conduct. When media attention is low, as in most cases of EU policies, it is a blunt sword right from the beginning.

Thus, the good news is that the EU succeeded in widening the political participation of civil society organisations by lowering the threshold of access; it has increased transparency and has lent support to the representation of weak interests. Furthermore, in principle the Commission and interest groups have reached an agreement that feedback mechanisms ought to be improved. But little has been done so far to put this agreement into practice.

Constrains on NGO Performance

When examining the capacities of NGOs to serve as agents of participatory democracy we also have to take a good look at what they consider to be their mission and how the institutional environment and the disposition of their members constrain their performance. Is democratic participation at the top of their list of priorities? How can they efficiently deal with the 'logic of influence' (Schmitter and Streeck 1999) and still advance democratic participation? Can they meet the requirements of a professional organization and how do organizational properties impact on their behaviour?

For an assessment of NGO priorities it is worthwhile to examine the statements of the Civil Society Contact Group (CSCG). The group was created by the largest and most important European NGO associations and networks to give civil society a firm common voice on constitutional and governance issues. CSCG strongly came out in favour of supporting participatory democracy and lobbied hard to insert the dialogue with civil society in the Constitutional Treaty. However, in spite of the sustained effort to push the agenda, neither the CSCG nor the Social Platform, which at the time played a catalytic role in the debate and was the main support of the CSCG, succeeded to forge a consensus on core concepts. They did not reach an agreement how best to define civil society and how to frame the civil dialogue. Thus, they were unable to formulate a coherent model to give substance to the vision of participatory democracy.

It was a matter of differing self-conceptions and organizational interests. Consequently, one should not expect that European NGOs put enhancing participatory democracy first. Rather, they have a cause and they want their concerns to prevail.

The question then is, will and can they represent their cause it in a way that maximizes citizens' involvement or at least gives members and supporters a fair and equal chance of participation? The institutional environment is not at all conducive to intensive cooperation between Brussels based NGOs and the grass roots. The European system of multi-level governance is mirrored in the organization of associations which makes for long and knotty ways of communication (Kohler-Koch and Buth 2009). Most EU level NGOs are federations of federations and for the sake of greater political impact they have gathered in sector specific platforms and networks. This has added an additional level to the long chain of interest representation. Furthermore, the organization of networks does not follow the logic of functional specialisation and does not produce a clear, hierarchical structure. Networks are characterized by heterarchy and multiple memberships. This facilitates communication on cross-cutting issues and has the advantage that NGOs themselves can take care of interest aggregation and do not have to leave it to the discretion of the Commission. The flip side of the coin is that communication structures are opaque and not transparent, which in turn keeps citizens at distance.

Brussels is, anyway, far removed from the grass roots, not just in geographic terms but also in terms of representing unfamiliar political cultures. In addition, language barriers, the fluidity of membership in recent years and frequent changes in administrative routines lead to difficult working conditions in Brussels and complicate communication with members. Obstacles are greater for NGOs with a mass membership than for trade associations or cause groups that operate as political entrepreneurs. Nevertheless, in recent years the European NGOs have become far more proficient in communicating with members and also the wider public. Still in 2006 the European NGO Confederation for Relief and Development (CONCORD) pioneered in conducting a survey among its members to better get to know its affiliates and the Platform of European Social NGOs (Social Platform) for the first time in the annual conference of 2008 organized a workshop to discuss the role of European NGO networks in bridging the gap between European and national levels. In the meantime also the newly established European NGOs have become far more experienced in dealing with members; it is generally agreed that internet presence and e-communication clearly facilitates communication.

However, the 'logic of influence' prevailing in Brussels impairs the transmission belt function of civil society associations. NGOs have to get organised in a way to meet the functional requirements of 'effective participation' and they have to play according to the rules. They have to be visible and influential for two reasons: the fight for attaining their objectives and the long-term survival of their organization. Only success averts the exit of members and the loss of resources, be it from supporters or the Commission. The Commission, increasingly, honours professional performance and provides funds on a project basis, which requires sophisticated administrative skills. Organising effective participation may come at the price of turning civil society organisations into a lobby groups like all the others, i.e., concentrating on particular interests and being — at best — a transmission-belt of established interests, instead of providing a space for reasoning and deliberation. The dangers are twofold: efficiency calls for elitism and effectiveness suggests specificity.

NGOs have done their best to meet the challenge under the constraining conditions of limited resources. Since most NGOs have a relatively small workforce, the site of offices and the work experience of the staff make a difference. Communication with EU institutions and with other NGOs is made easy because most offices are located close to the Commission in the same area and sometimes even in the same building as other NGOs. Informal contacts when participating in EU events are frequent so that staff members know each other and are well aware of their respective portfolios. Career patterns facilitate efficient cooperation: NGO staff mostly have EU or international experience, either gained in other European NGOs or in the Commission and the European Parliament. Previous work experience on the sub-national or local level is comparatively rare.

In short, the dominant picture is that of 'EU-level lobbying professionals'. Organisational properties such as career patterns, communication patterns emanating from proximity, the dependence on EU funding, etc, tend to support the formation of a self-referential European NGO community which has the best intention of working in the interest of citizens but gives citizens little say in its work (Kohler-Koch and Buth 2013). This holds true even though most federations have institutionalised mechanisms to give voice to their members and also communicate with lower levels of organisations. But detailed case studies show that sophisticated systems of mandating further a streamlining of policy preferences and generate middle-of-the-road positions (Strid 2009).

The greatest obstacles to democratic participation are, however, the institutional framework conditions. The EU system is designed to reach compromise solutions and the Commission, in particular, is committed to consensus building. This explains the technocratic framing of policy proposals and the reluctance to accept that policy-making is about hard choices concerning competing values, tastes, and interests. Politics is thus devoid of its political character. Accordingly, EU consultations are laid out as an exercise in information gathering and the collection of expert knowledge and demonstrate that the Commission is, first and foremost, looking for well-founded opinions supporting its position. Already in online consultations, the questions often suggest which answers are deemed to be appropriate, and the Commission's evaluation reports underline especially the favourable proposals and deal with opposing positions only in a summary fashion (Quittkat 2013b). Civil society organisations accept that they must play according to the rules in order to have influence. They voice their opposition not on political grounds but insist on representing public interests. They strive to be accepted as a partner in EU governance, knowledgeable, reliable and dedicated to the common European good.

The European Parliament is the only institution which is supposed to represent the diversity of public opinions, and due to its partisan composition ought to have an interest in engaging in political controversies. The Lisbon Treaty has reinforced the power of the European Parliament but with the paradoxical effect that the reform mitigated its representative function. 'In the interest of effectiveness' an 'informal trialogue' has been set up; it is celebrated as 'the true negotiating forum' where in small circle delegates of the Parliament, the Commission and the Council meet behind closed doors to reach a compromise.[15] The procedure ensures speedy agreements but it keeps decision-making out of the public view and conceals controversies. Consequently, civil society organisations have close to no chance to access the decision-making process at this important stage of decision-making and they lose a strong ally in their effort to bring out differences in political choice.

Conclusion and Outlook

Since Maastricht the qualitative change of the EU brought about a boost in NGO activities targeted at Brussels and inspired new ideas on how to make the EU more democratic. The democratic credentials of civil society ranked high in the debate and became firmly acknowledged in the Constitutional Treaty and later in the Lisbon Treaty. The commitment to an open and regular civil dialogue, which is considered to be a centrepiece of participatory democracy, strengthened the claim of NGOs to have a voice in EU affairs. A thorough examination of political reality shows a differentiated picture. According to our analysis the support for civil society organisations and the turn to more participatory governance have had the positive effect to expand the plurality of views in EU consultations and to give non-economic concerns presence. However, our final assessment is that despite all efforts increased NGO participation in EU governance did not render political representation in the EU more democratic. If we see democracy 'as a never-ending process of apportioning and publicly monitoring the exercise of power by citizens within polities marked by the institutionally distinct — but always mediated — realms of civil society and government institutions' (Keane 2010, 461) we have to conclude that civil society contributes little to the democratic legitimacy of the EU, because it does not bring about the democratic empowerment of citizens and hardly achieves equal and effective participation. Therefore, we have to ask if it is a matter of inappropriate means or if the EU due to its nature is unsuitable for democracy. In other words, if the dialogue with civil society organisations is not a promising way to achieve democratic participation, does the citizens' initiative have a greater potential to do so?

Under the 'Provisions on the Democratic Principles' (Title II) the Lisbon Treaty provided the legal basis for a European Citizens' Initiative (ECI). It allows one million citizens from at least seven out of twenty seven EU member states to raise their voice in EU governance. The ECI gives power to the citizens in so far as the initiative is not authority-controlled like a plebiscite. It does not, however, give citizens a right equivalent to a referendum. It does not constitute direct legislation by the people and does not even give them the control over the political agenda. The ECI can only invite the European Commission to bring forward proposals for legal acts and these are confined to areas where the Commission acts in accordance with the treaty.

As the drafting of the relevant regulations was a protracted process the first ECI could not be launched before April 2012. Nevertheless, more than two dozen pilot initiatives were started, which convey some comparable experiences.[16] That initiatives have a compelling cause and a strong emotional appeal does not guarantee success. Rather, what is required is efficient organisation to follow the procedure step-by-step and to meet the requirements of collecting and verifying the statements of support of a million people from at least seven EU countries with a given minimum number of signatories per member state. Only actors who can combine efficient transnational organisation and grass roots presence can undertake such an effort. So far it has turned out that the instrument is mainly of use to established EU or international NGOs and trade union confederations, European political parties and members of the European Parliament mostly in alliance with transnational operating NGOs. It is an attractive tool for NGOs to put pressure on the Commission and to demonstrate both to their membership and to EU-institutions that they can deliver. For the European Parliament it is a substitute for the missing agenda-setting power which is still denied to parliament.

Irrespective of the instrumental use to interested parties, the ECI might vitalize democratic participation. A recent initiative may serve as an example. The '8hours' campaign[17] aims at a revision of current EU legislation to the effect that it prohibits the transportation of animals destined for slaughter for more than eight hours. The initiative was first started by a member of the European Parliament and then joined by a German animal welfare organisation with many years of experience in working on the ground across borders.[18] The accumulated experience, which resulted in well-documented reports, made the NGO a trustworthy partner and the close cooperation with committed individuals and local groups in many European countries was essential for the mobilization of support. By the beginning of July 2012 more than 1,1 million signatures had been collected. Such a result could not have been achieved just by setting up a Facebook community and launching a website, even not if it is translated into 18 languages. Rather, the success is due to the engagement of animal welfare organisations and other voluntary groups at national and local levels as well as individual supporters. They spread participation by disseminating information material and contacting potential supporters and they organised the collection of signatures in the streets. In addition to the 8hours ECI campaign, supporters in the European Parliament have been rallied to sign a Written Declaration to support a review of existing legislation. This way a citizens' initiative managed to closely link direct citizens' participation with the political engagement of the democratic representatives. The initiative's only flaw is the biased representation in terms of country origin and political affiliation. When examining the list of supporters of the 8hours campaign — organisations and members of the

European Parliament[19] — numbers reflect both the geographic scope of the lead NGO (Germany and Italy) and the well-known centre-periphery difference in political participation.[20] The same seems to be true for media coverage, which is said to be best in Italy but low in Germany where the promoting NGO is located. So far the empirical basis is by far too small even for an educated guess as to what this means for the democratic credibility of such an initiative.

Only future experience will tell if the combination of a citizens' initiative with a significant and concurrent action in the European Parliament will make democratic participation happen.

Acknowledgements

I am deeply grateful to Harry Bauer, UCL for his stimulating comments.

Notes

1. One can only speak of a raise in civil society in the sense of a growth in organisations claiming to represent civil society. The Maastricht Treaty did not alter public dispositions; it did not create a community feeling that might induce citizens to be attentive to and participate in EU governance. It is highly contested as to which organisations qualify as civil society organisations. In accordance with the great majority of scholars working on the topic (Kohler-Koch and Quittkat 2009) we here focus on NGOs, voluntary autonomous organisations working for public purposes. For a theoretical treatment of the framing of civil society depending on how the EU is conceptualised see Kohler-Koch (2009).
2. For more details see Kohler-Koch and Buth (2013).
3. The most prominent example from the early days is the Commission's intervention in favour of a federated European Trade Union association in the late 1960s and early 1970s.
4. See Maastricht Treaty, Declaration on cooperation with charitable associations.
5. 'Working on European Social Policy: A report on the Forum', see http://www.actrav.itcilo.org/actrav-english/telearn/global/ilo/seura/euwok.htm (accessed 20 July 2012).
6. 'Turin European Council. Presidency Conclusions': (29 March 1996). See http://www.europarl.europa.eu/summits/tor1_en.htm (accessed 20 July 2012).
7. For a more detailed account see Kohler-Koch (2013a).
8. Most prominent are the publications by social scientists affiliated to ARENA and involved in the RECON project; see among others the edited volume by Eriksen and Fossum (2000) and RECON publications accessible under http://www.reconproject.eu/projectweb/portalproject/Publications.html (accessed 20 July 2012).
9. In a survey among scholars being experts in the field, an overwhelming majority (84,75 per cent) qualified NGOs adhering to the EU's Civil Society Contact Group as 'civil society organisations' (Kohler-Koch and Quittkat 2009).
10. For this and other quotes see Kohler-Koch (2008, 267).
11. This is the common denominator of the CSCG members; see http://www.act4europe.org/code/en/back.asp?Page=183 (accessed 20 July 2012).
12. For a comprehensive treatment of the theoretical reflections supporting our empirical research see Hüller (2010, 27–135).
13. The books by Kohler-Koch and Quittkat (2011, 2013) and Hüller (2010) present the consolidated findings; for a summary see Kohler-Koch (2013b). For a short project description and the complete list of publications see: http://www.mzes.uni-mannheim.de/projekte/pro_zeig_e.php?Recno=113 (accessed 20 July 2012).
14. Those were the policy fields we have analysed in depth.
15. See http://ec.europa.eu/codecision/stepbystep/text/index5_en.htm (accessed 20 July 2012).
16. For a short presentation of the first 25 initiatives see Kaufmann (2010).
17. See http://www.8hours.eu/8hours_en (accessed 20 July 2012).
18. For a summary report see http://campaignhandbook.gef.eu/1-million-european-citizens-for-better-animal-welfare/ (accessed 20 July 2012).
19. See the names listed on http://www.8hours.eu/supporters/ (accessed 20 July 2012).

20. The initiative is supported by 28 organisations and 33 EP parliamentarians from Germany and by 6:23 from Italy. Support in other large member states is far inferior: in France 5:3; Poland 3:1; Spain 4:2; the UK 9:11. Party affiliation is far more equally distributed.

References

Bellamy, R., and A. Warleigh. 2005. Introduction: the puzzle of EU citizenship. In *Citizenship and governance in the European Union*, ed. R. Bellamy and A. Warleigh, 3–17. London: Continuum.

Commission of the European Communities. 2001. *European governance – a White Paper*. Brussels: COM (2001) 428 final.

Conti, N., and V. Memoli. 2012. The multi-faceted nature of party-based Euroscepticism. *Acta Politica* 47, no. 2: 91–112.

Dahl, R.A. 1998. *On democracy*. New Haven: Yale University Press.

de Wilde, P., and H. J. Trenz. 2012. Denouncing European integration: Euroscepticism as polity contestation. *European Journal of Social Theory* (forthcoming), March 14, 2012, doi: 10.1177/1368431011432968.

Göhler, G. 1992. Politische Repräsentation in der Demokratie. In *Die politische Klasse in Deutschland*, eds. T. von Leif, H.J. Legrans, and A. Klein, 108–25. Bonn: Bouvier.

Greven, M. Th. 2000. NROs und die Informationalisierung des Regierens. Vorgänge, no. 151: 3–12.

Eriksen, E.O., and J.E. Fossum. 2000. *Democracy in the European Union: integration through deliberation?* London: Routledge.

Habermas, J. 1996. *Between facts and norms. Contributions to a discourse theory of law and democracy*. Cambridge: Polity Press.

Habermas, J. 2006. Political communication in media society: does democracy still enjoy an epistemic dimension? The impact of normative theory on empirical research. *Communication Theory* 16, no. 4: 411–26.

Hüller, T. 2010. *Demokratie und Sozialregulierung in Europa. Die Online-Konsultationen der EU-Kommission*. Frankfurt and New York: Campus Verlag.

Kaufmann, B. 2010. *The European citizens' initiative handbook. Your guide to the world's first transnational direct democratic tool*. Brussels: Green European Foundation.

Keane, J. 2003. *Global civil society*. Cambridge: Cambridge University Press.

Keane, J. 2010. Civil society, definitions and approaches. In *International encyclopedia of civil society*, eds. H.K. Anheier and S. Toepler, 461–4. New York: Springer.

Kohler-Koch, B. 2008. Does participatory governance hold its promises? In *Efficient and democratic governance in the European Union*, ed. B. Kohler-Koch and F. Larat, 265–95. Mannheim: CONNEX Report Series Vol. 5, http://www.mzes.uni-mannheim.de/projekte/typo3/site/fileadmin/BookSeries/Volume_Nine/CHAP%2017%20%28Kohler-Koch%29.pdf (accessed 20 July 2012).

Kohler-Koch, B. 2009. The three worlds of European civil society — what role for civil society for what kind of Europe? *Policy and Society* 28, no. 1: 47–57.

Kohler-Koch, B. 2010. How to put matters right — assessing the role of civil society in EU accountability. *West European Politics* 33, no. 5: 1117–41.

Kohler-Koch, B. 2013a. Governing with the European civil society. In *De-mystification of participatory democracy. EU governance and civil society*, ed. B. Kohler-Koch and C. Quittkat, Oxford: Oxford University Press (forthcoming).

Kohler-Koch, B. 2013b. Civil society participation: fostering democracy or furthering pluralism in EU lobbying? In De-mystification of participatory democracy. EU governance and civil society, ed. B. Kohler-Koch and C. Quittkat, Oxford: Oxford University Press (forthcoming).

Kohler-Koch, B., and V. Buth. 2009. Civil society in EU governance: lobby groups like any other? *TranState Working Papers 108*, Bremen: Transformations of the State. Collaborative Research Center 597, http://www.sfb597.uni-bremen.de/pages/pubApBeschreibung.php?SPRACHE=en&ID=148 (accessed 20 July 2012).

Kohler-Koch, B., and V. Buth. 2013. Squaring the circle: NGO professionalization and civic engagement. In *De-mystification of participatory democracy. EU governance and civil society*, ed. B. Kohler-Koch and C. Quittkat, Oxford: Oxford University Press (forthcoming).

Kohler-Koch, B., and B. Finke. 2007. The institutional shaping of EU–society relations: a contribution to democracy via participation? *Journal of Civil Society* 3, no. 3: 205–21.

Kohler-Koch, B., and C. Quittkat. 2009. What is civil society and who represents civil society in the EU? Results of an online survey among civil society experts. *Policy and Society* 28, no. 1: 11–22.

Kohler-Koch, B., and C. Quittkat. 2011. *Die Entzauberung partizipativer Demokratie. Zur Rolle der Zivilgesellschaft bei der Demokratisierung von EU-Governance*. Frankfurt and New York: Campus Verlag.

Kohler-Koch, B., and C. Quittkat. 2013. *De-mystification of participatory democracy EU governance and civil society*. Oxford: Oxford University Press.

Manin, B., A. Przeworski, and S. Stokes. 1999. Introduction. In *Democracy, accountability, and representation*, eds. A. Przeworski, S. Stokes, and B. Manin, 1–26. Cambridge: Cambridge University Press.

Quittkat, C. 2013a. Consultation in daily practice. An in-depth analysis. In *De-mystification of participatory democracy. EU governance and civil society*, ed. B. Kohler-Koch and C. Quittkat, Oxford: Oxford University Press (forthcoming).

Quittkat, C. 2013b. New instruments serving democracy: do online consultations benefit civil society? In *De-mystification of participatory democracy. EU governance and civil society*, ed. B. Kohler-Koch and C. Quittkat, Oxford: Oxford University Press (forthcoming).

Sabel, C.F., and J. Zeitlin. 2010. Learning from difference. the new architecture of experimentalist governance in the EU. In *Experimentalist governance in the European Union: towards a new architecture*, eds. C.F. Sabel and J. Zeitlin, 1–28. Oxford: Oxford University Press.

Schmitter, P.C., and W. Streeck. 1999. The organization of business interests. Studying the associative action of business in advanced industrial societies. MPfG Discussion Papers 99 (1). Köln: MPfG.

Strid, S. 2009. *Gendered interests in the European Union. The European Women's Lobby and the organisation and representation of women's interests*. Örebro: Örebro University Press.

Thaa, W. 2008. Kritik und Neubewertung politischer Repräsentation: vom Hindernis zur Möglichkeitsbedingung politischer Freiheit. *Politische Vierteljahresschrift* 49, no. 4: 618–40.

Urbinati, N. 2006. *Representative democracy: principles and genealogy*. Chicago: University of Chicago Press.

Young, I.M. 1997. Deferring group representation. In *Ethnicity and group rights*, eds. I. Shapiro and W. Kymlicka, 349–76. New York: New York University Press.

In the Face of Crisis: Input Legitimacy, Output Legitimacy and the Political Messianism of European Integration

J. H. H. WEILER

NYU School of Law, New York, NY, USA

ABSTRACT   European legitimacy discourse typically employs two principal concepts: input (process) legitimacy and output (result) legitimacy. But a third concept, political messianism, is central to the legitimation of Europe, though less commonly explored. In the current European circumstance, however, each of these three concepts is inoperable. Any solution to the crisis of Europe will have to draw upon the deep legitimacy resources of the national communities, the member states.

Prologue

Beauty is famously, or infamously, in the eyes of the beholder.

For some, Maastricht was finally the ushering forth of 'real' European integration. No longer merely the marketplace, but veritable economic and monetary union, the upgrading of the European Parliament (finally democracy!), human rights and the environment in the Treaty *expressis verbis* with the expectation of more than mere words to come, and European citizenship, no less. Even the old-fashioned 'Community' was upgraded to First with a term redolent with gravitas: 'Union'.

For others, Maastricht was a shill game, smoke and mirrors: a half-baked monetary union ('What will they do when the first asymmetric shock hits?' Marty Feldstein of Harvard warned at the time), an ever yawning democracy 'deficit' with the power shift to the EU not matched by veritable accountability and citizen impact, a vacuous concept of citizenship, with no duties and empty rights and an abandonment of the original and humane concept of Community for the hackneyed Union, a term recently vacated by the Soviets.

Citizens, let us remind ourselves, 'were not amused'. Maastricht was greeted by the typical indifference with which the elite-driven European construct was habitually met. Those who took an interest — the Danes and the French in whose countries commendably citizens were consulted — rejected it in one case, and barely passed it, with a wafer-thin majority in the other.[1] That, indeed, has always been the Achilles Heel of the European construct — the question whether the undoubtedly noble project enjoys popular legitimacy. The structure of this essay is simple enough. I will first outline the manner in which I plan to use the concept of legitimacy. Typically European legitimacy discourse employs two principal concepts: input (process) legitimacy and output (result) legitimacy. I will add a third, less explored, but in my view central legitimating feature of Europe — political messianism. I will explore, in turn, each of these forms of legitimacy in their European context, and in relation to each show why, in my view, they are exhausted, inoperable in the current circumstance. My conclusion is also simple enough. The crisis of Europe will require European solutions. But if these are to be successfully adopted, they will require an employment of legitimacy resources to be found with national communities, the member states, in some ways a very European outcome.

On Two Genres and Three Types of Legitimacy

Legitimacy is a notoriously elusive term, over-used and under-specified. So the first thing I will do is to explain the sense in which I plan to use 'Legitimacy' in this essay. Do not, please, argue with me and say: 'That is not legitimacy! It means something else!'[2] It is how I plan to use it, and I hope to convince you that it is a useful way for articulating something terribly important about the present crisis and the current state of European integration.

There are two basic genres — languages, vocabularies — of legitimacy: normative and social. The vocabulary of normative legitimacy is moral, ethical and it is informed by political theory. It is an objective measure even though there will be obvious ideological differences as to what should be considered as legitimate governance. Social legitimacy is empirical, assessed or measured with the tools of social science. It is a subjective measure, reflecting social attitudes. It is not a measurement of popularity, but of a deeper form of acceptance of the political regime.

The two types of legitimacy often inform each other and may even conflate, but not necessarily so. A series of examples will clarify. By our liberal pluralist normative yardstick, German national socialism of the 1930s and 1940s was a horrible aberration, the negation of legitimate governance. Yet, socially and empirically, for most Germans almost until the defeat in 1945 it was not only popular but considered deeply legitimate leadership.

By contrast, Weimer democracy would pass our normative test of legitimate government, yet for a very large number of Germans it was not merely unpopular, but considered illegitimate leadership, a betrayal of Germany.

However, in less extreme situations we do expect some measure of conflation between the two. One hopes that if a regime is normatively legitimate, because, say, it practices constitutional democracy, it will enjoy widespread social legitimacy, and that the opposite will be true too: in a regime which fails the normative tests, one hopes that the social legitimacy will be low too. One can imagine complicated permutations of these parameters.

Legitimacy, normative or social, should not be conflated with legality. Forbidding blacks to sit in the front of the bus was perfectly legal, but would fail many a test of normative legitimacy, and with time lost its social legitimacy as well. There are illegal measures which are considered, normatively and/or socially as legitimate, and legal measures which are considered illegitimate.

For the purpose of this essay, it is worth exploring briefly the relationship between popularity and legitimacy. If I am a life long adherent of the Labour party in the UK, I might be appalled by the election of the Tories and abhor every single measure adopted by the government of the Tory prime minister. But it would never enter my mind to consider such measures as 'illegitimate'. In fact, and this is critical for one of the principal propositions of this essay, the deeper the legitimacy resources of a regime, the better able it is to adopt *unpopular* measures critical in the time of crisis where exactly such measures may be necessary.

There is something peculiar about the current crisis. Even if there are big differences between the austerity and immediate growth camps, everyone knows that a solution has to be European, within a European framework. And yet, it has become self evident, that crafting a European solution has become so difficult, that the institutions and the Union decision-making process do not seem to be engaging satisfactorily and effectively with the crisis, even when employing the intergovernmental methodology, and that it is governments, national leaders, of a small club, who seem to be calling the shots. The problem is European, but Europe as such is finding it difficult to craft the remedies.

I would like to argue that in the present circumstance, the legitimacy resources of the European Union — referring here mostly to social legitimacy — are depleted, and that is why the Union has had to turn to the member states for salvation. Solutions will still have to be Europe-wide, but they will not be ideated, designed and crafted using the classical 'community method' but will be negotiated among and validated by the member states. They will require the legitimacy resources of the member states — in many countries close to depletion too — in order to gain valid acceptance in Europe.

Alan Milward famously and convincingly wrote on the European rescue of the nation state (Milward 2000). The pendulum has swung and in the present crisis it will be the nation state rescue of the European Union.

Moving from the genres of legitimacy to a typology I would like to suggest the three most important types or forms of legitimacy which have been central to the discussion of European integration. The most ubiquitous have been various variations on the theme of input and output legitimacy (for useful studies, see Boedeltje and Cornips 2004; Lindgren and Persson 2010).

- Process (or input) legitimacy — which in the current circumstance can, with some simplification, be synonymized with democracy. It is easier put in the negative: to the extent that the European mode of governance departs from the habits and practices of democracy as understood in the member states, its legitimacy, in this case both normative and social, will be compromised.
- Result (or output) legitimacy — which, again simplifying somewhat, would be all modern versions of bread and circus. As long as the Union delivers 'the goods' — prosperity, stability, security — it will enjoy a legitimacy that derives from a subtle combination of success *per se*, of success in realizing its objectives and of contentment with those results. There is no better way to legitimate a war than to win it. This variant of legitimacy is part of the very ethos of the Commission.
- Telos legitimacy or political messianism — whereby legitimacy is gained neither by process nor output but by promise, the promise of an attractive promised land. I will elaborate on this below.

I will now try and illustrate the collapse of all three forms of legitimacy in the current European circumstance.

Europe, the Current Circumstances

This is an interesting time to be reflecting on the European construct. Europe is at a nadir which one cannot remember for many decades and which, various brave or pompous or self-serving statements notwithstanding,[3] the Treaty of Lisbon has not been able to redress. The surface manifestations of crisis are with us every day on the front pages: the Euro crisis (Dinan 2011) being the most current. Beneath this surface, at the structural level, lurk more profound and long-term signs of enduring challenge and even dysfunction and malaise. Let us refract them through the lens of legitimacy.[4]

First, as regards process legitimacy, there is the persistent, chronic, troubling Democracy Deficit, which cannot be talked away. The manifestations of the so-called democracy deficit are persistent and no endless repetition of the powers of the European Parliament will remove them. In essence it is the inability of the Union to develop structures and processes which adequately replicate or, 'translate' (Walker 2003, 29), at the Union level even the imperfect habits of governmental control, parliamentary accountability and administrative responsibility that are practiced with different modalities in the various member states. Make no mistake: it is perfectly understood that the Union is not a state. But it is in the business of governance and has taken over extensive areas previously in the hands of the member states. In some critical areas, such as the interface of the Union with the international trading system, the competences of the Union are exclusive. In others they are dominant. Democracy is not about states. Democracy is about the exercise of public power — and the Union exercises a huge amount of public power. We live by the credo that any exercise of public power has to be legitimated democratically and it is exactly here that process legitimacy fails.

In essence, the two primordial features of any functioning democracy are missing — the grand principles of accountability and representation (Przeworski, Stokes, and Manin 1999; Schmitter and Karl 1991, 67; see also Mair 2005).

As regards accountability (Harlow 2003), even the basic condition of representative democracy that at election time the citizens can 'throw the scoundrels out' (Weiler 1999, 329; see also Shapiro 1996, 96) — that is replace the government — does not operate in Europe (Dehousse 1995, 123). The form of European governance (Allott 2002, 60), governance without government, is, and will remain for considerable time, perhaps forever, such that there is no 'government' to throw out. Dismissing the Commission by Parliament (or approving the appointment of the Commission President) is not quite the same, not even remotely so.

Startlingly, but not surprisingly, political accountability of Europe is remarkably weak. There have been some spectacular political failures of European governance. The embarrassing Copenhagen climate fiasco,[5] the weak (at best) realization of the much touted Lisbon Agenda (aka Lisbon Strategy or Lisbon Process) (see Begg 2008, 427; Begg 2004), the very story of the defunct 'Constitution' (Ward 2007, 461; Editorial Comments 2007, 561) to mention but three. It is hard to point in these instances to any measure of political accountability, of someone paying a political price as would be the case in national politics. In fact it is difficult to point to a single instance of accountability for political failure as distinct from personal accountability for misconduct in the annals of European integration. This is not, decidedly not, a story of corruption or malfeasance (on this aspect, see Mehde 2003, 423). My argument is that this failure is rooted in the very structure of European governance. It is not designed for political accountability. In similar vein, it is impossible to link in any meaningful way the results of elections to the European Parliament to the performance of the political groups within the preceding parliamentary session, in the way that is part of the mainstay of political accountability within the member states (Priestley 2010; Roa Bastos 2009; Audeoud 1999). Structurally, dissatisfaction with 'Europe' when it exists has no channel to affect, at the European level, the agents of European governance.

Likewise, at the most primitive level of democracy, there is simply no moment in the civic calendar of Europe where the citizen can influence directly the outcome of any policy choice facing the Community and Union in the way that citizens can when choosing between parties which offer sharply distinct programs at the national level. The political colour of the European Parliament only very weakly gets translated into the legislative and administrative output of the Union (Bogdanor 2007, 7–8; Follesdal and Hix 2006, 545).

The political deficit, to use the felicitous phrase of Renaud Dehousse (Dehousse 1995, 124; see also Ferry and Thibaud 1992), is at the core of the democracy deficit. The Commission, by its self-understanding linked to its very ontology, cannot be 'partisan' in a right–left sense, neither can the Council, by virtue of the haphazard political nature of its composition. Democracy normally must have some meaningful mechanism for expression of voter preference predicated on choice among options, typically informed by stronger or weaker ideological orientation (Follesdal and Hix 2006, 545). That is an indispensable component of politics. Democracy without politics is an oxymoron (Manent 2006, 59). And yet that is not only Europe, but it is a feature of Europe — the 'non-partisan' nature of the Commission — which is celebrated. The stock phrase found in endless student text books and the like, that the supranational Commission vindicates the European interest, whereas the intergovernmental Council is a clearing house for member state interest, is, at best, naïve. Does the 'European interest' not necessarily involve political and ideological choices? At times explicit, but always implicit?

Thus the two most primordial norms of democracy, the principle of accountability and the principle of representation are compromised in the very structure and process of the Union.

The second manifestation of the current European circumstance is evident in a continued slide in the legitimacy and mobilizing force of the European construct and its institutions. I pass over some of the uglier manifestations of European 'solidarity' both at governmental and popular level as regards the Euro-crisis or the near abandonment of Italy to deal with the influx of migrants from North Africa as if this was an Italian problem and not a problem for Europe as a whole. I look instead at two deeper and longer-term trends. The first is the extraordinary decline in voter participation in elections for the European Parliament. In Europe as a whole the rate of participation is below 45 per cent, with several countries, notably in the East, with a rate below 30 per cent. The correct comparison is, of course, with political elections to national parliaments where the numbers are considerably higher (Menon and Peet 2010; Magnette 2001). What is striking about these figures is that the decline coincides with a continuous shift in powers to the European Parliament, which today is a veritable co-legislator with the Council. The more powers the European Parliament, supposedly the *vox populi*, has gained, the greater popular indifference to it seems to have developed (Buzek 2011, 15; see also Weiler 1999, 266). It is sobering but not surprising to note the absence of the European Parliament as a major player in the current crisis. But the institutional crisis runs deeper. The Commission has excelled as a creative secretariat and implementor and monitor, but neither as the sources of ideas nor veritable political leadership. It has been faithful and effective as His Master's Voice. But most striking has been the disappearing act of the Council. No longer the proud leader of Europe according to the Giscardian design, but an elaborate rubber stamp to the Union's two Presidents — Merkel and Sarkozy (or now, Hollande). A double failure of institutional legitimacy, of Parliament and Council. Of supranationalism and intergovernmentalism. The resort to an extra-Union Treaty, as a centerpiece of the reconstruction, is but the poignant legal manifestation of this political reality.

The critique of the democracy deficit of the Union has itself been subjected to two types of critique itself. The first has simply contested the reality of the democracy deficit by essentially claiming that wrong criteria have been applied to the Union (Weiler 1995, especially page 225 onwards). The lines of debate are well known (Craig 1999, 25). For what it is worth, I have staked my position above. But I am more interested in the second type of critique which implicitly is an invocation of result or output legitimacy. Since the Union, not being a state, cannot replicate or adequately translate the habits and practices of statal democratic governance, its legitimacy may be found elsewhere (MacCormick 1997).

In analyzing the legitimacy (and mobilizing force) of the European Union, in particular against the background of its persistent democracy deficit, political and social science has indeed long used the distinction I have made between process legitimacy and outcome legitimacy (aka input/output, process/result, etc) (see, for example, Beitz 1989, chapters 2 and 4; Dahl 1991, 163; see also more specifically, Majone 1996; Scharpf 1999, especially page 7 onwards). The legitimacy of the Union more generally and the Commission more specifically, even if suffering from deficiencies in the state democratic sense, are said to rest on the results achieved — in the economic, social and, ultimately, political realms (Featherstone 1994, 150). The idea hearkens back to the most classic functionalist and neo-functionalist theories (Featherstone 1996, 155; Pentland 1981, 550 onwards; Rosamond 2000, 20 onwards; Mitrany 1966; Haas 1958, Haas 1976; Lindberg 1963; Lindberg and Scheingold 1971).

I do not want to take issue with the implied normativity of this position — a latter day *Panem et circenses* approach to democracy, which at some level at least could be considered quite troubling. It is with its empirical reality that I want to take some issue. I do not think that outcome legitimacy explains all or perhaps even most of the mobilizing force of the European construct. But whatever role it played it is dependent on the *Panem*. Rightly or wrongly, the economic woes of Europe, which are manifest in the Euro crisis are attributed to the European construct. So when there suddenly is no Bread, and certainly no cake, we are treated to a different kind of circus whereby the citizens' growing indifference is turning to hostility and the ability of Europe to act as a political mobilizing force seems not only spent, but even reversed. The worst way to legitimate a war is to lose it, and Europe is suddenly seen not as an icon of success but as an emblem of austerity, thus in terms of its promise of prosperity, failure. If success breeds legitimacy, failure, even if wrongly allocated, leads to the opposite.

Thus, not surprisingly there is a seemingly contagious spread of 'Anti-Europeanism' in national politics (Leconte 2010). What was once in the province of fringe parties on the far right and left has inched its way to more central political forces. The 'Question of Europe' as a central issue in political discourse was for long regarded as an 'English disease'. There is a growing contagion in member states in North and South, East and West, where political capital is to be made among non-fringe parties by anti-European advocacy (Harmsen and Spiering 2005, 13; Szczerbiak and Taggart 2008). The spill-over effect of this phenomenon is the shift of mainstream parties in this direction as a way of countering the gains at their flanks. If we are surprised by this it is only because we seem to have air-brushed out of our historical consciousness the rejection of the so-called European Constitution, an understandable amnesia since it represented a defeat of the collective political class in Europe by the *vox populi* (Fligstein 2008), albeit not speaking through, but instead giving a slap in the face to, the European institutions (for former examples, see Weiler, Haltern, and Mayer 1995, 4).

Europe as Political 'Messianism'

At some level the same could have been said 10 and even 20 years ago (see, for example, European Commission 2001; Bogdanor and Woodcock 1991, 492; Grimm 1995, 291 onwards; Hill 1990, 35). The democracy deficit is not new — it is enduring. And how did Europe legitimate itself before it scored its great successes of the first decades?

As I hinted above, at the conceptual level there is a third type of legitimation which, in my view, played for a long time a much larger role than is currently acknowledged. In fact, in my view, it has been decisive to the legitimacy of Europe and to the positive response of both the political class and citizens at large. I will also argue that it is a key to a crucial element in the Union's political culture. It is a legitimacy rooted in the '*politically messianic*'.

In political 'messianism', the justification for action and its mobilizing force derive not from process, as in classical democracy, or from result and success, but from the ideal pursued, the destiny to be achieved, the 'Promised Land' waiting at the end of the road. Indeed, in messianic visions the end always trumps the means.

Mark Mazower, in his brilliant and original history and historiography of twentieth-century Europe (Mazower 1998), insightfully shows how the Europe of monarchs and emperors which entered World War I was often rooted in a politically messianic narrative in various states (in Germany, and Italy, and Russia and even Britain and France). It then oscillated after the War towards new democratic orders, that is to process legitimacy, which then oscillated back into new forms of political messianism in fascism and communism. At the tale is usually told, after World War II Europe of the West, was said to oscillate back to democracy and process legitimacy. It is here that I want to point to an interesting quirk, not often noted.

On the one hand, the Western states, which were later to become the member states of the European Union, became resolutely democratic, their patriotism rooted in their new constitutional values, narratives of glory abandoned and even ridiculed, and messianic notions of the state losing all appeal. Famously, former empires, once defended with repression and blood, were now abandoned with zeal (Lacroix 2002, 949 onwards).

And yet, their common venture, European integration, was in my reading a politically messianic venture *par excellence*, the messianic becoming a central feature of its original and enduring political culture. The mobilizing force and principle-legitimating feature was the vision offered, the dream dreamt, the promise of a better future. It is this feature which explains not only the persistent mobilizing force (especially among elites and youth) but also key structural and institutional choices made. It will also give more depth to explanations of the current circumstance of Europe.

Since, unlike the democracy deficit which has been discussed and debated *ad nauseam* and *ad tedium*, political messianism is a feature of European legitimacy which has received less attention, I think it may be justified if I pay to it some more attention.

The Schuman Declaration as a Manifesto of Political Messianism

The Schuman declaration is somewhat akin to Europe's 'Declaration of Independence' in its combination of vision and blueprint. Notably, much of its text found its way into the preamble of the Treaty of Paris, the substance of which was informed by its ideas. It is interesting to re-read the declaration through the conceptual prism of political messianism. The hallmarks are easily detected as we would expect in a constitutive, magisterial document. It is manifest in what is in the Declaration and, no less importantly, in what is not therein. *Nota bene*: European integration is nothing like its European messianic predecessors — that of monarchies and empire and later fascism and communism. It is liberal and noble, but politically messianic it is nonetheless.

The messianic feature is notable in both its rhetoric and substance. Note, first, the language used — ceremonial and 'sermonial' with plenty of pathos (and bathos).

> World peace cannot be safeguarded without the making of creative efforts proportionate to the dangers which threaten it...

> The contribution which an organised and living Europe can bring to civilization is indispensable...

> ... a first step in the federation of Europe [which] will change the destinies of those regions which have long been devoted to the manufacture of munitions of war...

> Any war between France and Germany becomes not merely unthinkable, but materially impossible.

> This production will be offered to the world as a whole without distinction or exception...

It may be the leaven from which may grow a wider and deeper community between countries long opposed to one another by sanguinary divisions.

It is grand, inspiring, Churchillian one might even say with a tad of irony. Some old habits, such as the White Man's Burden and the missionary tradition, die hard: 'With increased resources Europe will be able to pursue the achievement of one of its essential tasks, namely, the development of the African continent'.

But it is not just the rhetoric. The substance itself is messianic: a compelling vision which has animated now at least three generations of European idealists where the 'ever closer union among the people of Europe', with peace and prosperity an icing on the cake, constitutes the beckoning promised land (Piodi 1999, 8).

It is worth exploring further the mobilizing force of this new plan for Europe. At the level of the surface language is its straight-forward pragmatic objective of consolidating peace and reconstructing European prosperity. But there is much more within the deep structure of the plan.

Peace, at all times an attractive desideratum, would have had its appeal in purely utilitarian terms. But it is readily apparent that in the historical context in which the Schuman Plan was put forward the notion of peace as an ideal probes a far deeper stratum than simple swords into ploughshares, sitting under ones' vines and fig trees, lambs and wolves — the classic Biblical metaphor for peace. The dilemma posed was an acute example of the alleged tension between Grace and Justice which has taxed philosophers and theologians through the ages — from William of Ockham (pre-modern), Friedrich Nietzsche (modernist) and the repugnant but profound Martin Heidegger (post-modern).

These were, after all, the early 1950s with the horrors of war still fresh in the mind and, in particular, the memory of the unspeakable savagery of German occupation. It would take many years for the hatred in countries such as The Netherlands, Denmark or France to subside fully. The idea, then, in 1950, of a Community of Equals as providing the structural underpinning for long-term peace among yesterday's enemies, represented more than the wise counsel of experienced statesmen.

It was, first, a 'peace of the brave' requiring courage and audacity. At a deeper level it managed to tap into the two civilizational pillars of Europe: the Enlightenment and the heritage of the French Revolution and the European Christian tradition (see for example, Habermas and Derrida 1987; Weiler 2007; Ferry 2010; Schuman 1963, 55 onwards).

Liberty was already achieved with the defeat of Nazi Germany — and Germans (like their Austrian bretheren-in-crime) embraced with zeal the notion that they, too, were liberated from National Socialism. But here was a project, encapsulated in the Schuman Declaration, which added to the transnational level both equality and fraternity. The post-WWI Versailles version of peace was to take yesterday's enemy, diminish him and keep his neck firmly under one's heel, with, of course, disastrous results. Here, instead was a vision in which yesteryear's enemy was regarded as an equal — Germany was to be treated as a full and equal partner in the venture — and engaged in a fraternal inter-dependent lock so that, indeed, the thought of resolving future disputes would become unthinkable (Munoz 2008, 44). This was, in fact, the project of the enlightenment taken to the international level as Kant himself had dreamt. To embrace the Schuman Plan was to tap into one of the most powerful idealistic seams in Europe's civilizational mines.

The Schuman Plan was also a call for forgiveness, a challenge to overcome an understandable hatred. In that particular historical context the Schumanian notion of peace resonated with, was evocative of, the distinct teaching, imagery and values of the Christian call for forgiving one's enemies, for love, for grace — values so recently consecrated in their wholesale breach. The Schuman Plan was in this sense, evocative of both confession and expiation, and redolent with the Christian belief in the power of repentance and renewal and the ultimate goodness of humankind. This evocation is not particularly astonishing given the personal backgrounds of the Founding Fathers — Adenauer, De Gaspari, Schumann, Monnet himself — all seriously committed Catholics.[6]

The mobilizing force, especially among elites, the political classes who felt more directly responsible for the calamities from which Europe was just exiting, is not surprising given the remarkable subterranean appeal to the two most potent visions of the idyllic 'Kingdom'— the humanist and religious combined in one project.[7] This also explains how, for the most part, both Right and Left, conservative and progressive, could embrace the project.

It is the messianic model which explains (in part) why for so long the Union could operate without a veritable commitment to the principles it demanded of its aspiring members — democracy and human rights. Aspirant states had to become members of the European Convention of Human Rights, but the Union itself did not. They had to prove their democratic credentials, but the Union itself did not — two anomalies which hardly raised eyebrows.

Note however, that its messianic features are reflected not only in the flowery rhetoric. In its original and unedited version the declaration is quite elaborate in operational detail. But you will find neither the word democracy, nor human rights, a thunderous silence. It's a 'Lets-Just-Do-It' type of programme animated by great idealism (and a goodly measure of good old state interest, as a whole generation of historians such as Alan Milward and Charles Maier among others have demonstrated; see Milward 2000; Maier and Bischof 1991).

The European double helix has from its inception been Commission and Council: an international (supposedly) a-political transnational administration/executive (the Commission) collaborating not, as we habitually say, with the member states but with the governments, the executive branch of the member states (Council), which for years and years had a forum that escaped in day-to-day matters the scrutiny of any parliament, European or national. Democracy is simply not part of the original vision of European integration.[8]

THE MAASTRICHT TREATY: SECOND THOUGHTS AFTER 20 YEARS

This observation is hardly shocking or even radical. Is it altogether fanciful to tell the narrative of Europe as one in which 'doers and believers' (notably the most original of its institutions, the Commission, coupled with an empowered executive branch of the member states in the guise of the Council and COREPER), an elitist (if well-paid) vanguard, were the self-appointed leaders from whom grudgingly, over decades, power had to be arrested by the European Parliament? And even the European Parliament has been a strange *vox populi*. For hasn't it been, for most of its life, a champion of European integration, so that to the extent that, inevitably, when the Union and European integration inspired fear and caution among citizens, (only natural in such a radical transformation of European politics) the European Parliament did not feel the place citizens would go to express those fears and concerns?

The politically messianic was offered not only for the sake of conceptual clarification but also as an explanation of the formidable past success of European integration in mobilizing support. They produced a culture of praxis, achievement, ever-expanding agendas. Given the noble dimensions of European integration one ought to see and acknowledge their virtuous facets.

But that is only part of the story. They also explain some of the story of decline in European legitimacy and mobilizing pull which is so obvious in the current circumstance. *Part of the very phenomenology of political messianism is that it always collapses as a mechanism for mobilization and legitimation*. It obviously collapses when the messianic project fails. When the revolution does not come. But interestingly, and more germane to the narrative of European Integration, even when successful it sows its seeds of collapse. At one level the collapse is inevitable, part of the very phenomenology of a messianic project. Reality is always more complicated, challenging, banal and ultimately less satisfying than the dream which preceded it. The result is not only absence of mobilization and legitimation, but actual rancor.

The original Promised Land, Canaan, was a very different proposition, challenging and hostile, to the dream which preceded it. Independent India, or Kenya, or even the US were very different to the dreams which preceded them and their like. Individually this is the story of many a courtship and love affair. The honeymoon is always better than the reality of marriage. Just as paradise becomes such, only when lost, the land itself always falls short of the promise. It is part of the ontology of the messianic.

The emblematic manifestation of this in the context of European integration is the difference between the 868 inspiring words of the Schuman dream and the 154,183 very real words of the (defunct) European Constitution now reinvented in the Treaty of Lisbon.

But in the case of Europe, there are additional contingent factors in the collapse of the messianic narrative as a mobilizing and legitimizing factor. At one level Europe is a victim of its own success. The passage of time coupled with the consolidation of peace, the internalization of the alternative inter-state discourse which Europe presented, has been so successful that to new generations of Europeans, both the pragmatic and idealist appeal of the Schuman vision seem simply incomprehensible. The reality against which their appeal was so powerful — the age-hold enmity between France and Germany and all that — is no longer a living memory, a live civilizational wire, a wonderful state of affairs in some considerable measure also owed to the European constructs.

At another level, much has changed in societal mores. Europe in large part has become a post-Christian society, and the profound commitment to the individual and his or her rights, relentlessly (and in many respects laudably) placing the individual in the center of political attention, has contributed to the emergence of the self-centered individual. Social mobilization in Europe is at its strongest when the direct interests of the individual are at stake and at their weakest when it requires tending to the needs of the other, as the recent Euro crisis, immigrant crisis and other such instances will readily attest. So part of the explanation of the loss of mobilizing force of the Schuman Vision is in the fact that what it offers either seems irrelevant or does not appeal to the very different idealistic sensibility of contemporary European society.

The result is that if political messianism is not rapidly anchored in the legitimation that comes from popular ownership, it rapidly becomes alienating and, like the Golem, turns on its creators.

Democracy was not part of the original DNA of European Integration. It still feels like a foreign implant. With the collapse of its original political messianism, the alienation we are now witnessing is only to be expected. And thus, when failure hits as in the Euro crisis, when the *Panem* is gone, all sources of legitimacy suddenly, simultaneously collapse.

This collapse comes at an inopportune moment, at the very moment when Europe of the Union would need all its legitimacy resources. The problems are European and the solution has to be at the European level. But for that solution to be perceived as legitimate, for the next phase in European integration not to be driven by resentful fear, the architects will not be able to rely, sadly, on the decisional process of the Union itself. They will have to dip heavily into the political structure and decisional process of the member states. It will be national parliaments, national judiciaries, national media and, yes, national governments who will have to lend their legitimacy to a solution which inevitably will involve yet a higher degree of integration. It will be an entirely European phenomenon that, at what will have to be a decisive moment in the evolution of the European construct, the importance, even primacy of the national communities as the deepest source of legitimacy of the integration project will be affirmed yet again.

Notes

1. The Brussels Mandarins like to wave (though not recently) Eurobarometer results as evidence of widespread support for Europe. But careful examination of the data seems to suggest that Europeans typically support that which Europe promises to do, not that which it actually does. Cf. Menon and Schain (2006, 9–10).
2. I found the following most useful, also as a demonstration of the breadth of the concept: Johnson, Dowd, and Ridgeway (2006), Levine (2005), Sadurski (2011), and Peter (2010).

3. See for example, 'Plenary session of the European Parliament, Strasbour, 20 February 2008: Treaty of Lisbon', which includes various statements from the members of the European Parliament, Janez Lenarcic, President of the Council and Margot Wallström, Vice-President of the European Commission, as well as the European Parliament resolution of 20 February 2008 on the Treaty of Lisbon (2007/2286(INI); 'Brussels European Council 14 December 2007', Brussels, 14 February 2008, 16616/1/07 REV 1, including the EU declaration on globalisation; European Commission, 'Your Guide to the Lisbon Treaty', http://ec.europa.eu/publications/booklets/others/84/en.pdf , President Buzek, News of the European Parliament, 1 December 2009, http://www.europarl.europa.eu/president/ressource/static/newsletter/newsletter-3/newsletter.html?ts=1277465318672). See also Barroso (2007).
4. The literature is rich. Here is a partial sample of some truly helpful studies: Thomassen (2009), Thomassen and Schmitt (1999), Beetham and Lord (1998), Haller (2009), Moravcsik (2002) and Guastaferro and Moschella (2012).
5. See European Parliament resolution of 10 February 2010 on the outcome of the Copenhagen Conference on Climate Change (COP 15), P78TA(2010)0019, Wednesday, 10 February 2010, especially points 5–6.
6. See Fimister (2008, 25): 'Schuman was an ardent Roman Catholic, and his views about the desirability of political unity in Western Europe owed much to the idea that it was above all the continent's Christian heritage which gave consistence and meaning to the identity of European civilization. And the Europe he knew and loved best was the Carolingian Europe that accorded with his religious faith and his experience of French and German cultures'. Also M. Sutton (2007, 34): 'It is with deep faith in our cause that I speak to you, and I am confident that through the will of our free peoples, with your support and with God's help, a new era for Europe will soon begin'. Extracts from a speech by Alcide De Gasperi at the Consultative Assembly of the Council of Europe in Strasbourg on 16 September 1952 — Volume 3, 1952 of the *Official Reports of Debates of the Consultative Assembly of the Council of Europe*.
7. One should add that the transnational reach of the Schuman Plan served, as one would expect, a powerful internal interest the discussion of which even today meets with resistance. The challenge of 'fraternity' and the need for forgiveness, love and grace was even more pressing internally than internationally. For each one of the original member states was seriously compromised internally. In post war Germany, to put it bluntly, neither state nor society could function if all those complicit in National Socialism were to be excluded. In the other five, though ostensibly and in a real sense victims of German aggression, important social forces became complicit and were morally compromised. This was obviously true of Fascist Italy and Vichy France. But even the little Luxembourg contributed one of the most criminally notorious units to the German army and Belgium distinguished itself as the country with the highest number of indigenous volunteers to the occupying German forces. The betrayal of Anne Frank and her family by their good Dutch neighbors was not an exception but emblematic of Dutch society and government who tidily handed over their entire Jewish citizenry for deportation and death. All these societies had a serious interest in 'moving on' and putting that compromised past behind them. If one were to forgive and embrace the external enemy, to turn one's back to the past and put one's faith in a better future, how much more so, how much easier, to do the same within one's own nation, society even family.
8. Featherstone (1994, 150), citing J. Delors, *Independent*, 26 July 1993.

References

Allott, P. 2002. European Governance and the re-branding of democracy. *European Law Review* 1, no. 27: 60–71.

Audeoud, O. 1999. Les partis politiques au niveau européen. Fédérations de partis nationaux. Les cahiers du GERSE, Nancy, 3 February.

Barroso, J.M.D. 2007. President of the European Commission, 'The European Union after the Lisbon Treaty', 4th Joint Parliamentary meeting on the Future of Europe, Brussels, 4 December 2007, SPEECH/07/793, 7 December 2007.

Beetham, D., and C. Lord. 1998. *Legitimacy and the European Union*. London and New York: Longman.

Begg, I. 2004. Facing the challenge. The Lisbon strategy for growth and employment. Report from the High Level Group chaired by Wim Kok, November.

Begg, I. 2008. Is there a convincing rationale for the Lisbon strategy. *Journal of Common Market Studies* 46, no. 2: 427–35.
Beitz, C.R. 1989. *Political equality: an essay in democratic theory*. Princeton: Princeton University Press.
Boedeltje, M., and J. Cornips. 2004. Input and output legitimacy in interactive governance. Technical report, October.
Bogdanor, V. 2007. Legitimacy, accountability and democracy in the European Union. *A Federal Trust Report*, 7–8. London: Federal Trust for Education and Research.
Bogdanor, V., and G. Woodcock. 1991. The European Community and sovereignty. *Parliamentary Affairs* 44, no. 4: 481–92.
Buzek, J. 2011. State of the Union: three cheers for the Lisbon Treaty and two warnings for political parties. *Journal of Common Market Studies* 49, no. S1: 7–18.
Craig, P. 1999. The nature of the community: integration, democracy, and legitimacy. In *The evolution of EU law*, ed. P. Craig and G. de Búrca, 1–50. Oxford: Oxford University Press.
Dahl, R.A. 1991. *Democracy and its critics*. New Haven: Yale University Press.
Dehousse, R. 1995. Constitutional reform in the EC. In *The crisis of representation in Europe*, ed. J. Hayward, 118–36. Abingdon: Frank Cass.
Dinan, D. 2011. Governance and Institutions: Implementing the Lisbon Treaty in the shadow of the Euro crisis. *Journal of Common Market Studies* 49, no. S1: 103–21.
Editorial Comments. 2007. What should replace the Constitutional Treaty? *Common Market Law Review* 44, no. 3: 561–66.
European Commission. 2001. European governance. A White Paper, COM (2001), 428 final, Brussels.
Featherstone, K. 1994. Jean Monnet and the democratic deficit in the European Union. *Journal of Common Market Studies* 32, no. 2: 149–70
Ferry, J.M. 2010. *La république crépusculaire. Comprendre le projet européen in sensu cosmopolitico*. Paris: Editions du Cerf.
Ferry, J.M., and P. Thibaud. 1992. *Discussion sur l'Europe*. Paris: Calmann-Lévy.
Fimister, A. 2008. Integral humanism and the re-unification of Europe. In S. Schirmann (ed.), *Robert Schuman et les pères de l'Europe: cultures politiques et années de formation*, ed. S. Schirmann, 25–37. Brussels: Peter Lang.
Finkielkraut, A. 1987. *La défaite de la pensée*. Paris: Gallimard.
Fligstein, N. 2008. *Euroclash. The EU, European identity, and the future of Europe*. Oxford: Oxford University Press.
Follesdal, A., and S. Hix. 2006. Why there is a democratic deficit in the EU: a response to Majone and Moravcsik. *Journal of Common Market Studies* 44, no. 3: 533–62.
Grimm, D. 1995. Does Europe need a constitution? *European Law Journal* 1, no. 3: 282–302.
Guastaferro, B., and M. Moschella. 2012. The EU, the IMF, and the representative turn: addressing the challenge of legitimacy. *Swiss Political Science Review* 18, no. 2: 199–219.
Haas, E.B. 1958. *The uniting of Europe*. Stanford: Stanford University Press.
Haas, E.B. 1976. Turbulent fields and the theory of regional integration. *International Organization* 30, no. 2: 173–212.
Habermas, J., and J. Derrida. 2005. February 15, or, what binds Europeans together: plea for a common foreign policy beginning in core Europe. In *Old Europe, new Europe, core Europe: transatlantic relations after the Iraq War*, ed. D. Levy, M. Pensky and J. Torpey, 3–13. London: Verso.
Haller, M. 2009. Is the European Union legitimate? To what extent? *International Social Science Journal* 60, no. 196: 223–34.
Harlow, C. 2003. *Accountability in the European Union*. Oxford: Oxford University Press.
Harmsen, R., and M. Spiering. 2005. *Euroscepticism: party politics, national identity and European integration*. Amsterdam: Rodopi.
Hill, C. 1990. European foreign policy: power bloc, civilian power — or flop? In *The evolution of an international actor: Western Europe's new assertiveness*, ed. R. Rummel. Boulder: Westview.
Hoerber, T. 2006. The nature of the beast: the past and future purpose of European integration. *L'Europe en formation* 1, February: 17–24.
Johnson, C., T.J. Dowd, and C.L. Ridgeway. 2006. Legitimacy as a social process. *Annual Review of Sociology* 32, no. 53–78.
Lacroix, J. 2002. For a European constitutional patriotism. *Political Studies* 50, no.
Leconte, C. 2010. *Understanding Euroscepticism*. London: Palgrave Macmillan.

Levine, B.B. 2006. Legitimacy. In International *Encyclopedia of Economic Sociology*, ed. J. Beckert and M. Zafirovski, 396–98. Abingdon: Routledge.

Lindberg, L.N. 1963. *The political dynamics of European economic integration.* Stanford: Stanford University Press.

Lindberg, L.N., and S.A. Scheingold. 1971. *Regional integration: theory and research.* Cambridge: Cambridge University Press.

Lindgren, K.O., and T. Persson, 2010. Input and output legitimacy: synergy or trade-off? Empirical evidence from an EU survey. *Journal of European Public Policy* 17, no. 4: 449–67.

MacCormick, N. 1997. Democracy, subsidiarity, and citizenship in the 'European Commonwealth'. *Law and Philosophy* 16, no. 4: 331–56.

Magnette, P. 2001. European governance and civic participation: can the European Union be politicized? *Jean Monnet Working Paper* 6/01.

Maier, C.S., and G. Bischof. 1991. *The Marshall Plan and Germany: West German development within the framework of the European Recovery Program.* Providence: Berg Press.

Mair, P. 2005. Popular democracy and the European Union polity. *European Governance Papers* (EUROGOV), no. C-05-03.

Majone, G. 1996. *Regulating Europe.* London: Routledge.

Manent, P. 2006. *La raison des nations, réflexions sur la démocratie en Europe.* Paris: Gallimard.

Mazower, M. 1998. *Dark continent: Europe's twentieth century.* London: Allen Lane.

Mehde, V. 2003. Responsibility and accountability in the European Commission. *Common Market Law Review* 40, no. 2: 423–42.

Menon, A., and J. Peet. 2010. Beyond the European Parliament: rethinking the EU's democratic legitimacy. *Center for European Reform Essays.* London: Center for European Reform.

Menon, A., and M.A. Schain. 2006. *Comparative federalism: the European Union and the United States in comparative perspective.* Oxford: Oxford University Press.

Milward, A. 2000. *The European rescue of the member state.* London: Routledge.

Mitrany, D. 1966. *A working peace system.* Chicago: Quadrangle Books.

Moravcsik, A. 2002. Reassessing legitimacy in the European Union. *JCMS: Journal of Common Market Studies* 40, no. 4: 603–24.

Munoz, A. 2008. L'engagement européen de Robert Schuman. In *Robert Schuman et les pères de l'Europe: cultures politiques et années de formation*, ed. S. Schirmann, 39–55. Brussels: Peter Lang.

Pentland, C. 1981. Political theories of European integration: between science and ideology. In *The European communities in action*, ed. D. Lasok and P. Soldatos, 545–69. Brussels: Bruylant.

Peter, F. 2010. Political legitimacy. In The Stanford Encyclopedia of Philosophy (Summer 2010 Edition), ed. E.N. Zalta, http://plato.stanford.edu/archives/sum2010/entries/legitimacy/ (last accessed 10 October 2012).

Piodi, F. 2010. From the Schuman Declaration to the birth of the ECSC: the role of Jean Monnet. European Parliament, Directorate-General for the Presidency, Archive and Documentation Centre, *CARDOC Journals*, no. 6, May.

Priestley, J. 2010. European political parties: the missing link. *Notre Europe*, Policy Paper 41.

Przeworski, A., S.C. Stokes, and B. Manin. 1999. *Democracy, accountability and representation.* Cambridge: Cambridge University Press.

Roa Bastos, F. 2009. Des partis politiques au niveau européen? Etat des lieux à la veille des élections européennes de juin 2009. *Etudes et Recherches* 71,

Rosamond, B. 2000. *Theories of European integration.* New York: Palgrave Macmillan.

Sadurski, W. 2011. Constitutional courts in transition processes: legitimacy and democratization. August 30, *Sydney Law School Research Paper No. 11/53*, http://ssrn.com/abstract=1919363 (last accessed 10 October 2012).

Scharpf, F.W. 1999. *Governing in Europe: effective and democratic?.* Oxford: Oxford University Press.

Schmitter, P.C., and Karl, T.L. 1991. What democracy is… and is not. *Journal of Democracy* 3, no. 2: 75–88.

Schuman, R. 1963. *Pour l'Europe.*

Shapiro, I. 1996. *Democracy's place.* Ithaca: Cornell University Press.

Sutton, M. 2007. *France and the construction of Europe, 1944–2007: the geopolitical imperative.* New York and Oxford: Berghan Books.

Szczerbiak, A., and P.A. Taggart. 2008. *Opposing Europe?* Vols. 1 and 2. Oxford: Oxford University Press.

Thomassen, J. 2009. *The legitimacy of the European Union after enlargement.* Oxford: Oxford University Press.

Thomassen, J., and H. Schmitt. 1999. Introduction: political legitimacy and representation in the European Union. In *Political representation and legitimacy in the European Union*, eds. H. Schmitt and J. Thomassen, 3–21. New York and Oxford: Oxford University Press.

Walker, N. 2003. Postnational constitutionalism and the problem of translation. In *European constitutionalism beyond the state*, ed. J.H.H. Weiler and M. Wind, 27–54. Cambridge: Cambridge University Press.

Ward, I. 2007. Bill and the fall of the Constitutional Treaty. *European Public Law* 13, no. 3: 461–88.

Weiler, J.H.H. 1995. Does Europe need a constitution? Demos, telos and the German Maastricht decision. *European Law Journal* 1, no. 3: 219–58.

Weiler, J.H.H. 1999. To be a European citizen: Eros and civilization. In *The Constitution of Europe, 'Do the new clothes have an emperor?' and other essays on European integration*, ed. J.H.H. Weiler, 324–57. Cambridge, MA: Harvard University Press.

Weiler, J.H.H. 2007. *L'Europe chrétienne: Une excursion.* Paris: Editions du Cerf.

Weiler, J.H.H., U.R. Haltern, and F.C. Mayer. 1995. European democracy and its critique. In *The crisis of representation in Europe*, ed. J. Hayward, 4–39. Abingdon: Frank Cass.

The Arc of Institutional Reform in Post-Maastricht Treaty Change

DESMOND DINAN

School of Public Policy, George Mason University, Arlington, VA, USA

ABSTRACT Though best known for its coverage of key policy areas, the Maastricht Treaty also introduced important institutional reforms. Building on the Single European Act, these pertained mainly to strengthening the legislative role of the European Parliament and extending the scope of qualified majority voting to more policy areas. Treaty-based institutional reform continued in the post-Maastricht period. Due to the twin challenges facing the EU in the aftermath of Maastricht — Central and Eastern European enlargement, and the gaping 'democratic deficit' — the focus of such reform shifted to the modalities of qualified majority voting and the size and composition of the Commission. The highly contentious nature of these issues thwarted effective institutional reform in the 1990s, overshadowed the work of the 2002–2003 Constitutional Convention, and dominated the intergovernmental conferences preceding the failed Constitutional Treaty and the subsequent Lisbon Treaty.

The Maastricht Treaty of 1992 stands out as a watershed in the history of European integration. It transformed the European Community (EC) in ways that seemed unimaginable less than a decade before. Building on the success of the single market program and Single European Act (SEA) in the late 1980s, the Maastricht Treaty launched the European Union (EU), built on an existing supranational pillar, covering socio-economic policy areas, and two new intergovernmental pillars, dealing with the Common Foreign and Security Policy (CFSP) and Justice and Home Affairs (JHA). Yet the treaty's most important policy innovation was not in the areas of foreign policy or internal security, but in an area firmly embedded in the supranational pillar: provisions for the preparation, realization, and operation of a single monetary policy and a single currency. It was the commitment to Economic and Monetary Union (EMU), an ambitious and potentially hazardous undertaking, which set the Maastricht Treaty apart from previous and future landmarks in the history of European integration.

Though best known for its policy innovations, the Maastricht Treaty contained a number of noteworthy institutional innovations as well. Some of these pertained to policy areas either introduced or amended by the treaty. For instance, management of monetary union required new institutional arrangements. Indeed, 'Institutionally, the key component of the Treaty on European Union [Maastricht Treaty] was the European Central Bank' (Mazzucelli 2012, 245). Yet most of the treaty's institutional reforms dealt with the general functioning of the EU in areas other than EMU, the CFSP, and JHA. Two stand out: the introduction of codecision for the Council and European Parliament (EP), and greater recourse to qualified majority voting (QMV) within the Council itself.

The rationale for these institutional reforms was hardly new. The principle of democratic legitimacy underlay efforts since the early days of the EC to strengthen the role of the Parliament in legislative decision-making, as well as in other activities normally associated with elected assemblies, such as providing oversight or scrutiny and authorizing the annual budget or multi-annual financial framework. Likewise, the principle of supranationality and the practicality of more efficient decision-making underlay successive efforts to extend the use of QMV, once again since the early days of the Community. Yet extending the power of the EP and the use of QMV had been highly contentious throughout EU history, given deeply divergent national positions on the desirability of such outcomes.

With the acceleration of European integration in the mid-1980s, the EP and sympathetic national governments pressed successfully for an extension of the EP's legislative authority. Their argument hinged on democratic accountability: as national governments transferred more sovereignty to the European level of governance, the EP, directly elected since 1979, merited an appropriate legislative role. The first breakthrough came in the SEA, when the EP acquired the right to a second reading of legislative proposals, through the cooperation procedure. The introduction of the codecision procedure in the Maastricht Treaty was a logical follow-on, given the additional transfer of sovereignty to the European level which the treaty brought about. Nevertheless the form of codecision introduced in the Maastricht Treaty privileged the Council over the Parliament; as far as legislative decision-making was concerned, the two institutions were equal in name only. The EP and its supporters would have to continue the struggle in the post-Maastricht period for a truly equitable co-decision procedure.

Extending the scope and use of QMV was even more contentious than increasing the EP's legislative power. Indeed, it was the anticipated extension of QMV in 1965 to additional policy areas that triggered the empty chair crisis, the most cataclysmic event in the history of the EC.

For ideological as well as practical reasons, the French government adamantly opposed greater use of QMV in Council decision-making. The Luxembourg Compromise of 1966, which ended the crisis, informally endorsed the national veto, thereby establishing unanimity as the overriding instrument of Council decision-making. As pressure grew in the early 1980s to intensify economic integration, the Luxembourg Compromise came to be seen as a major impediment to progress. Accordingly, calls to complete the single market led to calls as well for treaty change to affirm the use of QMV, effectively nullifying the Luxembourg Compromise. Despite lingering ideological concerns on the part of several national governments, a shared commitment to implementing the single market program resulted in provisions in the SEA pertaining to the greater use of QMV.

Reform of legislative decision-making — the introduction of the cooperation and codecision procedures, and the extension of QMV — represented continuity rather than change in the institutional evolution of European integration. Nevertheless, the SEA and Maastricht marked a decisive breakthrough. Building on the momentum generated by the single market program, the SEA and Maastricht greatly improved the power of the EP and the efficiency of the Council. Though best known for their provisions relating to key policy areas, the two sets of treaty changes also had a profound impact on the functioning of the EC and subsequently the EU. Institutionally as well as substantively, the Maastricht Treaty — as a successor to the SEA and in its own right — was indeed a watershed in the history of European integration.

Thanks to Maastricht, the nascent EU had a potentially powerful parliament and a Council in which legislative decisions could be taken by QMV in a relatively wide range of policy areas. The European Commission was a central actor whose fortunes had fluctuated since the launch of the EC, but whose role had not changed much as a result of treaty reform. The European Council had come into being in 1975 following a political agreement among national leaders, not because of a treaty change. Even though it had grown in importance over the years, not least because of its role in the SEA and Maastricht negotiations, the European Council was not yet recognized as a formal EU institution.

How would institutional arrangements in the EU evolve in the post-Maastricht period, specifically as a result of treaty change? Two key developments shaped the institutional agenda in the years following Maastricht: the growing challenge of democratic legitimacy and the prospect of enlargement on an unprecedented scale. First, the launch of the single market program and negotiation of the SEA had raised the EC's profile and generated considerable public interest. The initial reaction was generally favorable, though curiosity about the reanimated EC soon led to concern, initially vague and diffuse, about the EC's potential intrusiveness and dubious democratic credentials. Concerns about democratic legitimacy, already prevalent before the Maastricht Treaty, escalated soon afterwards, as the result of the June 1992 Danish referendum clearly showed. Second, the success of the single market program increased the EC's attractiveness to prospective member states. Even before the unexpected upheaval in Central and Eastern Europe in the late 1980s, the EC faced the possibility of enlargement in the not-too-distant future involving a number of members of the European Free Trade Association (EFTA). By the early 1990s, a plethora of newly-independent Central and Eastern European states was eager to join the queue for EU membership. The prospect of enlargement on a scale hitherto unimaginable stoked latent anxiety about the EU's institutional efficiency.

Faced with the twin pressures of unprecedented enlargement and questionable legitimacy, the EU would have to redouble earlier effort to strengthen its democratic credentials and improve its decision-making procedures. With the imminent and eventual accession of so many new, mostly small member states, the extension of QMV became linked to the characteristics of the system itself, as big member states attempted to redress what they saw as a growing decline in their relative voting weight. The big-small country divide emerged as well in a related institutional issue: the size and composition of the Commission in an EU likely to double in membership within 10 or 15 years. Accordingly, whereas the role of the EP and the scope of QMV had dominated the agenda of institutional reform before the Maastricht Treaty, questions relating to the modalities of QMV and the makeup of the Commission became paramount in the post-Maastricht period. Moreover, the increasing political salience of EU decision-making, due to the EU's expanded policy scope and substantial impact on citizens' everyday lives, enhanced the profile and importance of the European Council. The operation of the European Council therefore became another contentious item on the agenda of institutional reform.

This article traces the arc of institutional reform by means of formal treaty change in the post-Maastricht period, at a time of almost-continuous enlargement, a demanding policy environment, and widespread criticism of the EU's democratic legitimacy.[1] Institutional reform took place in two distinct, but overlapping, phases. First, in the 1990s, the EU attempted mostly to tackle the institutional implications of enlargement, culminating in the Nice summit of December 2000. Second, beginning even before the Nice summit took place, the discourse on institutional reform shifted from a narrow calculation of the implications of enlargement toward a broader discussion about the nature of EU governance, epitomized by the launch of the Constitutional Convention in 2003. Yet deeply-ingrained national obsessions with maximizing political influence overshadowed the constitutional discourse and brought the institutional agenda back to basics. As a result, institutional provisions in the Constitutional Treaty, and later the Lisbon Treaty, inevitably disappointed those who advocated far-reaching reform.

Institutional Reform in the Aftermath of Maastricht

The Maastricht Treaty stands out in the history of European integration not only for its inherent importance but also because of the public reaction that it generated, epitomized by the unexpected result of the Danish referendum in June 1992.[2] Although decided by a narrow margin — only 50.7 per cent against — Denmark's initial rejection of the Maastricht Treaty symbolized misgivings in many member states about the rapid acceleration of European integration. More ominously, the referendum energized Euroskeptics in Denmark and beyond. EU leaders grasped the seriousness of the situation for the fate of the Maastricht Treaty and the future of European integration. Their immediate concern was to assuage a sufficient number of Danish voters in order to ensure a positive result in the second referendum, scheduled for May 1993; hence the opt-outs from politically-contentious treaty obligations given to Denmark at the Edinburgh summit in December 1992. This maneuver had the desired effect: a reassuring 56.7 per cent voted in favor of ratification the second time around.

The lessons of the first Danish referendum result, and of the narrow approval of the Maastricht Treaty in the French referendum of September 1992 (only 51.05 per cent voted in favor), were not lost on EU leaders. Clearly, the Danish and French results signaled growing public unease with the nascent EU. Apart from nebulous concerns about the nature of supranational governance and possible loss of national identity, as well as disquiet about EMU and other policy areas, many Europeans expressed dissatisfaction with the institutional set-up in Brussels and Strasbourg. The Council seemed secretive and self-serving; the Commission remote and technocratic; and the Parliament expensive and irrelevant. More broadly, the EU failed to elicit affection or attachment. Far from seeing it as a novel political entity to which they could give their allegiance, citizens appeared to view the emergent EU with suspicion and distrust.

Alert to the extent of public alienation from the EU generally and its policies and institutions specifically, the European Council attempted to break the bureaucratic barrier surrounding Brussels, make the legislative process more transparent, and develop subsidiarity as the best way to ensure the EU's compatibility with the political aspirations of its citizens. Thus, the conclusions of the December 1992 European Council contained a lengthy section outlining the nature of subsidiarity, guidelines for its application, and concrete examples of existing legislation and pending proposals in light of the 'need for action' and 'proportionality' criteria (Commission 1992). The elucidation of subsidiarity went hand-in-hand with efforts to make the EU's decision-making procedures more transparent. These included the wider use of pre-legislative consultation documents (green papers), providing greater pubic access to the work of the Commission and the Council (including publishing the record of formal votes), and enacting clearer and simpler legislation. EU leaders' frantic efforts, undertaken in a series of summits in 1992 and 1993, to make the EU more comprehensible and acceptable to its citizens, testified to the profound impact of the Maastricht ratification crisis.

While these events unfolded, the new EU negotiated its first enlargement: the accession of Austria, Finland, and Sweden (Norway completed the negotiations but did not join) (Preston 1997, 87–112). What became known as the Eftan enlargement was soon overshadowed by the much more demanding and time-consuming EU expansion into Central and Eastern Europe. Nevertheless the Eftan enlargement was highly consequential institutionally for the EU. On the positive side of the ledger, Finland's and Sweden's accession strengthened traditions within the EU of participation, transparency and openness (hallmarks of Scandinavian democracy), a welcome development at a time of widespread public concern about accountability and legitimacy in EU governance. On the negative side, the Eftan enlargement sparked a bitter dispute not between the EU and the candidate countries but within the EU itself over the threshold for a blocking minority in the reweighted system of QMV.

Specifically, Britain and Spain objected to raising the number of votes required for a blocking minority from 23 to 26, in keeping with the arithmetic increase in the total number of Council votes due to the accession of three member states. Both countries were genuinely concerned about the diminution of power inherent in a having to form a blocking minority that required three additional votes, and the (Conservative) British government was sensitive to strong anti-EU sentiment within its own ranks. The impasse ended with the so-called Ioannina Compromise, a face-saving agreement whereby:

> ... if members of the Council representing a total of 23 to 25 votes indicate their intention to oppose the adoption... of a decision by a qualified majority, the Council will do all in its power to reach, within a reasonable time... a satisfactory solution that can be adopted by at least 65 votes [Britain's preferred qualified majority]. (Commission 1994)

The significance of the Ioannina Compromise was that it showed how disputes over institutional affairs, most notably over QMV, were likely to arise during future enlargement negotiations unless the EU tackled them beforehand in a comprehensive reform package. The EP had made that point loud and clear in a report adopted in January 1993, which urged national governments to undertake major institutional reform before proceeding with the Eftan enlargement (European Parliament 1992). The dispute over QMV strengthened the EP's conviction that large-scale institutional reform was pressing. Having the right — newly-conferred by the Maastricht Treaty — to grant its assent to enlargement gave the EP leverage to press its case. Although the EP overwhelmingly endorsed the Eftan enlargement in a series of votes in May 1994, individual parliamentarians emphasized during the preceding debate their dissatisfaction with the Ioannina Compromise and their determination to press for large-scale institutional reform.

Fortuitously for the EU, a pre-arranged IGC — mandated by the Maastricht Treaty to review the functioning of the CFSP — provided an ideal opportunity to negotiate institutional reform before beginning the next round of accession negotiations. Even before Austria, Finland, and Sweden joined the EU in 1995, the European Council had conceded the inevitability of further expansion to accommodate the Central and Eastern

European applicants, though without specifying a timetable. Accordingly, the institutional implications of enlargement came to dominate discussions about the impending IGC, scheduled to open in 1996.[3] A future EU of 20-something member states seemed unworkable without significant institutional adjustment.

The European Council decided in June 1994 to appoint a 'Reflection Group', consisting of national representatives, a Commissioner, and two Euro-parliamentarians, to prepare the ICG. In its final report, the Reflection Group identified the need for greater openness, accountability, simplification of decision-making procedures, and effectiveness in the EU's operations. Yet the report lacked specific proposals, serving instead to rehearse national and institutional positions in advance of the negotiations themselves. During the ICG, most national governments favored the idea of extending QMV to additional policy areas, which became bound up with the seemingly technical but politically-sensitive question of the reweighting of Council votes. This, in turn, led to friction between the big and small member states. Specifically, the big member states favored either an increase in the number of their votes or the introduction of a double majority, combining the traditional requirement of a qualified majority with a new demographic criterion. Without such a change, they argued, a qualified majority could be formed following Central and Eastern European enlargement by a group of countries that together did not represent a majority of the EU's population.

Negotiations about voting weights and the modalities of QMV soon became enmeshed in another controversial question: the size and composition of the Commission. At the time, each of the big member states appointed two Commissioners, while the small member states appointed one Commissioner each. Already, in an EU of 15 member states, the Commission (with 20 members) was arguably too large to be able to function well. France proposed breaking the link between the size of the EU and the size of the Commission: rather than having the right to appoint at least one Commissioner each, national governments should devise a system whereby the Commission would have substantially fewer members than the number of member states. Most small member states adamantly opposed the possible loss of 'their' Commissioner. With varying degrees of enthusiasm, most big member states expressed a willingness to give up at least their second Commissioner, but only in return for a re-weighting of votes in the Council.

EU leaders failed to reach a comprehensive agreement at the concluding summit of the IGC, in Amsterdam in June 1997. Various factors, including the touchiness of the institutional issues and the fractiousness of the European Council, account for the unsatisfactory outcome. Most important, perhaps, was that impending enlargement, the catalyst for large-scale institutional reform, was simple too distant to concentrate EU leaders' minds. Though foreseeable, enlargement was still far from imminent in 1997. As a result, the European Council deferred the day of reckoning on institutional reform, stipulating in a protocol attached to the Amsterdam Treaty that the Commission would comprise one Commissioner per member state as soon as the next enlargement took place, providing that Council votes were re-weighted in order to compensate big member states for the loss of a second Commissioner. The protocol also stated that at least one year before the EU enlarged to more than 20 member states, another IGC would be convened 'to carry out a comprehensive review of the provisions of the treaties on the composition and functioning of the institutions'.

With regard to institutionally affairs, the Amsterdam Treaty was more memorable for what it omitted than for what it included. Sorting out the modalities of QMV and the size of the Commission would have to await another day. Nevertheless the new treaty contained some significant institutional changes, such as capping the size of the EP, guaranteeing access to EU documents for any natural or legal person residing in the EU, and recognizing the role (however limited) of national parliaments in EU governance. The most noteworthy innovation undoubtedly was 'the first institutionalization of the concept of flexibility as a basic principle in the Treaties' (Stubb 1998, 1) Indeed, the debate about how to operationalize flexibility or differentiated integration — a debate sparked in part by the prospect of further enlargement — had dominated the IGC and the preparatory Reflection Group.

The EU tackled unresolved institutional issues — the so-called Amsterdam leftovers — in a follow-on IGC that took place three years later.[4] By that time Central and Eastern European enlargement was looming. Accordingly, the IGC that took place in 2000 also addressed institutional representation for the candidate countries, an issue that ordinarily would have been included in the accession negotiations. The narrowness of the agenda distinguished the new ICG from previous rounds of treaty reform.

The division between big and small member states, inherent in any negotiation about voting weights and Commission size, deepened as the ICG progressed. A French proposal for a radical reduction in the size of the Commission, involving a system for the selection of a smaller group of Commissioners that supposedly would ensure equality among all member states, exacerbated the divide. The small member states were skeptical, fearing that the big member states would skew the proposed new arrangement against them. The discussion over voting weights was equally divisive, not only between big and small member states. For instance, France was determined to keep the same number of Council votes as Germany, a much more populous country; and Belgium fought to retain parity with the Netherlands, despite having a substantially smaller population. EU leaders seemed far apart on the main agenda items when they convened in Nice for the concluding summit of the IGC, in December 2000 (Gray and Stubb 2001).

Not surprisingly, the Nice summit was one of the most acrimonious in EU history. As part of the deal to extend the number of policy areas subject to QMV, the big member states succeeded in getting more voting weight in the Council. Germany agreed to have the same number of votes as France, in return for the inclusion of a demographic criterion for the calculation of a qualified majority. The deal eventually struck on Council decision-making stipulated that a legislative proposal would pass if it received a qualified majority (about 72 per cent) of votes cast, representing an absolute majority of member states and, subject to a request by a national government, a qualified majority (62 per cent) of the EU's population. Having conceded more voting weight to the big member states, the small member states were more eager than ever to maintain national representation in the Commission. The big member states agreed to give up their second Commissioner, and all agreed to retain one Commissioner per member state until the EU expanded to 27 members (the existing 15; the 10 Central and Eastern European candidate countries; and Cyprus and Malta). The EU would then introduce a system to rotate Commission appointments among member states, with a view to ensuring fair representation over time.

Signed without much fanfare in February 2001, the Nice Treaty ended a chapter of EU history spanning the decade since the signing of the Maastricht Treaty, during which the EU struggled with the institutional implications of enlargement, first with regard to the Eftan countries, then with regard to the countries of Central and Eastern Europe. The EU's impending expansion would be unprecedented, qualitatively and quantitatively. Latent tension among existing member states over institutional issues, specifically relating to voting weights and Commission representation, had surfaced with a vengeance in the post-Maastricht period. Faced with growing public alienation from the EU, national governments were determined to get the best deal possible in the Amsterdam and Nice treaties. Yet the narrowness of the Amsterdam and Nice agendas, and the tenacity with which governments fought their corners, tarnished the image and utility of IGCs as a method of treaty reform (Gray 2000).

By 2001, the EU had successfully launched the third stage of EMU, whose participating countries were on the verge of introducing Euro notes and coins. Germany was celebrating more than ten years of unification, a costly but impressive endeavor. Most of the countries of Central and Eastern Europe had completed the arduous path to EU accession, with membership only a few years away. The Yugoslav wars, which had exposed the EU's weak will and capacity for conflict prevention and resolution, were over. Meeting in Tampere in October 1999, the Europeans Council had agreed on a number of measures to animate the increasingly important policy area of JHA. Despite these positive developments, however, the EU seemed mired in debates about arcane, though substantial, institutional issues that exacerbated rather than allayed public misgivings about the broader European project. Reaction to the Nice Treaty and the preceding IGC represented a turning point away from the post-Maastricht agenda of institutional leftovers and toward a loftier debate about better EU governance.

From Laeken to Lisbon: The Predominance of Institutional Issues

The debate began in 2000 with contributions by leading European statesmen, who were clearly frustrated with the narrowness of the Nice agenda.

The Commission made a seminal contribution in July 2001 with its White Paper on European Governance (Commission 2001). The European Council followed up at the end of the year with the Laeken Declaration, which called for 'European institutions... to be less unwieldy and rigid and, above all, more efficient and open'. Aware of the need to break away from debilitating IGCs, EU leaders decided in the Laeken Declaration to pave the way for the next round of treaty reform by opening up the process and convening a broadly-based convention to make concrete proposals (European Council 2001).

The Constitutional Convention, which opened in Brussels in February 2002, addressed a wide range of policy areas and institutional issues. Commission reform, QMV, the role of the EP, and the future of the European Council were all on the agenda. Given the free-wheeling nature of the debate and the variety of proposals tabled during the Convention, it seemed as if institutional reform was indeed being prepared in an entirely new way. In fact, national governments kept tight control over the debate about institutional arrangements, especially as the deadline of June 2003 approached for the Convention to produce a Draft Constitutional Treaty.[5]

The big-small country cleavage over institutional design soon resurfaced in the Convention. Many of the small member states mounted a fierce rearguard action to scrap the provision in the recently-concluded Nice Treaty breaking the link between the number of EU members and the size of the Commission, asserting their right always to appoint a Commissioner. With the support of the big member states, the Convention's presidium (governing body) nonetheless pushed through a provision for a college of 13 Commissioners, selected on the basis of equal rotation among member states, plus the Commission president and the proposed new position of EU foreign minister and Commission vice-president. Similarly, the debate over the modalities of QMV reopened old wounds. Acutely aware of their relative loss of power as a result of enlargement, France and Germany pressed for a new voting system whereby half the number of member states representing at least 60 per cent of the EU's population would constitute a qualified majority. Using their considerable powers of political persuasion, the two countries succeeded in having the new voting formula included in the Convention's Draft Constitutional Treaty.

A proposal to reform the rotating presidency, one of the most distinctive features of the Council and the European Council, also split the big and small member states. The European Council had long since become the most important political body in the EU, where decision on such key questions as enlargement, treaty reform, and EMU ultimately were made. Though cherished as a symbol of equality among member states, the system whereby the presidency of the European Council rotated every six months from one member state to another was inherently inefficient. In an ever-expanding EU, the lengthening interval between each member state's turn in the presidency robbed the rotational system of much of its appeal. However, the fact that the big member states proposed replacing the rotating presidency with the election by the European Council of a president who could remain in office for up to five years raised concerns among the small member states, which feared that the standing president would always come from a big country and would undermine the influence of the Commission president, traditionally a champion of the small countries. Many small member states had similar misgivings about the proposal for an EU foreign minister/Commission vice-president, who would preside over meetings of the Foreign Affairs Council.

Though intended as a novel and more inclusive means of conducting treaty reform, the Constitutional Convention was merely a prelude to yet another IGC, still the only means by which the treaty could be changed. Decision-making in IGCs remained the exclusive preserve of national governments, though the Commission and the EP also had a voice. Understandably, national governments used the post-Convention IGC to achieve their objectives, especially in institutional affairs, provoking sharp differences among them on the same issues that had bedeviled the pre-Amsterdam and pre-Nice IGCs.

Thus France and Germany now denounced the Nice agreement on QMV, which they had so recently had spearheaded, as unfair for the EU's most populous member states, advocating instead the new, double-majority system.[6] Though considerably less populous than France and Germany, Poland and Spain had benefited considerably from the Nice arrangement and were eager to keep it. As for reform of the Commission, most of small member states — existing and prospective — saw the IGC as an opportunity to reverse the Nice decision to reduce the number of Commissioners to far fewer than number of EU member states.

The tenacity with which the Polish and Spanish governments resisted French and German pressure to change from the traditional system of weighted votes, recently recalibrated at Nice, to the radically different double majority system reflected genuine concern about lost of voting power and the domestic political salience of the issue. Indeed, it was domestic developments unrelated to the IGC — changes of government in Poland and Spain—that facilitated an agreement on QMV. Less constrained by political pressure than their predecessors, and sensitive to the broader implications of an ongoing row with France and Germany over institutional affairs, the new governments in Poland and Spain acquiesced in the double majority system, though not along the lines originally proposed in the Draft Constitutional Treaty.

Influenced partly by the new formula for a double majority, which was not as advantageous to France and Germany as their original proposal in the Constitutional Convention, the small member states agreed in the IGC to a Commission greatly reduced in size, beginning in 2014. Ultimately, the rationale of institutional efficiency and the more persuasive power of the big member states overcame resistance to the loss of permanent national representation in the Commission, a loss that many small member states would keenly feel. Indeed, lingering resentment in Ireland against the Nice agreement and subsequent formula in the Constitutional Treaty for a smaller Commission emerged with a vengeance only a short while later, during the referendum on the Lisbon Treaty.

The Lisbon Treaty was the eventual outcome of the rejection by French and Dutch voters of the Constitutional Treaty, in referendums in 2005.[7] Institutional issues hardly featured in the referendum campaigns, either on the positive or negative side. The substance of the treaty itself seemed irrelevant to the referendum debates in both countries, which hinged on widespread dissatisfaction with the EU and domestic political and economic concerns. Nevertheless the outcome of the two referendums made ratification of the Constitutional Treaty politically impossible. Determined to salvage as much as possible of the treaty's content, which represented more than two years of deliberation in the Constitutional Convention and negotiation in the IGC, EU leaders retreated from the politically-charged rhetoric of constitutionalization, focusing instead on the necessity of treaty change in light of EU enlargement and the EU's inability under existing treaty arrangements to achieve its full potential as a global actor.

Yet in order to recast the Constitutional Treaty in a more acceptable — or at least less alarming — form, national governments once again had to convene an IGC. Despite their best efforts to organize the shortest possible IGC that would merely rubberstamp uncontroversial changes, such as to the name of the treaty, inevitably the requirement for unanimity in an IGC gave governments leverage to revisit what were, for them, unsatisfactory aspects of the Constitutional Treaty. The most spectacular example at the new IGC, culminating in a tense standoff at June 2007 summit, was a renewed Polish effort, orchestrated by the country's Euroskeptical president, to retain the Nice arrangement for QMV. By that point, reopening the debate about QMV was anathema to the other national governments. Eventually, the Polish government was able again to accept the double majority system, though only in return for an agreement to delay its entry into force until 2014. Once again, the political sensitivity of institutional issues had overshadowed a post-Maastricht IGC (European Policy Center 2007)

The negative result of the Irish referendum on the Lisbon Treaty, in June 2008, was less damaging to the treaty's prospects than the negative results of the Dutch and French referendums had been for the Constitutional Treaty, largely because Ireland was the only country holding a referendum on Lisbon and a second referendum would likely be won if EU leaders managed to assuage particular Irish concerns. One of these was a long-standing institutional issue: the size and composition of the Commission. Given widespread though vague concern in Ireland about the prospect of not always having an Irish Commissioner, the government pressed its counterparts in the EU to scrap the provision for a smaller Commission than one Commissioner per member state (O'Brennan 2008). Considering the effort made over the years to bring this reform about, maintaining one Commissioner per member state, which had first been implemented in 2004, seemed like a retrograde step. Nevertheless other national governments acceded to the Irish request, which was part of a package of measures agreed to by the European Council in order to facilitate holding, and winning, a second referendum in Ireland on the Lisbon Treaty, which duly happened in October 2009.

Implementation of the Lisbon Treaty in December that year ended a lengthy process of institutional reform via treaty change, which began eight years earlier with the Laeken Declaration. During that time, the EU had almost doubled in size, with the accession in 2004 and 2007 of 12 new member states. The enlarged EU operated reasonably well under the rules of the Nice Treaty, which had been negotiated to accommodate an EU of nearly 30 member states. The post-Lisbon EU is nonetheless more coherent and comprehensible, and strikes a reasonable balance between institutional efficiency and democratic legitimacy. The double majority system of QMV, due to come into operation in 2014, is more equitable than its predecessor, which was based on a somewhat arbitrary allocation of votes per member state. The EP, the EU's only directly-elected body, has additional budgetary authority and a greater legislative role. Keeping the size of the Commission at one Commissioner per member state is arguably preferable than reducing it drastically. A Commission of 27 members — or more after future enlargements — is undoubtedly unwieldy, though a strong Commission president can organize the college in ways that minimize its ineffectiveness. Moreover, it may be better to have a Commission in which every member state is represented than a smaller Commission from which, at any given time, some countries are excluded and whose people, as a result, may feel alienated.

The institutional innovations in the Lisbon Treaty heralded an improvement in EU policy-making, especially in CFSP and JHA, as long as national governments were willing to integrate more closely in those areas. The treaty formally recast the balance between the institutions, with the European Council clearly emerging in the ascendant. Apart from acquiring responsibility for decision-making in specific, politically-sensitive areas other than legislation, the creation of the elected presidency was particularly significant for the institution's future. Despite the concerns of the small member states, the European Council presidency did not become a sinecure for the big member states. Indeed, rivalry among the big member states ensured that someone from a small member state would be elected to the office. Nevertheless, given traditional Franco-German domination of the European Council, the new European Council president's freedom of maneuver was bound to be constrained, regardless of country of origin. Overall, the Lisbon Treaty reinforced the post-Maastricht trend within the EU toward the emergence of a commanding European Council, a confident Council and Parliament sharing legislative responsibility, and a politically-constrained Commission.

Conclusion

Questions about EU governance are again at the forefront of the discourse on European integration. The issue now, in light of the Eurozone crisis, is economic governance. Specifically, EU governments and institutions are grappling with how best to strengthen the rules and arrangements that underpin the single currency. Following the exhausting trek from Laeken to Lisbon, EU leaders have no intention of embarking once more on an ambitious round of treaty reform. A provision in the Lisbon Treaty establishing a simplified amendment procedure obviates the need for a Convention, followed by a full-fledged IGC, in order to make relatively minor modifications, even if such modifications are politically controversial. Thus, France and Germany advocated recourse to the simplified procedure when they sought, in December 2011, to include a fiscal pact in the Lisbon Treaty. Having already acquiesced in the use of this procedure to make other EMU-related treaty changes, the EP was reluctant to allow another, more far-reaching change to take place in the same way. Instead, the EP wanted the European Council to convene a Convention, in which the EP would be well-represented and correspondingly influential. National governments feared opening a Pandora's Box — who knew what other items would pop up on the Convention's agenda? — and running the risk of potentially fraught ratification procedures. In the event, Britain's refusal to participate in the negotiations meant that the proposed pact would have to be concluded as an intergovernmental treaty among the other member states, outside the EU's own treaty framework (Dinan 2012).

The response to the Eurozone crisis demonstrated the reality of the EU's institutional arrangements in the post-Maastricht era. Meetings of the heads of state and government, whether under the auspices of the European Council or in Eurozone summits, were at the apex of the EU's institutional architecture. The growing frequency of these meetings attested to the seriousness of the crisis and the extent to which 'the European Council has emerged as the centre of political gravity' in the EU (Puetter 2012, 161). The predominance of the Franco–German tandem made the work of Herman Van Rompuy, the EU's first elected President of the European Council, especially challenging. Based on his performance since coming to office in December 2009, particularly in the difficult circumstances of the Eurozone crisis, the switch in the Lisbon Treaty from a rotating to a standing European Council presidency nevertheless seems like a worthwhile innovation. Van Rompuy himself is confident that having a standing president benefits the European Council. 'Thanks to the new continuity of my function', he wrote in his report on the operation of the European Council in 2011, '[the presidency] is better equipped to steer change, to give orientations or quite practically to follow-up earlier decisions' (Council 2012, 16).

Despite treaty changes since the early 1990s that sought to shore up the Commission presidency, the political influence of that office has declined steadily over time. Tussles among member states over the selection of Commission presidents, together with sometimes bruising battles in the EP over their appointments, have reduced the standing of successive Commission presidents. The establishment of an elected European Council presidency was a further blow. The relationship between the two offices is inherently prickly, given that the Commission President had more to lose institutionally from the establishment of a standing European Council President than the standing European Council President had from the existence of the Commission President. By elevating the importance of the European Council and its president, the onset of the crisis further diminished the political effectiveness of the Commission President. Despite being an *ex officio* a member of it, the European Council is not a congenial environment for a Commission President, who lacks the stature and political heft of a national leader, especially if the Commission President comes from a small member state.

The limited political influence of its president does not mean that the Commission itself lacks influence or authority, however. The Commission played an important part in Eurozone governance before the recent reforms, whether in budgetary surveillance or the 'Europe 2020' process. Nor is the community method, which privileges the role of the Commission, a thing of the past. Apart from specific legislative responses to the crisis, such as the 'Six Pack' of legislative proposals submitted early in 2011 to reinforce surveillance of fiscal policy in the Eurozone, the Commission remains front and center of other EU business, such as efforts to strengthen the single market — a work perpetually in progress. The Commission's most potent weapon is still its exclusive right to initiate legislation, though pressure from the Council and the EP increasingly limits the Commission's freedom of maneuver.

The EP continued to grow in formal power and informal influence in the post-Maastricht period. With the reform of codecision in the Amsterdam Treaty and the extension of its use in the Amsterdam and subsequent treaties; the expansion of the assent procedure; and the strengthening of its budgetary authority, the EP has become a far more formidable actor in the last 20 years. As well as using other institutional reforms to bolster its political position, the EP exploited a major confrontation with the Commission in 1999, which precipitated the resignation of the Santer College, to tilt the balance between the two institutions irrevocably in its favor. Under astute leadership, especially in the Conference of Presidents, which represents the political group leaders, the EP has pushed its institutional interests relentlessly in relation to the Commission and the Council. In view of the growing prominence of the European Council, relations between the EP and the European Council are likely to be the next battleground in the EP's war for institutional ascendancy.

As for formal treaty changes, the modalities of QMV and the size and composition of the Commission were the two most discordant institutional issues in the post-Maastricht period, dividing member states largely along big-small lines. The year 2014 is when the Commission should have been reduced to 15 members and when the new system of QMV will come into operation. Such is the nature of inter-governmental bargaining that the system of QMV about to be put into operation is not the system originally proposed in the Draft Constitutional Treaty. The story of QMV and Commission reform in the post-Maastricht period illustrates not only the unpredictability of IGCs but also, more fundamentally, the inherently untidy nature of formal institutional change in the ever-evolving EU, as well as the vagaries of any possible constitutional settlement.

Notes

1. On the nature of treaty reform, see Christiansen, Falkner, and Jørgensen (2002).

2. On ratification of the Maastricht Treaty, see Laursen and Vanhoonacker (1994).
3. On the 1996–1997 IGC and ensuing Amsterdam Treaty, see Laursen (2002).
4. On the 2000 IGC and ensuing Nice Treaty, see Laursen (2006).
5. On the Constitutional Convention, subsequent IGC, and the Constitutional Treaty, see Beach (2012) and Laursen (2008).
6. On the debate over QMV, see Cichocki and Życzkowsk (2002).
7. On the Lisbon Treaty, see Ziller (2012).

References

Beach, D. 2012. The Constitutional Treaty: the failed formal constitutionalization. In *Designing the European Union: from Paris to Lisbon*, ed. F. Laursen, 350–92. London: Palgrave Macmillan.

Christiansen, T., G. Falkner, and K.E. Jørgensen. 2002. Theorizing EU treaty reform: beyond diplomacy and bargaining. *Journal of European Public Policy* 9, no. 1: 12–32.

Cichocki, M.A., and K. Życzkowsk. 2002. *Institutional design and voting power in the European Union*. Ashgate: Farnam.

Commission. 1992. European Council Conclusions, Edinburgh, 11–12 December 1992, *Bulletin EC*, 12–1992.

Commission. 1994. *Bulletin EC*, 3–1994, point 1.3.27.

Commission. 2001. European governance. A White Paper. Brussels, 25 July 2001, COM(2001) 428 final.

Council. 2012. *The European Council in 2011*. General Secretariat of the Council. Luxembourg: Publications Office of the European Union.

Dinan, D. 2012. Governance and Institutions: impact of the escalating crisis. *Journal of Common Market Studies*, Annual Review, Vol. 50, S.1, September 2012, pp. 85–90.

European Council. 2001. Laeken Declaration on the future of the European Union, http://european-convention.eu.int/pdf/lknen.pdf (accessed 12 August, 2012).

European Council. 2006. Brussels European Council, June 15–16, Presidency Conclusions, 10633/1/06, REV 1, Brussels, July 17.

European Parliament. 1992. Report of the Committee on Institutional Affairs on the structure and strategy for the EU with regard to enlargement, PE 152.242 final, May 21.

European Policy Center. 2007. A midsummer night's treaty, http://www.epc.eu/pub_details.php?pub_id=416&cat_id=5 (accessed August 12, 2012).

Gray, M. 2000. Negotiating EU treaties: the case for a new approach. In *Rethinking the European Union: IGC 2000 and beyond*, ed. E. Best, M. Gray, and A. Stubb, 263–80. Maastricht: European Institute of Public Administration.

Gray, M., and A. Stubb. 2011. The Treaty of Nice. negotiating a poisoned chalice? *Journal of Common Market Studies* 39, Annual Review: 5–23.

Laursen, F. 2002. *The Amsterdam Treaty: national preference formation, interstate bargaining and outcome*. Odense: Odense University Press.

Laursen, F. 2006. *The Treaty of Nice. actor preferences, bargaining and institutional choice*. Leiden: Nijhoff/Brill.

Laursen, F. 2008. *The rise and fall of the Constitutional Treaty*. Leiden: Nijhoff/Brill.

Laursen, F., and S. Vanhoonacker. 1994. *The ratification of the Maastricht Treaty: issues, debates, and future implications*. Dordrecht: Martinus Nijhoff Publishers.

Mazzucelli, C. 2012. The Treaty of Maastricht: designing the European Union. In *Designing the European Union: from Paris to Lisbon*, ed. F. Laursen, 244–86. London: Palgrave Macmillan.

O'Brennan, J. 2008. Ireland and the Lisbon Treaty: quo vadis? *CEPS Policy Brief No. 176*, October.

Preston, C. 1997. *Enlargement and integration in the European Union*. London: Routledge.

Puetter, U. 2012. Europe's deliberative intergovernmentalism: the role of the Council and European Council in EU economic governance. *Journal of European Public Policy* 19, no. 2: 161–78.

Stubb, A. 1998. The Amsterdam Treaty and flexible integration. *ECSA Review* 11, no. 2: 1–2.

Ziller, J. 2012. The Treaty of Lisbon: Constitutional Treaty, Episode II. In *Designing the European Union: from Paris to Lisbon*, ed. F. Laursen, 393–412. London: Palgrave Macmillan.

Index

References in **Bold** refer to figures.
References in *Italics* refer to tables.

absolute veto 55
accountability: democracy 145
Ad Hoc Group on Immigration 36
Adonnino Committee 35
agenda setting: conditional 55, 56
agricultural policy 53, 72
Alcidi, C. 90
Amsterdam IGC (1997) 165
Amsterdam Treaty (1999) 19–20, 166; co-decision procedure 55; Petersberg tasks 26; third pillar 5
animal welfare 137
anti-trust law 89
apartheid 128
Area of Freedom Security and Justice (AFSJ) 5, 40
asylum 5, 36, 39; applications 35
Austria 104n, 163

banking: contagious 110; failure 89; internationalization 94; liquidity 114; union 118
Beger, N. 129
Belgium 166
Berlusconi, S. 99
border: controls 35; management 39
Brandt, W. 72
Bretton Woods system 72
Bundesbank 108, 111, 112, 113

capital: flow imbalances 93; markets 86; outflows 109
Caporaso, J. 9
Castren, O. 93
civil rights 128
civil society 125–38; assessing democratic value of participation 130–1; EU governance participatory turn 132–3; Europeanization 126–30; NGO performance constraints 133–6; outlook 136–8; reality test 131
co-decision procedure 51–64; Code of Conduct (Conference of Presidents 2008) 62; early agreements and normative implications 61–3; institutional functioning 54–5; interinstitutional implications 55–8; intrainstitutional implications 58–61; predecessors 53–4
Cold War (1947–91) 2, 11
Comité européen de la lutte anti-drogue (CELAD) 36
Common Commercial Policy 20, 22
Common Foreign and Security Policy (EU CFSP): creation 2, 3–4; missions 5; QMF 19
communitarization 40, 46, 70
competitive authorization 29n
competitiveness 97, 109
conciliation committee 57, 58
Conference of Presidents 173; Code of Conduct for Negotiating Codecision Files (2008) 62; guidelines for adoption of reading agreements (2004) 62
Constitution for Europe Treaty: draft 80
Constitutional Convention (2003) 162, 168, 169
Convention on Future of Europe (EC 2001): draft Constitution for Europe Treaty 80, 168, 169, 173
Convention Implementing Schengen Agreement (CISA 1995) 35
convergence criteria 94, 110
Cooper, R. 87, 89
cooperation 88: 103n
Copenhagen accession criteria (1993) 72
Copenhagen summit (1973) 73
corruption 145
council model 70
credit booms 93
criminal procedural law 49n
current account transactions **97**

Dahl, R.A. 130, 132
de Gaulle, C. 74
debt 92; brakes 117; Greece 86, 104n; public 86

INDEX

deficits 109
Dehousse, R. 146
Delors III Commission (1993–4) 45
Delors, J. 38, 76
democracy 18, 146; defective 29n; deficit 144–5, 147
democratic participation 130
Denmark: opt-outs 6, 110; referendum (1992) 161, 163; TEU ratification 3, 12, 41, 127, 142
devaluation 94
differentiation 110
Dinan, D. 3, 6, 11, 12
diplomacy 25–6
Dooge Committee 35
double majority system 170; QMV 171
Drafts: Constitutional Treaty 80, 168, 169, 173; Europol Convention 46
drug addiction 39
Dyson, K. 10

early agreements 61–3
EC pillar 78
economic constitution failure 110
Economic and Monetary Union (EMU) 9–11, 90–100, 160, 167; unsuitability of economic constitution 108–9
Economic Semester 117
Edinburgh: European Council (1992) 49n
Eftan enlargement 163, 167
Eichel, H. 113
Eichengreen, B. 92
8 hours campaign 137
elections: participation rate 146
Elgström, O. 21
empty chair crisis 160
enlargement 163–4; big bang (2004) 6, 80; implications 162; institutional implications 165
EU-17: openness 93
Euro Plus Pact 117
Euro-bonds 110
Euro-crisis 146
euro-zone crisis 7, 12, 13, 85–103, 104n, 171; break-up cost 101; dynamics 98–100; dynamics of divergence 94–8; fiscal deficits, capital flows and market spillovers 92–4; Greek tragedy 90–1; market spillovers and policy externalities 88–9; perverse incentives and institutions 90; risk and moral hazard 89–90; TEU structural flaws and Stability and Growth Pact (SGP) 91–2; theoretical approach 87–8
Eurojust 6
Europe 2020: process 173
Europe des patries 70
Europe without frontiers 76

European Arrest Warrant (2002) 6, 48
European Banking Authority (EBA) 118
European Central Bank (ECB) 10, 79, 85, 99, 160; quantitative easing 108; stability culture 111
European Citizens' Initiative (ECI) 8–9, 136–8
European Coal and Steel Community (ECSC) 22
European Commission (EC): president 75
European Convention of Human Rights (ECHR) 151
European Council 7, 69–82, 161; Compact for Growth and Jobs (2012) 104n; creating institutional opportunities for ambitious multi-level players 81–2; creation 71–3, 76; Edinburgh (1992) 49n; Fontainebleau (1984) 35; highest instance of appeal 78; JHA 79; Maastricht and revisions 77–9; major functions 76; Paris to Maastricht 76–7; presidency creation 25, 75, 172–3; Rome (1990) 37; Seville agreement (2002) 79; shaping Idée Directrice 74–6; Stuttgart Summit (1983) 76, 78, 81; TEU exclusion 77; TEU Nice (Article 4) 78; via constitutional convention to Lisbon Treaty 80–1
European Court of Justice (ECJ) 4, 100
European Economic Community (EEC) 22
European External Action Service (EEAS) 5, 25, 26
European Financial Stability Facility (EFSF) 99, 116, 118
European Free Trade Association (EFTA) 162
European identity 8, 12
European Monetary System (EMS): demise (1992) 12
European NGO Confederation for Relief and Development (CONCORD) 134
European Ombudsman 126
European Parliament (EP) 64n; codecision and QMV 160–73; influence 58; institutional ascendency 173; Rule 62 (Rules of Procedure) 56; Rule 70 (Rules of Procedure) 62; second reading amendments 55–6; Single European Act (SEA) 53, 76–7, 82, 161, *see also* Conference of Presidents
European Police Office (Europol) 6, 38, 41, 43, 46, 47; Convention (1995) 49n
European Political Cooperation (EPC) 4, 24
European Political Union 2
European Security and Defence Policy (ESDP) 2, 20, 23
European Social Policy (ESP): Forum 127; Green Paper (1993) 127

INDEX

European Stability Mechanism (ESM) 99, 112, 118
European Systemic Risk Board (ESRB) 116
European Union (EU): Civil Society Contact Group 129, 133; Common Foreign and Security Policy (EU CFSP) 5, 19, **II** 3–4; conflicts and tensions of roles 28; Convention on Extradition (1996) 48; governance participatory turn 132–3; -NGO cooperation 127
Europeanization 121; civil society 126–30
Europol 6, 38, 41, 43, 46, 47; Convention (1995) 49n
Euroscepticism 127, 147
Eurostat 104n, 112, 115
Eurosystem 114
Excessive Deficit Procedure (EDP) 110
Excessive Imbalance Procedure (EIP) 116
Exchange Rate Mechanism (ERM) 114
exchange rates 96, **96, 98**
export growth: negative 97
external relations 15–29; EU roles in world arena 21–8; Maastricht as root stock 17–19; negotiation of hybridity: from Amsterdam to Lisbon 19–21
extradition: EU Convention (1996) 48

Farrell, H. 55, 60
Feldstein, M. 141
financial trilemma 101
Finland 104n, 122; enlargement 163
fiscal compact treaty 117
flexibility concept 167
Flynn, P. 45
Fontainebleau European Council (1984) 35
France: EU size 165; euro-zone strategy (1969) 72; QMV 161, 169, 172; TEU referendum 3, 12, 127, 142, 163
fraud 39
Frieden, J. 88

Garrett, G. 57
GATT Uruguay Round 2, 18
Germany 172; Bundesbank 108, 111, 112, 113; isolation 122; limiting liabilities 108; national socialism 142; parallelism 109; QMV 161, 169; TEU ratification 3; unification 3, 11; unification and asylum 37; voting weights 166
GIIPS 93–8, 103; trade *93*
Giscard d'Estaing, V. 73, 75, 80
Gradin, A. 45
Grauwe, P. De 92
Greece: boom 85–6; credit 93; debt 86, 104n; and euro-zone crisis 90–1; fiscal data 115; tragedy 90–1; Troika 119
Greek tragedy: transnational 90–100

Gros, D. 90
Gulf conflict (1990–1) 18

Habermas, J. 128, 131
Hagemann, S. 57
Héritier, A. 55, 60
High Contracting Parties 77, 78
High Representative/Vice-President (HRVP): introduction 4, 19, 21; role 25
Hill, C. 25
Hix, S. 55
Hoyland, B. 57
human rights 128, 151
Hungary 104n
hybrid: third-generation 17, 21
hybridity 29n; EU external affairs 16; institutionalized 18; Maastricht Treaty 4–5; negotiation 19–21; root of problems 17

Iceland 104n
identity: European 8, 12
immigration 5, 36, 39
inflation 111
input legitimacy 144
institutional ascendency: European Parliament 173
institutional reform 7–9, 159–73; Laeken to Lisbon 167–71; in Maastricht aftermath 162–7
institutionalized hybridity 18
integration 16
intellectual property (IP) 22
Intergovernmental Conference (IGC: 1995–7) 19
Internal Market 2
International Monetary Fund (IMF) 119
internationalization: banking 94
Involving Civil Society (EC 2001) 127
Ioannina Compromise (1994) 164
Ireland: bail-out 99; credit 93; debt ratios 92; Lisbon Treaty referendum 170; opt-outs 6; Troika 119
Italy 99; credit 93; North African migration 146

Joint Declarations 54, 59
justice: social 128
Justice and Home Affairs (JHA) 4, 5, 24, 33–48; budget 40; communitarization option 38; compromise in negotiations 37–8; fields of common interest 39; government positions 37–8; IGC (1996) 38; institutional framework and decision-making 43–6; joint actions 43; K.1 TEU 38; K.3 TEU 42, 43; K.4 TEU 44; K.6 TEU 46; K.9. 40; legal basis and instruments 41–3; Luxembourg presidency 38; Maastricht *Third Pillar*

177

precursors 34–7; parliamentary and judicial control 46–7; wide gate opened - but without further directions 38–41

Kavonius, I.K. 93
Keohane, R.O. 88, 90
Kohl, H. 76
Kohler-Koch, B. 8
König, T. 57
Kosovo conflict (1999) 20
Kreppel, A. 56

labour: productivity per hour **95**
Laeken Declaration (2001) 80, 168, 171
Larosière, J. De 116
law enforcement cooperation 35
legitimacy: current circumstances of Europe 144–8; Europe as political Messianism 148–9; popularity 143; prologue 141–2; Schuman declaration (1950) 149–53; two genres and three types 142–4
Lehman Brothers: collapse 108
liquidity: banking 114
Lisbon Treaty: Principle of Participatory Democracy 128
Lisbon Treaty (2008) 4–5, 170; economic policy 112; European Council institutional features 80–1; HRVP 25–6; Ireland referendum (2009) 170; Provisions on Democratic Principles (Title II) 136
longer-term refinancing operation (LTFO) 114
Luxembourg Compromise (1966) 161

Maastricht Plus 107–23; crisis management 118–19; crisis prevention 116–18; crisis prevention and management 115–16; excessive imbalances and sovereign creditworthiness 108–11; limited liability and collective insurance 121–3; supreme emergency 119–21; theory and practice 111–14
Maastricht Treaty: historical context 2–3; introduction 1–2; legacy 11–14; structural flaws 90–103, *see also* Treaty on European Union (TEU)
Manners, I. 27
markets: capital 86; spillovers 88–9
Marzinotto, B. 86, 97
Mazower, M. 148
Merkel, A. 99, 113, 121
Middle East Peace Process 2
migration: North African to Italy 146
Milward, A. 13, 143
Min-hyung Kim 9
Mitterrand, F. 76
mixed actor system 4, 16

Monar, J. 5
monetary union: lack of political infrastructure 87
Moravcsik, A. 16
Mutual Assistance Group (GAM) 36

Napel, S. 57
national socialism: Germany 142
Netherlands 122, 170; voting weight 166
NGOs (non-governmental organizations) 8; development 126; performance constraints 133–6
Nice Summit (2000) 162, 166
Nice Treaty (2001) 20, 167, 168
no bail-outs 108, 118
normative legitimacy 142
normative power 27
North Atlantic Treaty Organization (NATO) 23

openness: import shares *93*
opt-outs 3, 6, 110; UK 3, 6, 110
Optimal Currency Area (OCA) 109
output legitimacy 144

Padoa-Schoppa, T. 87
Papandreou, G. 86
parallelism: Germany 109
Pareto superior outcomes 103n
Paris Summits: (1972) 73; (1974) 73, 74–5
Patten, C. 25
peace 150
peace-building 26
peace-keeping 26
Petersberg tasks (Amsterdam Treaty) 26
PIIGS (Portugal, Italy, Ireland, Spain) 86
pillarization 3–6
Pisani-Ferry, J. 86, 97
Poland 170; opt-outs 6; QMV 169
Police Chiefs' Task Force 6
police cooperation 39
Police and Judicial Cooperation on Criminal Matters (PJCCM) 5
political deficit 146
Political Messianism 144, 148–9; Schuman declaration (1950) 149–53, 154n
Pompidou, G. 72
popularity: legitimacy 143
Portugal: bail-out 99; credit 93; Troika 119
presidency model 7, 70, 79
President of European Council: creation 25, 75, 172
process legitimacy 144
proportionality 163
prosperity 18
public debt 86

INDEX

Qualified Majority Voting (QMV) 7–8, 53, 77, 79, 160–73; reverse 100, 116
quantitative easing: ECB 108

Raunio, T. 54
referendums: Denmark (1992) 161, 163; France on TEU (1992) 3, 12, 127, 142, 163; Ireland 170
Reflection Group 19, 41, 43, 165, 166
reform: institutional (2009) 159–73
result legitimacy 144
reverse qualified majority voting 100, 116
Rhodes' Coordinators' Group on Free Movement 36
rights: civil 128; human 128, 151
risk 89–90, 115
road transport sector: Working Time Directive 57
Rome European Council (14/15 December 1990) 37
Rompuy, H. van 7, 76, 172
Ross, G. 11

Sapir, A. 9, 86, 87, 94, 97
Sarkozy, N. 99
Scharpf, F. 13
Schengen Agreement (1985) 35, 39
Schengen Information System (SIS) 36
Schlesinger, H. 107
Schmidt, H. 75
Schröder, G. 113
Schuman declaration (1950) 149–53, 154n
security policy 23–4
securocrats 24
Seville agreement: (European Council 2002) 79
Shackleton, M. 54
Single European Act (SEA) 53, 76–7, 82, 161
Single Market Programme 22
Six Pack: SGP 100, 104n, 116–17, 173
Smith, M. 4
smuggling 36
social justice 128
social legitimacy 142
social platform 127, 133
Solana, J. 25
Solemn Declaration: Stuttgart Summit (1983) 76, 78, 81
Soviet Union: collapse 2
Spain: blocking minority 164; credit 93; debt deflation 86; debt ratios 92; QMV 169
stability 18; culture 111, 113
Stability, Coordination and Governance in EMU (2012) 112, 117

Stability and Growth Pact (SGP) 9, 86, 92, 102, 110; Six Pack 100, 116–17
state liquidity 110
Stuttgart Summit (1983): Solemn Declaration 76, 78, 81
subsidiarity 163; principle 6
summitry: institutionalized 74
Sweden: enlargement 163–4; opt-outs 6

Tampere (1999) 167
TARGET2 payment system 114
tax collection 86
taxation 53
Telos legitimacy 144
third-generation hybrid 17, 21, 28
trade: deficits 93; GIIPS *93*; openness 93, *93*
transfer union 110, 121
Transferable Securities (COD 1995 188) 56–7
Treaty on European Union (TEU): first pillar 18; second pillar two 18; third pillar 5, 18, 24, 34–43; agreement 3; Article C 43; convergence criteria 103n; ratification 3; Title IV (old pillar 3) 34, 38, 41, 42, 45, *see also* Justice and Home Affairs (JHA)
TREVI 34–6, 39, 42, 45, 48n; Group of Coordinators 44
trialogues 54
Troika 119
Tsebeli, G. 53, 55, 56, 57

United Kingdom (UK): blocking minority 164; JHA 38; opt-outs 3, 6, 110

veto 55
Vitorino, A. 45
voice telephony (COD 1994 437) 56
voting weights 166, 167

wage costs: manufacturing industry **95**
Wallace, W. 25
Walzer, M. 120
Weiler, J. 13
Werner negotiations (1970–1) 109
Werner Plan 72
Wessels, W. 7
Westlake, M. 19
Widgren, M. 57
Working Time Directive: road transport sector 57

Yugoslavia: break-up 2